The Islamic State: How Viable Is It?

Yoram Schweitzer and Omer Einav, Editors

iNSS Institute for National Security Studies

The Institute for National Security Studies (INSS), incorporating the Jaffee Center for Strategic Studies, was founded in 2006.

The purpose of the Institute for National Security Studies is first, to conduct basic research that meets the highest academic standards on matters related to Israel's national security as well as Middle East regional and international security affairs. Second, the Institute aims to contribute to the public debate and governmental deliberation of issues that are – or should be – at the top of Israel's national security agenda.

INSS seeks to address Israeli decision makers and policymakers, the defense establishment, public opinion makers, the academic community in Israel and abroad, and the general public.

INSS publishes research that it deems worthy of public attention, while it maintains a strict policy of non-partisanship. The opinions expressed in this publication are the authors' alone, and do not necessarily reflect the views of the Institute, its trustees, boards, research staff, or the organizations and individuals that support its research.

The Islamic State: How Viable Is It?

Yoram Schweitzer and Omer Einav, Editors

iNSS

המכון למחקרי ביטחון לאומי

THE INSTITUTE FOR NATIONAL SECURITY STUDIES

INCORPORATING THE JAFFEE
CENTER FOR STRATEGIC STUDIES   TEL AVIV UNIVERSITY
אוניברסיטת תל-אביב

המדינה האסלאמית
דגל שחור מתנוסס מעליה

יורם שוייצר ועומר עינב, עורכים

Editor: Judith Rosen
Graphic design: Michal Semo-Kovetz, Yael Bieber
Cover design: Michal Semo-Kovetz, Adva Lubrani
Printing: Elinir

Institute for National Security Studies (a public benefit company)
40 Haim Levanon Street
POB 39950
Ramat Aviv
Tel Aviv 6997556

Tel. +972-3-640-0400
Fax. +972-3-744-7590

E-mail: info@inss.org.il
http://www.inss.org.il

ISBN: 978-965-550-572-6

Table of Contents

Preface

Historical developments and processes generally evolve gradually and below the surface of public scrutiny, and it is difficult to foresee starting points and often equally difficult to identify end points. In contrast, dramatic moments that are seared into collective memory can be pinpointed. One such moment, in effect a watershed, was recorded in June 2014, when the Islamic State in Iraq and Syria (ISIS) seized a dominant position in the global consciousness with its occupation of the city of Mosul in Iraq, and thereafter with its announcement of the establishment of the Islamic State headed by Caliph Abu Bakr al-Baghdadi.

The conflation of impressive military achievements and the challenge to the hundred-year-old state order that existed in the areas occupied by the Islamic State and in the greater region, along with the radical ideology painted in bright shades of Salafi jihadi Islam that drives Islamic State activity, took the Middle East and the international arena by surprise. Since then, there have been numerous attempts to understand the origins of the Islamic State; the essence of this particular phenomenon; its characteristics; its growth; and the various implications of its actions. In tandem, there have been increasing efforts to devise ways to cope with the challenges it poses.

The Islamic State currently lies at the heart of international discourse, researched and analyzed by decision makers and intelligence bodies, academics, and journalists alike. This may be attributed, inter alia, to the fact that the Islamic State is understood to be a multifaceted challenge – security-military, political, economic, legal, ideological, cultural, and moral – on national and regional levels, as well as a challenge to the stability of the entire world.

This volume is part of the intellectual effort currently underway at many research institutes throughout the world that are closely following the phenomenon of the Islamic State in order to offer plausible interpretations of its nature and contribute to the efforts to eradicate it. More specifically, the objective of this volume is twofold, incorporating two complementary dimensions. First, it represents an attempt to establish a rich research foundation and knowledge base on the Islamic State that will help advance further research in this area. Second, it enables an understanding of the complexity and difficulties inherent in the Islamic State challenge, which should assist in the examination and selection of ways toward an informed and effective response.

The book is a compilation of articles written by researchers at the Institute for National Security Studies (INSS) and experts from other research institutes in Israel. The structure of the volume reflects the various and diverse aspects that the Islamic State phenomenon represents. The articles present a broad and comprehensive picture: an explanation and analysis of the historical, religious and geopolitical context for the growth of the Islamic State, the characteristics of the entity, how it acts, its effects on various states, the challenge that it presents to regional and world powers, its possible future directions and development, and the types of action required for weakening and even obliterating it.

The book is divided into eight sections. The first section includes articles that examine the ground from which the Islamic State sprouted forth: the growth of the Salafi jihadi stream, the development of the concept of the caliphate in Islam, the theoretical geopolitical context of the breakdown of the nation state in the Middle East, and the practical background for the rise of the Islamic State from the radical camp. The second section deals with the various aspects that define the Islamic State primarily since its establishment, the many levels on which it operates, and the challenges that it presents for its rivals. To this end, the military and intelligence contexts that pertain to the patterns of action by Islamic State are analyzed, and issues of governance, economy, and law, as well as the use of media and social networks – a significant component in Islamic State activity – are probed as well.

The following four sections of the volume address the geopolitical level and geographical context of the Islamic State phenomenon, broken down by states and organizations. The analyses look at the various actors and their respective attitudes toward the Islamic State, and deal with the impact of the Islamic State on particular states within their borders, as well as each response to the Islamic State in its areas of operation. The third section looks at the region where the Islamic State first emerged and its immediate surroundings, namely, Syria, Iraq, the Kurdish areas, Lebanon, Jordan, and among the Sunni population in the State of Israel and areas of the Palestinian Authority. The next section relates to the leading regional powers in the Middle East – Iran, Saudi Arabia, Turkey, and Israel – vis-à-vis the challenge. The fifth section examines the expansion of the Islamic State's sphere of influence to areas beyond the primary territories that it captured – Egypt, Libya, Central Africa, and South Asia. The sixth section observes the developments from the wider prism of the superpowers, and attempts to analyze the relationship between the Islamic State and the actors that largely dictate the international agenda: the United States, Russia, the European Union, and China.

The seventh section of the volume explores the intensity of the threat that emerges from the direction of Islamic State, and the strategic vision with which to address this threat. The section's two articles present various perspectives for analysis of the phenomenon and ways of dealing with it. The final section presents insights that derive from the preceding articles' examination and analysis of the Islamic State, in an attempt to contribute both to the discourse on the phenomenon and the choice of the most effective alternatives for dealing with the challenges it presents.

An important issue, ostensibly semantic, in fact has material significance in the context of this compilation. The terminology chosen for the entity under examination is specifically "the Islamic State," rather than ISIS. In our view, the reluctance of world leaders and others dealing with this subject to use the term Islamic State due to a fear of strengthening the "brand," or alternatively, because of their reservations about identifying the phenomenon with Islam in general, is mistaken. In point of fact, use of the name adopted by the Islamic State as a title that embodies it clarifies its nature, vision, and perception of itself as a preparation for the caliphate. Its definition as "Islamic" accurately reflects its nature, ambitions, and guiding ideology. The Islamic State is also not defined as a terror organization in this volume, because we believe that this designation does not reflect the greater dimensions of the phenomenon, and using it is liable to diminish the sense of the Islamic State's full power and multiple dimensions and the potential risk it poses.

Predictably, the articles included here include numerous expressions and names from foreign languages, primarily Arabic. The phrases and transliteration that were selected conform to the style in INSS publications. The goal is to adhere strictly to a common language and uniform style, even if it causes a certain deviation from official customary transliteration rules.

Furthermore, the subject is part of the broad spectrum of studies about the intellectual and operational streams behind the Islamic State. In this context, several terms can be used, with each symbolizing a slightly different meaning, e.g., radical/extreme Islam, fundamentalist Islam, Islamists, and jihadists. We have chosen the term Salafi jihad, in its various forms, in order to describe this stream. Clearly the choice of this term is subject to debate, but for purposes of the discussion, this is the vocabulary that we feel is best suited to reflect the phenomenon. While occasional use may be made of other terms for lack of a suitable alternative, in general, and for the sake of uniformity, we have adhered to use of the term Salafi jihad.

Several restrictions have shaped this volume. Despite the many and far ranging topics included here, there are additional aspects of the Islamic State phenomenon that are either not covered at all or are not dealt with comprehensively. In addition, practical considerations forced us to limit the scope and length of the articles. The desire to produce an integrated, clear, and relevant study dictated the relatively restricted framework for each article. Furthermore, the articles reflect the situational reality at the time of their writing, but clearly a highly dynamic struggle is at work. There will no doubt be changes in the relevant regional and international environment of the Islamic State following publication of the volume, as there have been even in the period of time between when the articles were completed and their publication (the terror attack in Paris on November 13, 2015, for example). Consequently, we have tried to refrain from time dependent interpretations, and have chosen instead to deal with the phenomenon through a long term, process-oriented view and not make do with a description of specific events that have occurred since the Islamic State was established.

We would like to thank the authors of the articles for their contributions to this volume. Sincere thanks also go to Anat Kurz, Director of Research at the Institute for National Security Studies; Moshe Grundman, Director of Publications at the Institute; and Judith Rosen, Editor of INSS English publications, for their contribution to the preparation and publication of the volume.

Yoram Schweitzer and Omer Einav
December 2015

Part I

Background

A State Is Born:
What Lies behind the Establishment of
the Islamic State

Kobi Michael

The Islamic State, whose establishment was announced over a year ago by its leader Abu Bakr al-Baghdadi, started out as a quirky peculiarity, but has since turned into an influential element in the region as well as a challenge to the international community. The process of its establishment and expansion seems to have been facilitated by a convergence of four major trends: upheavals that led to the collapse of the region's Arab nation states and their decline into a state failure process; an ideological vacuum initiated by disillusionment with pan-Arabism and the stinging inability of the Muslim Brotherhood and political Islam, particularly in Egypt, to fill that vacuum; the reluctance of the West to intervene in any substantive sense, combined with a lack of global leadership and an irrelevant US strategy;[1] and the unwillingness of moderate opposition groups in Syria to cooperate and formulate a joint vision. These trends unfolded while jihadist organizations were present and active in the region.[2]

From an historical perspective, one can view the Islamic State as a product of the region's chronic structural instability. Over the last century, the Middle East experienced four major upheavals, each of which led to the formation of a political structure at odds with the social framework that was based primarily on ethnic, tribal, or religious affiliations. This incompatibility inevitably eroded the legitimacy of the various regimes and heightened the potential for opposition and subversion. In most cases, the nation-state model survived, thanks to an authoritarian rule dependent on effective security and intelligence services.

The fragility of the political model was evident in the difficulty with which most of the regimes have withstood the shockwaves of Arab upheavals, the weakening of central governments, and the acceleration of statehood failures. Political Islam – the chief ideological rival of nationalism – failed the first test it faced (the Muslim Brotherhood in Egypt). As it faded, it left behind an ideological vacuum that Salafist jihadist movements rapidly tried to fill. The conditions created by state failures throughout the region were exploited by radical Islamic currents, the most prominent being ISIS, which led to the establishment of the Islamic State.

This chapter surveys the sociopolitical features of the chronic structural instability of the region from an historical perspective. It examines the significance of the failed state and the recurrence of this phenomenon throughout the region. It also analyzes the connection between the expansion of the failed state phenomenon and the growing strength of ISIS and the establishment of the Islamic State.

Chronic Structural Instability from an Historical Perspective

Historically, the region was long organized along local, extended family, tribal, ethnic, and religious lines with a clear correlation between identity and territory.[3] Defined territories were home to distinct homogeneous ethnic, tribal, and religious groups. Most of these were backward societies (i.e., with low literacy rates and no modern infrastructure and industrialization). Any change in the traditional power structure was considered foreign, provocative, or rebellious and thus illegitimate; as such, it aroused opposition, which in some cases translated into counterrevolution. Subsequently, upheavals in the Arab region called into question the geopolitical logic that defined the modern region, which involved states with a central authoritarian government and well-defined borders drawn by the Sykes-Picot agreement. Since their inception, most of these nations have experienced instability that led to extreme political crises and threatened their survival – but survive they did, thanks to oppression and intimidation. Indeed, they maintained their political structure through regime changes until the shockwaves of the Arab Spring.

The first upheaval in the region came with the spread of the Ottoman Empire, which organized the area politically and administratively (*sanjaks*) in a way that was supposed to grant it efficient administrative control. Ottoman rule managed to institute moderate and long term processes of modernization without rousing serious antagonism, and was capable of putting down any manifestation of such with a brutal hand. The Turkish sultans enjoyed a form of legitimacy due to their religious background, and in many respects the Ottoman Empire served as a kind of Islamic caliphate.

The second significant upheaval came with the fall of the Ottoman Empire at the end of World War I and the division of the spoils among the victors – Great Britain and France – via the Sykes-Picot agreement in 1916. As part of the agreement, the region was divided into areas of influence and artificial political state units. These units amassed together various ethnic groups, rival religions, and even speakers of different languages into single states with loose identities and no shared national or historical ethos. Borders were drawn to frame state entities that were modeled on nation states prevalent in Europe at the time.

The ouster of the monarch by the Free Officers Movement during the Egyptian revolt of 1952 followed by the Baath Revolutions in Syria and Iraq marked the third major upheaval. The Officers revolt introduced a political ideological alternative – pan-Arabism – that peaked with the establishment of the United Arab Republic led by former Egyptian President Gamal Abdel Nasser. In Iraq, Syria, and Libya, despotic regimes became the norm, as these were successful in preserving the multi-ethnic, multi-tribal, and multi-religious entities by force and through the relentless oppression of their opponents. In these three cases, the rulers were members of a minority and nurtured members of "their own" sect as well as particular ethnic, religious, or tribal groups at the expense of everyone else. The power structure they created was corrupt, lacking any real public legitimacy.

Oppression, frustration, and changes in the international arena – particularly the dissolution of the Soviet Union, which was the strategic support of these rulers, and the growth of globalization, mass media, social media, and the impressive successes of al-Qaeda – paved the way for the fourth upheaval. The butterfly effect that began in late 2010 in a Tunisian marketplace became an all-encompassing regional upheaval that led to the collapse of several Arab nation states and an impressive, albeit short-lived surge of political Islam in the region. Concurrently, the area saw the meteoric rise of Salafi jihadist Islam. In the case of the Islamic State, this became manifest in the conquest of extensive territories in northwest Iraq and eastern Syria, the obliteration of established international borders, and the founding of an entity that – in the eyes of its leader and followers – was the basis of the great Islamic caliphate. More than any of its predecessors, this fourth upheaval was attended by a deepening of the bitter Sunni-Shiite rift. The religious struggle now grew into a political conflict between Saudi Arabia, which saw itself as the leader of the Sunni world, and Iran, the leader of the Shiites.

The fourth upheaval has been a sharp reminder that the Arab nation states never succeeded in becoming political units with an adequate legitimacy base or institutionalized mechanisms to resolve conflicts and manage social change. With power structures that were never legitimate, they achieved stability – as became fully evident in Syria and Iraq – through force. The Arab Spring, the moment for those seeking change, steered these countries onto the path of state failure. The weakness of many Arab nation states, their rapid decline – in which central governments lost their authority and ability to govern – and particularly their monopoly on the use of force, created the conditions for the rise of other, non-state actors,[4] such as the Islamic State. These movements have exploited the absence of government while conquering territories and populations, appropriating state functions, and presenting alternate ideologies in order to reshape the region.

The Islamic State and the rising number of failed states are thus interconnected. The failed states are no longer mere local events or human tragedies limited to one state or one people at a time. As arenas of conflict, they have become a regional and international challenge due to the instability that they export.[5] With its decentralized network, the Islamic State too is no longer a local phenomenon limited to areas in Iraq and Syria. Present throughout the Middle East,[6] proxies are gradually and continuously formed and nurtured in East Asia, Western Europe, and North America as part of its effort to change the global order and challenge the West's fundamental values.

What is a Failed State, and How Did It Become an International Challenge?

A failed state[7] is defined or diagnosed as such by its non-existent or limited ability to provide its citizens with minimal personal security.[8] Weakened governance stems from blatant weakness in a central government and the loss of a state's monopoly on the use of force. "Governance" reflects how well state institutions function by virtue of the government's "stateness"[9] and the extent to which law enforcement and regulatory bodies can do their job in a way that allows the state to manage the economy, realize its sovereignty, and provide its citizens with adequate (domestic and external) security, law and order, and health and educational services.[10]

In failed states, ungoverned outlying areas expand and become arenas that allow and encourage activity by external actors, both state and non-state. The latter further destabilize the principle of "stateness," increase chaos, and help export violence and instability to the territory of the failed state. Non-state actors manage to seize control of locales and populations, and then undergo a process of institutionalization in order to improve their mechanisms of control over land and people. Such processes of institutionalization turn non-state actors into semi-state actors, for example, Hamas in the Gaza Strip, Hezbollah in southern Lebanon, and the Islamic State in Iraq and Syria.[11]

Countries suffering from internal fragmentation and weak or non-functional institutions are liable to become failed states. Michael Hudson has classified various nations on a continuum from fragile to stable to dynamic, with reference to these two variables. According to his conclusions, when effectivity is low and fragmentation high, a state's stability is threatened.[12]

	Low political-identity fragmentation	High political-identity fragmentation
High government effectivity	Dynamic: China, Turkey, Chile	Fragile but controlled: Saudi Arabia, Syria (the latter before 2011)
Low government effectivity	Stable but sluggish: Armenia, Bangladesh, Tanzania	Fragile and unstable: Nigeria, Somalia, Libya, Iraq, Syria (the latter 3 states after 2011)

Many nations around the world lie somewhere along the continuum of different degrees of state failure.[13] The uniqueness and degree of state failure in each case are a consequence of the connection between the seriousness of the threat and internal and external challenges on the one hand, and the performance level of state institutions, or "state quality,"[14] on the other. The lower the level of performance of a state's institution, and the lower the level of legitimacy that the public attributes to its institutions and the government in general, the greater the distress and impact of internal and external conflicts, and the higher the state's level of failure. The higher the state's level of failure, the greater the possibility of the spread and takeover of non-state and other – usually violent – entities that view themselves as alternatives to the state.[15]

Solid evidence of this lies in the Islamic State's seizure of northwest Iraq and eastern Syria and the establishment of the caliphate in June 2014. Ramifications of this will affect the stability and future of Iraq, Jordan, and Syria (the latter no longer constitutes a state), and the entire region's stability and security. The Islamic State generates shockwaves that, like falling dominoes, affect events in distant locations by encouraging subversive elements in the form of terrorist organizations and Salafist jihadists that share its ideology and methods. Examples of such groups are those operating within Libya, the Palestinian Authority, and the Sinai Peninsula, as well as terrorist infrastructures in Western Europe and Northern Africa.

Ethnic and religious divisions and the absence of a unifying national ethos is another significant feature of failed states. A striking example of this is Afghanistan: a multi-national state with various ethnic groups forced to live together. Ongoing friction and conflict have turned the country into a killing field of armed militias fighting each other despite the fact that all are Muslim.[16] Syria and Iraq, like Libya, Yemen, and even Lebanon, are similar. While each country has its own unique ethnic and tribal makeup, each suffers from ethnic and religious rifts and lacks a unifying national ethos.

This corresponds to what Benjamin Miller observes about the lack of correlation between the state and the nation – what he calls the state-to-nation imbalance – as a cause of instability and both internal and regional conflict. Such a condition differs from a coherent state in which the state correlates with the nation and in which borders and sovereignty are not disputed, government institutions are stable, and the government maintains a monopoly on the use of force.[17] According to Miller, even when elites in non-cohesive states try to reach a settlement, internal and external pressures eventually undermine their efforts.[18] There is no doubt that Iraq and Syria are prominent examples that lend weight to his claim. The Islamic State has exploited the processes of state failure in Syria and Iraq – both non-cohesive states – in order to spread, seize control, and entrench itself, and thus establish a caliphate. As David Reilly observes, the failed state phenomenon is not about to disappear, and the clash between functional, cohesive states and failed ones is inevitable.[19] The inevitability of the clash is partly due to the security threat generated by failed states. Organizations that export violence and terrorism to cohesive functional states operate in and from failed states even if they have no common borders. Globalization, technology, and accessibility to state weapons, including WMD, allow these organizations to operate cross-border terrorism and sow chaos at low cost with relative ease. Therefore, notes Reilly, "weak states, like Afghanistan, can pose as great a danger to our national interests as strong states."[20] This insight is equally valid for Syria and Iraq, where the Islamic State – an entity that is becoming both a regional and international threat – has set up shop.

Failed states are incapable of enforcing their authority within and around their borders. This leads to the creation of outlying areas of lawlessness that become preferred environments for the activity of terrorist organizations. Global order and balance rely on the ability of states to preserve law and order within their borders. Therefore, every failed state upsets the world order to some degree or another. The results are global terrorism, mass civilian flight, and the creation of new refugees,[21] genocide, violations of basic human rights, local and international corruption, and rising crime.

Iraq is a conspicuous contemporary example of the processes of state failure. The deep rift between Sunnis and Shiites, coupled with Kurdish isolationism, affects the central government's legitimacy and performance. The central government's weakness is likewise manifest in the poor quality of the military and the frequent low level of discipline and loyalty in soldiers and units. All these factors weaken the state's hold on areas distant from the capital and create highly favorable conditions for the Islamic State. The Islamic State strengthens its hold by using terrorism and brutality against local residents while exploiting the Sunni population's hostility toward the Shiite government. These processes further weaken the central government, granting ethnic groups, such as the Kurds, opportunities to rid themselves of the state and establish independent entities that take turns seizing economic resources so as to further weaken the central government and its institutions.

In the post-Cold War era, internal security challenges, such as civil war, guerrilla warfare, and terrorism – all of which are associated with failed states – have been on the rise and become the chief threat to global as well as regional security in various arenas. Since World War II, more people have died as a result of these factors than from conflicts between regular armies.[22] Terrorist attacks, particularly 9/11, have made it clear to the international community that it cannot ignore a phenomenon that threatens the security of the entire globe. There are also far-reaching implications if several states designated as failed to some extent or other are in possession of ABC weapons (Pakistan, for example). The concern here is that nuclear weapons will fall into undesirable hands. In Iraq, for example, stores of low enriched uranium were seized by the Islamic State in July 2014.[23]

Failed States and the Islamic State against the Backdrop of the Arab Upheaval

The increase in the number of failed states following the regional upheaval is an intensifying threat to the stability of the Middle East due to the growing impact of radical Islamic organizations in the area and the increased involvement of external actors in the affairs of failed states. External players may be states – as is Iran in Syria, Iraq in Yemen, or Saudi Arabia in both Yemen and Syria – or non-state actors, such as the Islamic State in Iraq, Syria, Egypt, Libya, and the Gaza Strip.

What at first glance seems to be a conflict among armed groups and government forces, as in Syria, Iraq, Libya, or Yemen, is in fact a conflict between regional and global powers, between Sunnis and Shiites, and even between moderate and radical Sunnis, as in the case of Syria, Libya, and the Gaza Strip. This means that Arab regimes are ever less capable of enforcing their will in their own territories, while the strength of the Islamic State grows and its influence spreads throughout the region and beyond. Confronting this phenomenon requires high levels of cooperation, the reinforcement of moderates in the region, determination, and global and regional leadership. Regional players have a crucial role to play; without them, the regional system will not be able to stabilize even if the world powers decide to invest tremendous resources into fighting the Islamic State and rebuild failed states.

After five years of upheavals, many states are on the brink of collapse or about to reorganize themselves according to diverse federal models. Independent state entities (such as the Kurds and the Islamic State) may be able to exist without recognition from a central government or the international community. It may be that the nation state is not the ideal model for certain areas of the Middle East. Perhaps models with specific federal features are more relevant to states divided by deep tribal, regional, and religious rifts, as are Libya, Syria, Iraq, Yemen, and the Palestinian Authority. While the international community opposes border changes and the collapse of existing states because it fears for the regional and global stability predicated on the building blocks of sovereign nation states, Arab peoples today seek the freedom to live in political settings that match their identities.[24]

Nation states such as Iraq and Syria are losing control of vast tracts of land that are falling into the hands of Salafist jihadist organizations, which desire to build the foundations of the new Islamic caliphate there and threaten to expand toward Jordan, Saudi Arabia, and the Gulf states. On the other hand, the survival of the Islamic State is not preordained; its future hinges on its ability to spread and seize control despite opposition. The military power of the Islamic State seems limited. It cannot win a military confrontation against state armies, such as the Turkish army, and certainly not a confrontation against a coordinated military action organized by an alliance or coalition of Arabs armies with Turkish backing and international assistance. Iraq and Syria cannot meet the challenge on their own unless a dramatic change occurs in Iran's position or its involvement in present day affairs. The Kurds will continue to fight for their region and fend off Islamic State troops each time the latter try to breach Kurdish lines.

Thus with no regional coalition enjoying international support, the current situation is liable to become permanent and turn the Syrian-Iraqi expanses into a killing field for years to come.

Notes

The author wishes to thank Yoel Guzansky, his co-author of a research study about failed states. Portions of that work proved very helpful in the preparation of this chapter.

1   For an in-depth discussion of the failures of US strategy and its irrelevance, see Linda Robinson, Paul D. Miller, John Gordon IV, Jeffrey Decker, Michael Schwille, Raphael S. Cohen, *Improving Strategic Competence: Lessons from 13 Years of War* (Santa Monica, CA: RAND Corporation, 2014), http://www.rand.org/content/dam/rand/pubs/research_reports/RR800/RR816/RAND_RR816.pdf. See also Michael Eisenstadt, "Aligning Means and Ends, Policies and Strategy in the War on ISIL," Testimony submitted to the House Armed Services Subcommittee on Emerging Threats and Capabilities, Washington Institute, June 24, 2015, https://www.washingtoninstitute.org/policy-analysis/view/aligning-means-and-ends-policies-and-strategy-in-the-war-on-isil; Michael Eisenstadt, "The War Against ISIL: In Search of a Viable Strategy," Washington Institute, June 15, 2015, http://washin.st/1LaOWJt; "CIA Reorganizes for the Long War against Violent Extremism," *Middle East Briefing*, http://mebriefing.com/?p=1627; James F. Jeffrey, David Pollock, Robert Satloff, and Andrew J. Tabler, "The ISIS Fight and the State of the Union Address," *PolicyWatch 2358*, Washington Institute, January 21, 2015, http://www.washingtoninstitute.org/policy-analysis/view/the-isis-fight-and-the-state-of-the-union-address; Tina Kaidanow, "Expanding Counterterrorism Partnerships: U.S. Efforts to Tackle the Evolving Terrorist Threat," Washington Institute, January

26, 2015, http://www.washingtoninstitute.org/policy-analysis/view/expanding-counterterrorism-partnerships-u.s.-efforts-to-tackle-the-evolving.

2   Udi Dekel, Nir Boms, and Ofir Winter, *Syria: New Map, New Actors - Challenges and Opportunities for Israel*, Memorandum No. 151 (Tel Aviv: Institute for National Security Studies, December 2015).

3   On the importance of the correlation between identity and territory, and the instability that arises in the absence of this correlation, see Benjamin Miller, "When and How Regions Become Peaceful: Potential Theoretical Pathways to Peace," *International Studies Review* 7, no. 2 (2005): 229-67.

4   On the conditions in which non-state entities seize control of state functions, see Robert I. Rotberg, "Failed States in a World of Terror," *Foreign Affairs* (July-August 2002), https://www.foreignaffairs.com/articles/2002-07-01/failed-states-world-terror.

5   For more on the problematic global ramifications of failing states, see Amy Zegart, "Stop Drinking the Weak Sauce," *Foreign Policy,* February 23, 2015, http://goo.gl/amVuyz.

6   For more on the spread of jihadist organizations and the Islamic State, see Yoram Schweitzer, "Egypt's War in the Sinai Peninsula: A Struggle That Goes Beyond Egypt," *INSS Insight* No. 661, February 3, 2015, http://www.inss.org.il/index.aspx?id=4538&articleid=8667.

7   The literature uses interchangeable terms such as "fragile state," "collapsed state," and "state failure." It is beyond the scope of this essay to analyze the reasons behind these various terms. For the sake of the current discussion, this chapter uses the term "failed state."

8   As stated in paragraph 143 of the 2005 World Summit Outcome (A/RES/60/1), entitled "Human Security," the heads of state and governments stressed "the right of all people to live in freedom and dignity, free from poverty and despair," and recognized that "all individuals, in particular vulnerable people, are entitled to freedom from fear and freedom from want, with an equal opportunity to enjoy their rights and fully develop their human potential."

9   Francis Fukuyama, *State Building: Governance and World Order in the Twenty-First Century* (London: Profile Books, 2005), pp. 1-3.

10   For more, see Fukuyama, *State Building*, pp. 3-7.

11   Carmit Valensi, "The Ruler and the Ruled: The Civilian Components in the Entrenchment of the Islamic State," *Shorty Blog*, Institute for National Security Studies, June 28, 2015, http://heb.inss.org.il/index.aspx?id=5193&Blogid=9948.

12   Michael Hudson, *Arab Politics: The Search for Legitimacy* (New Haven, CT: Yale University Press, 1977), p. 391.

13   The Annual Fragile States Index, the Fund for Peace, 2014, http://ffp.statesindex.org/.

14   Fukuyama, *State Building*, p. 5.

15 Yoel Guzansky and Amir Kulick, "The Failed State: Ramifications for Israel's Strategic Environment," *Strategic Assessment* 13, no. 2 (2010): 39-54, http://www. inss.org.il/uploadimages/Import/(FILE)1283414450.pdf.

16 Mordechai Kedar, "America Leaves, Terrorism Enters," *Maraah Magazine for State, Society and Culture* 351, March 2014, http://www.maraah-magazine.co.il/ show_item.asp?levelId=65470&ItemId=27&katavaId=3537&itemType=0.

17 Miller, "When and How Regions Become Peaceful: Potential Theoretical Pathways to Peace."

18 This claim recalls Azar's theory on internal forces that preserve the conflict in terms of the normal relations range (NRR). See: Edward E. Azar, Paul Jureidini, and Ronald McLaurin, "Protracted Social Conflict: Theory and Practice in the Middle East," *Journal of Palestine Studies* 8, no. 1 (1978): 41-60.

19 David Reilly, "The Two-Level Game of Failing States: Internal and External Sources of State Failure," *Journal of Conflict Studies* 28 (2008): 17.

20 Cited in Ibid. See "The National Security Strategy of the United States of America, 2002," http://www.whitehouse.gov/nsc/nss.pdf.

21 For more on the refugee problem and its humanitarian significance and severe implications for regional security, see Benedetta Berti, "Syrian Refugees and Regional Security," *SADA Middle East Analysis*, February 5, 2015.

22 James Fearon and David Laitin, "Ethnicity, Insurgency and Civil War," *American Political Science Review* 97, no. 1 (2003): 75.

23 Michelle Nicholas, "Exclusive: Iraq tells U.N. that 'Terrorist Groups' Seized Nuclear Materials," *Reuters*, July 9, 2014.

24 Guzansky and Kulick, "The Failed State: Ramifications for Israel's Strategic Environment."

The Islamic Caliphate:
A Controversial Consensus

Ofir Winter

The institution of the caliphate is nearly as old as Islam itself. Its roots lie in the days following the death of Muhammad in 632, when the Muslims convened and chose a "caliph" (literally "successor" or "deputy"). While the Shiites recognize ʿAli b. Abi Talib as the sole legitimate heir of the prophet, the Sunnis recognize the first four "rightly guided" caliphs (*al-Khulafa al-Rashidun*), as well as the principal caliphates that succeeded them – the Umayyad, Abbasid, Mamluk, and Ottoman. The caliphate ruled the Sunni Muslim world for nearly 1,300 years, enjoying relative hegemony until its abolition in 1924 by Kemal Ataturk, the founder of modern Turkey.

Although Sunni commentators have defined the essence of the caliphate differently in different periods, they tend to agree that the caliphate was founded for the purpose of managing Muslim affairs in accordance with the laws of God and organizing the lives of their people according to the principles of Islamic religious law.[1] In practice, the caliphate has experienced highs and lows over the course of its history. In some periods, it exerted authority over political, administrative, financial, legal, and military affairs; in others, it was reduced to the symbolic and spiritual realm, such as leading mass prayers, much in the manner of the modern Catholic papacy.[2]

The Islamic State's 2014 announcement on the renewal of the caliphate showed that the institution is not only a governmental-religious institution of the past, but also a living and breathing ideal that excites the imagination of present day Muslims. The secret of the caliphate's appeal is twofold: first, it contains a nostalgic promise to correct the modern political order – perceived by many as oppressive and corrupt – and restore the original and just order of Islam. This is accomplished through the unification of Muslims in a framework that will revive their honor and bring them national and economic prosperity. Second, it is a concept that is embedded in the culture and history of Islam, one that enjoys a broad consensus among scholars from various Sunni sects. Yet alongside the shared belief that the caliphate is an exalted aspiration, the Islamic religious clerics hotly dispute its substance, the proper timing for its renewal, the manner in which its leader should be appointed, and its reciprocal relations with modern Arab nation states. From this perspective, the internal Muslim debate over the caliphate is yet another facet of the struggle for hegemony and religious authority between rival forces in contemporary Sunni Islam.

The Islamic State as the Realization of the Caliphate Vision

On June 29, 2014, Islamic State spokesman Abu Muhammad al-ʿAdnani announced the restoration of the caliphate and the appointment of Abu Bakr al-Baghdadi as caliph. His announcement aroused enthusiasm among multitudes of Muslims in Arab and Western countries, who began thronging to the battlefields of Syria and Iraq and dedicating – and in many cases sacrificing – their lives for the consolidation and expansion of the newly established caliphate. Suddenly, ninety years after Ataturk abolished the institution, arguing that it was an anachronistic and disastrous system for Muslims in general and Turks in particular, its vitality reemerged. What had symbolized the backwardness and impotence of Islam vis-à-vis the West to the nationalistic forces operating in the Middle East in the early twentieth century now became the wave of the future, while the Arab nation states, which had symbolized the future as well as the realization of independence and modernity to those same secular forces, found themselves on the defensive.

Time, it appears, has made people forget the miserable downfall of the most recent caliphate, the Ottoman Empire. The weakness of the Arab nation states, as well as the failure of the secular ideologies of the twentieth century to fulfill their promises, has thus brought the caliphate back to life. The vision of a union of the faithful under a single leader, who will impose Islamic law upon all, was once again regarded by many Muslims as an alternative that reflects their beliefs and values, and will achieve their goals. In the internal arena, the caliphate will be able to reconstruct the organic legal and political order that prevailed since ancient times. In the international arena, the caliphate will combat the injustices of both the Arab-Muslim regimes that have strayed from the righteous path and the infidel Western superpowers, and restore Islamic civilization, the Islamic nation, and all Muslims to their rightful place.[3]

At the center of the announcement on the caliphate stands al-Baghdadi, who has become an integral part of the Islamic State brand thanks to his much emphasized kinship with the tribe of Muhammad and his religious education. The Salafi jihad organizations that have recognized the caliphate have sworn personal allegiance to al-Baghdadi, thereby demonstrating the impressive power of the caliph and his enterprise, even though doubts still linger concerning the Islamic State's ability to maintain its unity and choose an heir after his departure. The announcement promises that al-Baghdadi will establish institutions, dissolve oppression, impose justice, and replace the current state of destruction, corruption, oppression, and fear with security. It declares that the time has come for the nation of Muhammad to cast off its disgrace and resume its glory. According to the announcement, the signs of victory are already apparent: the Islamic State flag flies high while the heretical nation states see their flags lowered, their borders breached, and their soldiers killed, taken prisoner, and defeated. Such signals awaken the dream deep in the heart of every Muslim believer as well as the hope of a rejuvenated caliphate that beckons every jihad fighter.[4]

The Debate over the Caliphate in Current Sunni Islam

The announcement of the caliphate prompted a sharp internal debate between the Islamic State and its Muslim enemies, and reflects the struggle between the newly proclaimed entity and traditional forces for hegemony over Islamic religious law. The caliphate does not merely aim to build a new reality; it is at war with everything that preceded it. Al-'Adnani made it clear that the reestablishment of the caliphate denies the legitimacy of every other Islamic organization. The duty of all Muslims is to swear allegiance to Caliph al-Baghdadi; those who do not are guilty of dividing the Islamic nation. This divisive pronouncement was aimed above all at Jabhat al-Nusra, the al-Qaeda branch in Syria and the Islamic State's direct rival representation of the Salafi jihad vision in that territory. It likewise posed a challenge to religious authorities deemed heretical by the Islamic State, such as the Muslim Brotherhood and the religious establishments associated with Arab regimes.

Opposition to the caliphate has thus united sworn enemies, who now find themselves on the same side of the fence against the Islamic State. It has compelled religious clerics of all stripes to tackle the seductive notion of the caliphate among large Muslim audiences, especially youth. At the same time, the counter arguments offered by opponents of the Islamic State vary. The Salafi jihad forces and the Muslim Brotherhood, for whom the caliphate is an ultimate objective, have resorted to convoluted apologetics in order to reconcile their denunciation of the Islamic State with their support (in principle) for the establishment of the caliphate. On the other hand, those Arab regimes that regard the rise of the caliphate as a direct existential threat to their countries have had to explain why, from the perspective of religious law, modern Arab nations are in no way inferior to a rooted Islamic institution such as the caliphate. The religious legal debate on the caliphate has also revealed strategic differences of opinion over the future of the Islamic nation, tactical arguments on the proper and effective means of realizing its goals, and splits regarding the prevalent modern state order in the Middle East.

The announcement of the caliphate reflects the anticipation by the Islamic State of three possible religious critiques of its action, and therefore took pains to provide possible answers: (1) to the argument that the caliphate was established without a Muslim consensus (*ijma*), the Islamic State ridiculed the demand for general agreement among the factions, brigades, divisions, coalitions, armies, fronts, movements, and organizations of the Islamic nation; (2) to the argument that the caliphate was established with no consultation (*shura*) with religious establishments in Arab countries, the Islamic State pointed to the absurdity of demanding that it consult with its enemies, who do not recognize it; (3) and to the argument that circumstances were not ripe for a move of this type, the Islamic State replied that any delay in forming the caliphate once its essential elements are in place – in other words, its possession of large tracts of land in Iraq and Syria – is deemed a sin under religious law.[5]

The response by al-Qaeda, which opposed the declaration and vigorously demanded that the Islamic State retract it, was politically sound but ideologically complex. The organization's founders, Osama Bin Laden and Ayman al-Zawahiri, had discussed and studied the possibility of a caliphate and cited it as a goal, but had done virtually nothing to bring it about. For al-Qaeda, a caliph able to unite Muslims under the flag of Islam and institute a moral and pious society is described as a desirable ideal, one that the organization uses for propaganda purposes when recruiting Muslims to global jihad against the

United States and its allies. Yet although its leaders regard the Arab nation states as the possible core of a united Islamic entity, they have not directed their immediate struggle at dissolving these countries and eliminating their borders. Instead, they have focused on ousting the heretical governing elite, attacking its supportive external forces, and creating the conditions necessary for promoting the political, religious, and social reforms that they preach.[6] For example, Jabhat al-Nusra, the Syrian branch of al-Qaeda, has been engaged in the struggle to overthrow the Assad regime and establish an emirate in Syria, in the belief that the caliphate can be established only at a later stage, after a victory in Syria is achieved.

A positive attitude to a caliphate, along with reservations to its establishment by the Islamic State, was thus reflected in Jabhat al-Nusra's response to Al-'Adnani's announcement. In an article in *al-Risalah*, Jabhat al-Nusra acknowledges the hope that the caliphate may offer to a younger generation of Muslims, who live in the discouraging and depressing reality of Western hegemony over the territory of Islam and who are "grasping at any ray of light as if it were the dawn." The article also expresses appreciation for certain aspects of al-Baghdadi's actions in Iraq and Syria, such as his release of prisoners from jail and recruitment of the faithful to the path of jihad. At the same time, it emphatically rejects the declaration of the caliphate on the basis of three reasons. First, the process is unacceptable because al-Baghdadi neither consulted with the sages of Islamic religious law nor was selected by them. Second, the religious education of the appointed caliph is inadequate; he purports to manage the affairs of Muslims without having written a single religious text of any significance. Third, the Islamic State is undermining the Salafi jihad project. The article also alleges that the brutal executions conducted by the organization not only invited an international coalition against it, but also gave Islam the reputation of being a barbaric and merciless religion, and have thus alienated believers from the path of jihad, which has seemingly become a synonym for bloodbath, slaughter, and murder. Thus, instead of uniting Muslims under the flag of Islam, al-Baghdadi has divided them and concentrated on antagonizing the heretics at the expense of true Muslims. The article concludes that al-Baghdadi is not the long hoped-for caliph who will lead the Muslims from darkness to light, but is instead leading the nation toward catastrophe.[7]

The announcement of the caliphate caught the Muslim Brotherhood in a similar apologetic trap. Like the Islamic State, it promotes a revolution, whose ultimate goal is the establishment of an Islamic caliphate and the nation of Islam as a concrete political framework. Yet whereas the Islamic State regards this as an immediate objective and attempts to achieve it by force wherever possible, the Muslim Brotherhood treats it as an undefined long term goal to be reached gradually, at some unknown point in the future. Furthermore, while the Islamic State rejects nationalism, the Muslim Brotherhood sees no wrong in harboring nationalist feelings for a particular territory, provided that they remain secondary to a profound commitment to the Islamic nation.[8]

Although the Muslim Brotherhood's response to the Islamic State's declaration of the caliphate is notable for its ambivalence, its conclusion is unequivocal: the caliphate of the Islamic State is totally invalid under Islamic law. Indeed, Yusuf al-Qaradawi, today's unofficial spiritual leader of the Muslim Brotherhood, published an announcement in the name of the International Union of Muslim Scholars that opened with fundamental ideological support for the idea of a caliphate, but continued with objections to any attempt to realize it before conditions are ripe. In the spirit of the teachings of Hassan al-Banna, the founding father of the Muslim Brotherhood, al-Qaradawi noted that these conditions included the establishment of countries that would be governed by *sharia*, enjoy reciprocal relations, wield material, spiritual, and human power, and possess an internal unity that would make them immune to external attack. According to al-Qaradawi, al-Baghdadi's declaration of the caliphate also fails to meet other criteria in Islamic law. It was issued unilaterally, without the backing of a general Islamic consensus and with no consultation, as required by the Qur'an (Sura 3: verse 159). It does not advance Muslim goals; it gives the caliphate a bad name and encourages the enemies of Islam to join forces against the rebels fighting for legitimate rights in Syria and Iraq. Finally, it leaves an opening for anarchy in Islamic rulings by creating a situation in which any organization can assume the authority to rule on a key issue such as the caliphate.[9]

The official religious establishment of Egypt, which is headed by al-Azhar University and Dar al-Iftaa al-Misriyyah (the Egyptian House of Fatwa) subject to it, is highly influential at the local level as well as in the Sunni Arab world in general. After the announcement of the caliphate, it began taking vigorous action to delegitimize the Islamic State, as did religious establishments in other Sunni Arab countries. A special body was established to counter the Islamic State's rulings and prevent the spread of its ideas.[10]

Unlike al-Qaeda and the Muslim Brotherhood, it expressed substantive doubts – not only about the timing, form, and expectations of the caliphate – but also about the institution itself. The principal challenge facing Egypt vis-à-vis the formation of the Islamic State and the allegiance it has won from the Sinai-based Ansar Bait al-Maqdis organization in November 2014, was how to anchor the legitimacy of the nation state at the expense of the historical institution of the caliphate. Its position reflects a political shift rather than a change in the concept of regular religious law, since until the Islamic State's declaration, Dar al-Iftaa al-Misriyyah was careful to avoid questioning the idea of the caliphate. In a *fatwa* (religious ruling) published in May 2011 it even defined the caliphate as a religious commandment, noting that modern nation states – temporary substitutes for the caliphate at a time of weakness – have not stopped yearning for a caliphate; indeed, the dissolution of the caliphate in 1924 and its division into countries according to the Sykes-Picot agreement was a disaster for Muslims. Nonetheless, as the leaders of modern nation states have prevented anarchy and provided stability for believers, they should therefore be obeyed; rebellion against their rule is thus forbidden.[11]

After the announcement of the caliphate, Dar al-Iftaa al-Misriyyah too modified its views. It now stated that the legitimacy of the nation state was based on more than the mere absence of a caliphate, and provided other reasons for upholding this idea. In November 2014, Shawqi ʿAllam, Grand Mufti of Egypt and head of Dar al-Iftaa al-Misriyyah, published a book in English targeting young Muslims in the West entitled *The Ideological Battle: Egypt's Dar al-Iftaa Combats Radicalization*. Opposing the claim of the Islamic State, he ruled that the caliphate was not a holy institution derived from religious texts, and that the Prophet Muhammad had not commanded it at all; rather it was a governmental framework that had developed out of the political, social, and religious circumstances of the period. According to this narrative, a replacement was needed to help Muslims maintain their unity and spread their views after Muhammad's death. This, however, does not signify that Islam is a static religion that demands the restoration of a fixed form of government and a return to the Middle Ages. Quite the contrary; flexibility is the soul of Islam, and "the *fatwas* represent the bridge between the legal tradition and the contemporary world in which we live. They are the link between the past and the present, the absolute and the relative, the theoretical and the practical."[12] According to ʿAllam, this means that Muslims are allowed to choose any form of government that serves their interests in any given period, and that there is no religious objection to the definition of Egypt as a modern and democratic nation state.

Conclusion

Although the caliphate is an historic institution, it is also a concept that resonates among many Muslims and continues to affect political, religious, and ideological discourse in contemporary Sunni Islam, all the more since the Islamic State announcement. The debate over the caliphate between the Islamic State, al-Qaeda, the Muslim Brotherhood, and national religious establishments is not exclusively a religious legal dilemma; rather it is a political struggle about who the legitimate interpreter of the holy texts and their significance ought to be. It is a struggle between an entity that is disseminating a radical, subversive, and incendiary message that eradicates the borders of nation states, and forces of a territorially particular nature; between a religious leader with no recognized institutional authority who has appointed himself caliph and attracted masses of believers, and Islamic legal scholars who hold official status and are fighting to preserve their religious hegemony; between an organization that appeals to young Muslims in the language and media tools familiar to them, and older institutions that are being forced to adjust to a dynamic reality and operate beyond their natural comfort zone in order to maintain their influence. The struggle over the status of the caliphate is expected to continue in the coming years and will be decided not only by an overthrow of al-Baghdadi and the defeat of his combatants, rather – and perhaps most of all – in the struggle over the ideology and values in the political and religious fields.

Notes

1   Assad al-Qassam, *The Crisis of the Caliphate and the Imamate and its Modern Consequences* (Beirut: al-Adir, 1997), pp. 21-25; Fauzi M. Najjar, *The Islamic State: A Study in Traditional Politics* (Darien: Monographic Press, 1967), pp. 13-15.
2   "Khalifa," in *Encyclopedia of Islam: New Edition* (Leiden: Brill, 1978), pp. 937-53.
3   Abu Mohammad al-'Adnani, "This is God's Promise," Mu'assasat al-Battar al-I'lamiyya, http://goo.gl/hfLcFV.
4   Al-'Adnani, "This is God's Promise."
5   Ibid.
6   Reza Pankhurst, *The Inevitable Caliphate?* (London: Hurst & Company, 2013), pp. 133-60, 202.

7   Abu Faruq al-Muhajir, "Khilafa One Year On," *al-Risalah* 1 (July 2015): 21-25.

8   Pankhurst, *The Inevitable Caliphate?* pp. 194, 199.

9   ʿAli Muhyi al-Din al-Qurra Daghi and Yusuf al-Qaradawi, "The International Union of Muslim Scholars emphasizes that the declaration of the caliphate by the Islamic State organization in Iraq is illegitimate and unrealistic," International Union of Muslim of Muslim Scholars (July 3, 2014), http://goo.gl/94vCvR.

10   For example, Mirsad al-Iftà, "The pamphlet 'The Takfir of the Arab States' is a new means by the Islamic State to recruit fighters and destabilize the Arab states," Dar al-Iftaa al-Misriyyah, April 10, 2015, http://goo.gl/Kiak4S.

11   The Fatwa Council, "The Caliphate and the Islamic Countries," Dar al-Iftaa al-Misriyyah (May 18, 2015), http://goo.gl/RqTFIs.

12   Shawki Allam, *The Ideological Battle: Egypt's Dar al- Iftaa Combats Radicalization*, 2014, pp. 102-8, http://dar-alifta.org/BIMG/The%20Ideological%20Battle%20(2).pdf.

Radicalism and Islamic Terror: Historical Background

Meir Litvak

Islamic fundamentalism is part of a worldwide phenomenon of an activist and often belligerent response to perceived threats from modernity and globalization – originating in the West – to the religious and cultural identity of various societies. In addition, the resort to religious activism was and remains a response to the severe socioeconomic upheavals these societies have experienced as a result of modernization, especially among those who were not fortunate enough to enjoy its benefits. The Islamic State is the most extreme and violent manifestation of Islamic fundamentalism in the modern era.

Distress and concern over the loss of religious and cultural identity have been especially strong in Muslim societies and particularly in the Arab Middle East since the middle of the nineteenth century. They are rooted in the deep gulf between the Islamic self-perception of the proper status of Islam, deemed as superior to all other civilizations, on the one hand, and the political, economic and technological inferiority of the Muslim world in the modern era compared to the West, on the other. This gulf is especially blatant given the fact that unlike Judaism and Christianity, Islam as a religion and civilization was immensely successful at the outset. It outshone Europe and its achievements were not far less impressive than those of India and China. This historical accomplishment nourished the belief that Islam's success in this world was one of the proofs of its theological veracity. Therefore, the weakness and inferiority of Muslim societies in the modern era and the dominance of Western civilization aroused both psychological and theological distress due to the difficulty in bridging the gap between belief and reality.

One of the main responses to the crisis was reformist Salafism identified with Muhammad 'Abduh (d. 1905), the Grand Mufti of Egypt. The basic premise of this movement was the prevalent belief that Islam at the time of its " righteous forefathers" (al-salaf al-salih), i.e., the era of the prophet Muhammad and the next three generations, was at the peak of its glory and must therefore serve as a model for Muslims for all generations. To this, 'Abduh added the assertion that Islam was from its outset a rational religion that advanced and developed thanks to its ability to adapt to circumstances while retaining its core and essence. However, Islam lost that ability in its third century of existence because of reprehensible collaboration in systems run by tyrannical rulers, corrupt clergymen, and Turkish military commanders who retained their pagan customs. His solution to the problem was to rejuvenate Islamic law by applying ijtihad, i.e., independent reasoning and rational tools to reinterpret religious law in order to provide religious answers to legal and ethical questions and problems that emerged in the modern era, while taking into consideration the needs of the new era and the best interests of the public (masalha). In practice, 'Abduh proposed to integrate a range of methods and ideas borrowed from Western culture into Islam in a controlled fashion, in order for Islam to adapt to the modern age while maintaining its identity.[1]

Muhammad Rashid Ridda (d. 1935), 'Abduh's disciple, followed this path, but the post-World War I upheavals radically changed his attitude and the orientation of Salafism as a whole. The dissolution of the Ottoman Empire, the last Muslim empire in history; the West's conquest of most Islamic countries and the Middle East in particular; the abolition in 1924 by Kemal Ataturk of the caliphate, the symbol of cultural and political unity of the Islamic world; and the rise of secular nationalism profoundly affected Ridda and his followers and generated a sense of intense crisis. They found it impossible to separate Europe's culture from its imperialism. In fact, Western culture itself suffered from an acute crisis due to the horrific death toll of the Great War, after which the values that it espoused seemed more hollow than ever. Ridda's conclusion was to continue to support the modernization of Islam but to oppose unequivocally any attempt to adopt Western values.[2]

In many ways Ridda's ideas continue the writings of the great Islamic jurist Taqi a-Din Ibn Taymiyyah (1263-1328) and the teachings of Muhammad Ibn 'Abd al-Wahhab (1703-1792), the founder of the conservative Wahhabi branch of Islam. Both espoused a rigid purist line in their scholarship and advocated the practice of violence against anyone who deviated from pure Islam. But unlike prior religious purism, generated when religion dominated the cultural and intellectual arena, contemporary Islamic fundamentalism is a response to modernity and secularism, which are viewed as endangering the very existence of Islam.

Ridda was a theoretician who preached through the journal *al-Manar*, which was published in Cairo and disseminated among most if not all Muslim communities in the world. But the person most responsible for the transition from theory to practice was Hassan al-Banna (1906-1949), who in 1928 founded the Muslim Brotherhood in Egypt and shaped its philosophy and mode of operation. Born into a rural religious family and having received a modern education, Banna was himself a product of modernization. He was sent to work as a teacher in Ismailiya, where most of the residents were recent arrivals from village communities who had no social frameworks to replace what they had lost when they moved to the city. By contrast, the urban elite consisted of a large European community that dictated the city's Westernized life style. Banna did not differ from his intellectual predecessors in diagnosing the problem: for hundreds of years, Islam had absorbed foreign influences that had distorted its original message and corrupted the Muslims. In addition, Islam became stagnant and was unable to provide answers to religious and social problems rooted in modernization and cultural Westernization, and the result was a chasm driven between the believers and religion.

The solution he offered was two-pronged: the modernization of Islam and the Islamization of modernity, i.e., the rejuvenation of Islam by means of *ijtihad* – while rejecting Western values and bringing believers back to the correct religious path – together with the imposition of Islamic values on modern reality. The great innovation lay in the method he proposed for bringing believers back to the religious way of life and the centrality of politics in his doctrine. Banna developed the *da'wa* strategy, which combined religious preaching with the construction of a network of welfare services that at the time the state was either incapable or unwilling to provide. In exchange for receiving services such as preschools, medical care, and charity, people were obligated to participate in the movement's religious activity and adopt an Islamic way of life. The Islamization of society was intended to be a bottom-up movement and culminate in the establishment of an Islamic regime (*nizam islami*). Banna explained that politics is an essential component of Islam and that the establishment of a state that would function on the basis of *sharia* – Islamic religious law – was a key Islamic value. He rejected liberal democracy as a foreign idea whose aim was to split the believers to rival sects. Still, understanding the appeal of democracy, he spoke of an Islamic democracy as a model for the future in which only Islamic movements incorporating the Qur'an and *sharia* as the basis of their platforms would be able to participate. Banna attributed great importance to the idea of jihad, coining the phrase, "Allah is our goal, the Prophet is our leader, the Qur'an is our constitution, jihad is our way, and death for Allah is our most exalted wish." Nonetheless, he postponed the realization of jihad to a future time.[3]

At the outset, Banna rejected the use of political violence against Muslims, though by the end of World War II he authorized young activists who wanted to expedite the formation of the desired Islamic state to found secret terrorist cells within the Brotherhood. In 1946-1948 activists assassinated several pro-British politicians, and the Muslim Brotherhood sent volunteers to help the Palestinians in the war against the Zionists in 1948. The acts of terrorism led to the banning of the movement in 1948. In revenge, a Brotherhood member murdered Egyptian Prime Minister Mahmoud al-Nuqrashi in December 1948, and in a countermove, the police killed Banna in February 1949.

Although it was outlawed, the Muslim Brotherhood continued to operate and even supported Abdel Nasser when he assumed power in the military coup on July 23, 1952, hoping to serve as his spiritual guide. But by 1954, a rift grew among them because of Nasser's authoritarianism, his refusal to allow the movement any influence, and his decision to form a secular regime. Following an assassination attempt on Nasser's life in 1954, the Egyptian regime banned it again. Nasser continued to persecute the Muslim Brotherhood until his death in 1970.

The Nasser regime's secular policy and the suppression of the Muslim Brotherhood generated the Salafist jihadi stream in Islam. The founder of that stream was Sayyid Qutb (1906-1966), a chief ideologue of the Muslim Brotherhood until his arrest in 1964. Lying on his prison hospital bed after having suffered severe torture, he wrote his book *Milestones* (*Ma'alim fi al-Tariq*), which is considered the Salafist manifesto. According to Qutb, human reality allows two possible situations: *hakimiyya*, which means God's sovereignty and the absolute rule of the laws of Islam, while anything less is a regression to *jahiliyya*, the era of barbarism and ignorance preceding Islam.

According to Qutb, Egypt and other Muslim countries had entered a new era of *jahiliyya*, because they had voluntarily subordinated themselves to human laws and ideas such as nationalism and socialism, and their inhabitants were Muslims in name alone. Qutb despaired of the Muslim Brotherhood's gradual Islamization of society from the ground up, saying that no modern Arab state would allow the true adherents of Islam to disseminate their teachings, either by applying rigid suppression or by indoctrinating the masses via the regime's schools and media. The only choice left to the true defenders of Islam was to withdraw from society into a self-imposed ghetto where they could live according to Islamic law and concurrently amass weapons and attract more supporters to the cause. Once they were strong enough, the true believers would seize the reins of government by force, whereupon they would use the means of the modern state to impose Islam on society. In order to justify the revolt against the rulers – an idea antithetical to Muslim tradition – Qutb cited Ibn Taymiyyah, who said that a ruler who does not obey the laws of Islam is a heretic against whom one must declare jihad.[4]

Qutb was executed in 1966, but while in prison he exerted great influence on young Islamic activists who were jailed with him and adopted his philosophy. Two events – the Six Day War in 1967 and Nasser's death in 1970 – invigorated Islamist movements and ideas. The defeat to Israel revealed the failure of Nasser's socialist pan-Arab vision, and Islam was seen as the best option for filling that ideological void. Islam was presented as an all-encompassing system offering solutions to problems in this world and the next, and as the only way of realizing Arab and Islamic revival and empowerment.

The Islamists' ideas were expressed in general terms and did not go into details, which would have exposed their impracticality, and their vagueness enhanced their popular appeal. The Islamic solution was presented as authentic, rooted in local culture and most suitable to local conditions, unlike imported solutions like liberalism or socialism whose foreign sources were presented as the key to their failure in the region. The Islamic way was presented as one that had gained great success in the past, but unlike other alternatives, which had all failed, had not been tried in the present.[5] In the 1970s, the failure of Arab socialism to extricate Arab countries from their backwardness was glaring; especially acute was its failure to provide employment for hundreds of thousands of young high school and university graduates. The Islamic movements' slogan – "Islam is the solution" – held tremendous lure, particularly for young people whose chances for finding jobs and housing and even getting married were limited.

President Anwar el-Sadat, Nasser's successor, released thousands of Islamists from jail and allowed the Muslim Brotherhood to renew its activity, albeit with some restrictions. Sadat's policy of economic openness, which widened social gaps, increased the appeal of the Muslim Brotherhood's welfare system among broad segments of Egyptian society. At the same time, some of the newly released young activists established several organizations that strove to topple the Egyptian regime. Three were particularly important: al-Takfir wal-Hijra, headed by Shukri Mustafa, which was comprised of several dozen students and in 1977 kidnapped and killed a former minister in the Egyptian government; Jama'at al-Muslimin, led by Tah al-Samawi, whose members torched mosques they felt were insufficiently religious; and al-Jihad, headed by 'Abd al-Salam Faraj, whose members assassinated Sadat in October 1981.[6] The Egyptian authorities eliminated all of these organizations, arrested hundreds of supporters, and executed dozens. But the phenomenon did not disappear.

The Soviet invasion of Afghanistan in December 1979 was an important milestone in the development of Salafist movements. Until then, these groups focused on battling the near enemy, i.e., the rulers of their nations, based on the belief that these rulers were a threat to the Muslim community from within and were preventing it from realizing its religious and political goals. But the Soviet invasion produced a change in priorities and a new focus on the distant enemy threatening Islam from without. Consequently, thousands of young men from the Middle East flocked to Afghanistan to take part in the jihad and, for the first time in history, created an Islamic version of the international brigades. Among those who came to Afghanistan was Osama Bin Laden from Saudi Arabia, who stood out as a gifted organizer, and the Palestinian radical theorist 'Abdullah 'Azzam; the meeting between the two resulted in the establishment of the Office for Mujahidin Services, which recruited Muslim volunteers, and later, the founding of al-Qaeda.

'Azzam promoted jihad to the second most important religious duty in Islam after the belief in the unity of God; it was, he said, the personal obligation incumbent upon every Muslim. But unlike other thinkers and probably because he was Palestinian, he focused on the obligation to restore to Islamic rule all lands conquered by Islam's external enemies – from Palestine through Kosovo to Sicily and Spain – solely through jihad. He explained that warriors of Islam must establish priorities; accordingly, they were to focus on one arena as the primary aim for jihad but would choose another arena as their secondary target. After liberating the primary target and establishing an Islamic emirate there, they would go onto the secondary target, at which point they would pick a tertiary target, and so on. Thus jihad would continue until the liberation of all Islamic lands and the establishment of the caliphate, which would stretch from Indonesia in the east to Morocco and Spain in the west. Although he was a Palestinian, 'Azzam maintained that Afghanistan should be the primary jihad target rather than Palestine, because the prospects of victory were greater and because Palestinian society had undergone a process of Westernization and corruption through contact with Israel, whereas Afghan society remained truer to Islam, and it would therefore be easier to establish the utopian Islamic state there first. It was essential to wage jihad on the land where conflict prevailed between oppressed Muslims and their non-Muslim rulers (e.g., the Philippines) simultaneously and to the degree possible in the Islamic lands destined to be liberated (e.g., Egypt and Algeria) until the liberation of all Islamic lands.[7]

'Azzam laid the foundations for the establishment of al-Qaeda and was Bin Laden's spiritual guide throughout the war in Afghanistan. Based on the notion *al-qaeda al-sulba* ("the solid base") conjured by 'Azzam, Bin Laden announced the formation of al-Qaeda in late November-early December 1989 in Peshawar, thus beginning a new chapter in the history of global terrorism. A key factor that hastened the establishment of al-Qaeda was the failure of the Salafist jihadist organizations in Egypt, Syria, and Algeria to topple the existing regimes. There were several reasons for this failure: the Arab regimes succeeded in applying the lessons of the revolution in Iran and applied brutal and sophisticated means of oppression to neutralize the Salafists. At the same time, the vicious terrorist means employed by the Salafists – including indiscriminate murder of innocent civilians, dismemberment of live people, and damage to the local economy – alienated many of their potential supporters, who preferred corrupt regimes to barbaric terrorists.[8] The failure to topple the Arab regimes led Bin Laden to the observation that American support was the key to the survival of these regimes and hence to the conclusion that it was necessary to oust the United States from the region through terrorism. In other words, unlike other Salafist organizations, al-Qaeda focused its activity on the distant enemy and turned to international terrorism.

Al-Qaeda's terrorist activity against the United States, culminating in the 9/11 attacks in 2001, encouraged US President George W. Bush to invade Afghanistan that same year and Iraq in 2003. This move provided al-Qaeda with renewed momentum, and volunteers from all over the world rushed to Iraq to participate in the jihad. The first leader identified with al-Qaeda in Iraq was Abu Mus'ab al-Zarqawi, a criminal from Jordan who was "born again" in prison and turned to jihad. Diverging opinions regarding the struggle's priorities developed between al-Zarqawi and Ayman al-Zawahiri, Bin Laden's right hand man. Al-Zarqawi focused on terrorism and mass killings of Shiites, whom he called heretics and traitors to Islam, whereas Bin Laden preferred to focus on the fight against the United States. Al-Zarqawi was killed by US forces in 2006; his successors – Abu Ayub al-Masri (also known as Abu Hamza al-Muhajer) and Abu 'Umar al-Baghdadi – were likewise killed by the Americans in April 2010. This time, the heir was Ibrahim 'Awwad Ibrahim 'Ali al-Badri, better known as Abu Bakr al-Baghdadi, who changed the name of the organization to the Islamic State in Iraq and, in its present incarnation, the Islamic State.

This brief overview of the history of Islamic fundamentalism shows an almost linear progression of radicalization and transition from rhetoric to violence. The process is rooted in several factors, the most important being the profound socioeconomic and political crisis of the Arab world, which created fertile ground for extremism and raised generations of desperate young people clinging to the radical message as a solution to the regional ills. Furthermore, the sense that their culture is threatened has intensified with globalization. In addition, the Muslim Brotherhood's failure to gain political influence via preaching and elections drove many Islamists to violence. Since the 1970s, the radicals shifted from battling Arab rulers to fighting the United States – the leader of the world of heresy – but turned inward with the outbreak of the Arab Spring in 2011.

Despite the common ideological base of Islamic organizations, radicalism usually leads to schisms and power struggles among leaders and groups claiming to lead and save the world of Islam. The combination of a radical ideology, which views the world in stark black and white terms, with the inherent difficulties of realizing their ideals has led these organizations to adopt murderous methods, most of whose victims are Arabs and Muslims whose conduct was not pure enough for the radicals. Not only has this violence not resolved what ails Muslims in the modern era; but it has greatly exacerbated their plight.

Notes

1   Albert Hourani, *Arabic Thought in the Liberal Age, 1789-1939* (Cambridge: Cambridge University Press, 1983), pp. 103-60.
2   Ibid, pp. 171-209.
3   Ephraim Barak, ed., *Islam Is Our Message and Jihad Is Our Path: Hassan al-Banna – Collected Letters* (Tel Aviv: Dayan Center for Middle East Studies, 2012), pp. 17-48.
4   Uriya Shavit, "Jihad and the New Jahaliya of Sayyid Qutub," in *Jihad: Ideological Roots,* ed. Yosef Kostiner (Tel Aviv: Dayan Center for Middle East Studies, 2012), pp. 29-40.
5   Meir Litvak, "Introduction," in *Islam and Democracy in the Arab World*, ed. Meir Litvak (Tel Aviv: Hakibbutz Hameuhad, 1997), p. 16.
6   David Sagiv, "The Ideology of Egyptian Jihadist Organizations," *The New Middle East* 36 (2004): 132-47.
7   Asaf Maliach and Shaul Shay, *From Kabul to Jerusalem: al-Qaeda, Global Islamic Jihad, and the Israeli-Palestinian Conflict* (Tel Aviv: Matan, 2010).
8   Emmanuel Sivan, "Why Radical Muslims Aren't Taking Over Governments," *MERIA* 2, no. 2 (1998).

The Internal Conflict in the Global Jihad Camp

Yoram Schweitzer

The founding of the organization known as the Islamic State in the spring of 2013, and its June 2014 announcement of the establishment of the Islamic State under the leadership of the caliph Abu Bakr al-Baghdadi, caused a split among all organizations belonging to and identifying with the global jihad camp – a camp that until then had been led by al-Qaeda. The dispute began in April 2013 with al-Baghdadi's unilateral declaration of a union between the Islamic State of Iraq (ISI), an organization under his leadership that was a branch of al-Qaeda, and the Jabhat al-Nusra organization in Syria, led by Abu Mohammad al-Julani. The decision, which al-Baghdadi made without consulting al-Julani, set the two at odds; al-Julani quickly rejected the unification, while declaring his loyalty to al-Zawahiri, the emir of al-Qaeda and his supreme commander. For his part, al-Zawahiri tried unsuccessfully to mediate between the hostile parties and preserve unity. Thus in May 2013 he ruled that al-Baghdadi would remain responsible for Iraq, while al-Julani would be responsible for Syria. He also announced that Jabhat al-Nusra would become the Syrian branch of al-Qaeda and an official member of its cluster of alliances.[1] After a year of additional but futile attempts at mediation and compromise, accompanied by grave mutual accusations by spokesmen of ISIS and al-Qaeda supporters, the feud reached a peak with al-Zawahiri's declaration of February 2014, in which he disclaimed all responsibility for ISIS activity in Iraq and Syria, and the consequent expulsion of the organization from the al-Qaeda cluster of alliances.[2]

These events were followed by the announcement in late June 2014 by Islamic State spokesman Abu Muhammad al-'Adnani of the founding of the Islamic State and the self-appointment of al-Baghdadi as caliph. This amounted to a coup d'état within the global jihad camp, and catapulted al-Baghdadi to the top of the leadership – over al-Zawahiri – by granting him the status of a mortal successor to the Prophet Muhammad. Caustic disputes and power struggles ensued between supporters of both the Islamic State and al-Qaeda, who were required to choose between adherence to the old leadership or loyalty to the new caliph. The unique step of appointing a caliph outraged senior Muslim religious figures, who denied the legality and legitimacy of this appointment in particular, as well as Islamic State policies in areas under its control.[3] They responded in a letter in September 2014, addressed directly to al-Baghdadi and signed by 126 leading religious figures. They listed their main criticism of the Islamic State's injustices and its distorted interpretation of the commandments of Islam. The authors emphasized that the use of religious concepts outside the context of the Qur'an and the Hadith was forbidden.[4] They also noted that 24 prohibitions in the Qur'an and Hadith were regularly violated by the Islamic State, including the ban on religious legal rulings (*fatwas*) without a proper knowledge of the Islamic texts, and the ban on declaring individuals to be non-Muslim unless they openly declare disbelief. Other violations include slavery, harm to Christians or any people of the Scripture (*ahal al-dhimmi*), forced conversions to Islam, and elimination of the rights of women and children. The Islamic State ignored this general condemnation, declaring that it was of little importance to al-Baghdadi's caliphate.[5]

The most important result of the steps taken by al-Baghdadi was a tremendous upheaval in the ranks of global Islam. Until the establishment of the Islamic State, al-Qaeda had managed to retain the loyalty of its main partners – al-Qaeda in the Arabian Peninsula, al-Shabaab in Somalia, Jabhat al-Nusra (which replaced al-Qaeda in Iraq after al-Zawahiri expelled al-Baghdadi), and al-Qaeda in the Indian subcontinent (AQIS)[6] – despite a series of setbacks caused by the loss of many of its principal commanders, including its leader, Bin Laden.[7] Once the Islamic State was established, however, splits began within organizations, and loyalties began shifting from al-Zawahiri to Caliph al-Baghdadi, mainly among organizations that had regarded al-Qaeda and above all its supreme commander as a supreme guide, a model for imitation, and a source with whom to identify.

For example, since its establishment, the Islamic State has succeeded in recruiting organizations and factions that had formerly identified with al-Qaeda, and some were joined in thirty-four provinces (*wilayats*) operating in Iraq,

Syria, Egypt, Libya, Yemen, Algeria, Saudi Arabia, Khorasan (Afghanistan-Pakistan-Central Asian republics), the northern Caucasus, and Nigeria. Various organizations in these countries swore allegiance to al-Baghdadi after a long process, during which they were carefully evaluated by the Islamic State and found suitable to be accepted as subordinate partners. The criteria considered included their potential contribution to promotion of Islamic State interests, their operational capability, their control of sizable territories, their ability to unite other organizations under their leadership, and their utter loyalty to the idea of the Islamic caliphate. These organizations had previously identified chiefly with al-Qaeda; some had even expressed loyalty to that organization, which they now redirected to the Islamic State. Among the most prominent of these is Ansar Bait al-Maqdis, an Egyptian Salafi organization operating mainly in the Sinai Peninsula but also in Egypt itself. Having expressed loyalty to Bin Laden and al-Zawahiri, his successor, when it was founded in late 2011, it swore allegiance to the Islamic State in November 2014. Noteworthy too is that certain factions active in Egypt have not changed their affiliation, as in the case of al-Murabitun, led by Hisham Ashmawi, who shifted its affiliation with Ansar Bait al-Maqdis to operate independently with leanings to al-Qaeda.[8]

Another organization in a different geographical region that once sided with al-Qaeda without officially belonging to its cluster of alliances but has since joined the Islamic State is Boko Haram in Nigeria. Its close connections to al-Qaeda and its partners, mainly in the Maghreb and Somalia, were reflected in the training of its operatives and its financing by al-Qaeda partner organizations. Boko Haram gradually came to cooperate with the Islamic State, with which it was officially united in March 2015, when its leader, Abubakar Shekau, swore allegiance to al-Baghdadi. A similar process took place with groups such as Okba ibn Nafaa in Tunisia and Ansar al-Sharia in Libya, combatants who had left the Caucasian Emirate in Chechnya and Dagestan, and factions that had left the Taliban and its partners in Afghanistan and have now been recognized as "Wilayat Khorasan." Other groups, including al-Ansar al-Dawla al-Islamiya and Battalions of Omar al-Hadid in the Gaza Strip, and organizations in Southeast Asia such as Abu Sayyaf in the Philippines and Jamaah Ansharut Tauhid (JAT) in Indonesia have likewise made this move. Particularly noteworthy was the shift in allegiance by the Islamic Movement of Uzbekistan (IMU), which for many years had been one of al-Qaeda's most prominent allies and closest collaborators in

Afghanistan and Pakistan. Following the announcement of the death of Mullah Omar, the original leader of the Taliban and the emir of al-Qaeda and its partners, IMU swore allegiance to al-Baghdadi on July 31, 2015.[9]

The prevailing sentiment in the public and institutional discourse – within the intelligence community, academia, and media – on the conflict between the two camps assigns a clear victory to the Islamic State. The most unequivocal and pessimistic assessment of al-Qaeda's chance of surviving its conflict with the Islamic State has come from no other than al-Qaeda authoritative supporters, whose names were conspicuous among the signatures in the letter against the appointment of al-Baghdadi. In a rare interview with the *New York Times* in June 2015, Abu Muhammad al-Maqdisi and Abu Qatada – two of al-Qaeda's most important religious guides and advocates – asserted that the organization had reached the end of the road and had lost its struggle against the Islamic State.[10] Their assessment was based on an image of the Islamic State as an invincible successful terrorist entity with military achievements and the ability to conquer and control large swaths of land, mainly in Iraq and Syria, and enjoy unprecedented worldwide media coverage – in contrast to al-Qaeda, which is having difficulty mobilizing material support and finding new recruits among young Muslims.

At the end of 2015, a year and a half after the establishment of the Islamic State and the declaration of the caliphate, the names ISIS and Islamic State appear on Google more than 240 million times, as compared to some 50 million references to al-Qaeda. The Islamic State's sophisticated strategy is based on operations in cyberspace, which it conducts through its media division on social media channels: YouTube, Facebook, Twitter, Tumblr, and others. In addition to this activity, admirers and supporters of the organization engage in independent media activity and promote the organization's interests on social media; together they are creating an effective system of non-military "soft" power.[11] Al-Qaeda and its partners, on the other hand, who were once perceived as masters in the use of the "old media" to promote their agenda of global jihad and who are in fact active in "modern" social media, are at this point either too busy or incapable of competing with the Islamic State, due to constraints in means and manpower. Instead, they are focusing their efforts mainly on fortifying their position in various theaters of conflict, where they are again competing with Islamic State operatives for dominance among the supporters of global jihad.

The military struggle between the two camps is conducted on various fronts, with its clearest expression in Syria, currently a key jihad arena. Jabhat al-Nusra, in cooperation with organizations that are members of local coalitions, such as Jaish al-Fatah and Ansar al-Sharia, are fighting the Islamic State (and the regime's forces) in the provinces of Idlib, Daraa, and Aleppo.[12] In Libya, the organizations supporting al-Qaeda, including Majlis Shura Derna, which has joined the Abu Salim Martyrs Brigade, are fighting the partners of the Islamic State. In the Caucasus, enmity exists between the Caucasus Emirate, which swore allegiance to al-Qaeda in the summer of 2014,[13] and other members of the Emirate that swore allegiance and were accepted into the Islamic State in June 2015. In Afghanistan, the new Taliban leader, Mullah Akhtar Mohammad Mansoor, reaffirmed his support for al-Qaeda after receiving an oath of allegiance from al-Zawahiri in August 2015.[14] As for Yemen and Saudi Arabia, it appears that al-Qaeda in the Arabian Peninsula has not yet spoken its final word in the campaign against the Islamic State. Despite a number of showcase terrorist attacks by organizations identifying with the Islamic State in these two countries, it appears that jihad adherents are more inclined to support al-Qaeda and its partners in this region. In Africa, too, neither party has an advantage at this stage; in Nigeria, Boko Haram supports the Islamic State, while in Somalia, al-Shabaab is a supporter and representative of al-Qaeda.

Despite the momentum and victorious image enjoyed by the Islamic State as an independent entity with the grandiose ambitions of conquering territory and establishing a caliphate, it is only at the beginning of its road, especially as it is facing a coalition of over sixty Arab and Western countries. On the other hand, al-Qaeda – which until recently was perceived by many as the most dangerous terrorist threat of all – is benefiting from the distraction of the international coalition, and behind the smokescreen created by the Islamic State, is taking advantage of the opportunity to rebuild and consolidate its infrastructure in various locations throughout the world. It thus appears that despite the decisiveness with which the Islamic State has been crowned as the new undisputed leader of the global jihad camp, it is still premature to discount the influence of al-Qaeda and its cluster of alliances on the global terrorism map.

The rivalry between al-Qaeda and its partners and the Islamic State and its supporters is caused by a dispute not about vision, but rather about the strategy and the most effective pace and method to achieve it. The bitter feud between them is to a great extent the result of personal and organizational competition over prestige and power. It is entirely possible that at some point, after the leaders of al-Qaeda and the Islamic State are no longer active, and especially given the possibility that the two camps will suffer severe setbacks at the hands of the international coalition operating against them, the two organizations will revert to cooperative action in order to defend themselves and promote their dream of reclaiming Islam's glory and supremacy. Most likely the current bitter struggle for the allegiance and support of admirers will continue in the short term. In the future, however, they are liable to act as a team, thereby aggravating the international jihad terrorist threat, both individually and in tandem. The leaders of the international coalition against terrorism should therefore continue to attack both camps, which despite their antagonism, embrace the same ideology and espouse similar goals, even if their current paths are different and subject to internal dispute. As both sides are of the same nature, the campaign against al-Qaeda and its allies must continue in full force, side by side with present efforts to halt the spread of the Islamic State. The rivalry between them is fertile ground for divide-and-conquer tactics. Herein lies an opportunity for operational intelligence warfare to pitch the two camps against each other by recruiting their operatives and conducting operational psychological warfare in order to exacerbate the conflict. The extreme cruelty of the Islamic State, which overshadows that of al-Qaeda and its partners, must not be allowed to create the illusion that any understanding can be reached with either organization. The leaders of the campaign against them must be responsible for achieving victory over both.

Notes

I would like to thank Tali Rotschild, a research assistant in the Terrorism and Low Intensity Conflict Program, for her help in writing this article.

1   Basma Atassi, "Qaeda Chief Annuls Syrian-Iraqi Jihad," *al-Jazeera*, June 9, 2013, http://www.aljazeera.com/news/middleeast/2013/06/2013699425657882. html?utm=from_old_mobile mergerle.

2   Liz Sly, "Al-Qaeda Disavows any Ties with Radical Islamist ISIS Group in Syria, Iraq," *Washington Post*, February 3, 2014, https://www.washingtonpost.com/world/ middle_east/al-qaeda-disavows-any-ties-with-radical-islamist-isis-group-in-syria-iraq/2014/02/03/2c9afc3a-8cef-11e3-98ab-fe5228217bd1_story.html; Thomas Joscelyn, "Al-Qaeda's General Command Disowns the Islamic State of Iraq and

the Sham," *Long War Journal*, February 3, 2014, http://www.longwarjournal.org/archives/2014/02/al_qaedas_general_co.php.

3   Agence France Presse-Amman, "Jordan's Abu Qatada Says Caliphate Declaration 'Void,'" *al-Arabiya,* July 16, 2014, http://english.alarabiya.net/en/News/middle-east/2014/07/16/Jordan-s-Abu-Qatada-says-caliphate-declaration-void-.html; Tariq Abd al-Halim and Hani al-Sibai, "A Declaration of Innocence so as to Allow Both Those Who Die and Those Who Live [to] Be Aware," *Jihadology*, April 19, 2014, http://jihadology.net/2014/04/19/new-audio-message-from-dr-%E1%B9%ADariq-abd-al-%E1%B8%A5alim-and-hani-al-sibai-a-declaration-of-innocence-so-as-to-allow-both-those-who-die-and-those-who-live-be-aware.

4   Samuel Oakford, "Muslim Scholars Make the Theological Case Against the Islamic State," *Vice News*, September 25, 2014, https://news.vice.com/article/muslim-scholars-make-the-theological-case-against-the-islamic-state.

5   Ibid.

6   Al-Qaeda in the Indian Subcontinent was founded and joined the al-Qaeda alliance in September 2014.

7   Yoram Schweitzer, "Al-Qaeda and Global Jihad in Search of Direction," in *Strategic Survey for Israel 2012-2013*, eds. Anat Kurz and Shlom Brom (Tel Aviv: Institute for National Security Studies, 2013), http://www.inss.org.il/uploadImages/systemFiles/INSS2012Balance_ENG_Schweitzer.pdf.

8   "Muhammad Jamal Network (MJN) al-Qaeda in Egypt Jamal Network," Global Security, n. d., http://www.globalsecurity.org/military/world/para/mjn.htm; Ahmed Eleiba, "What is the Sgnificance of al-Qaeda's Presence in Sinai?" August 2, 2015, *al Ahram*, http://english.ahram.org.eg/News/136788.aspx.

9   Jund Allah Studios, "Jund Allah Studios Presents a New Video Message from the Islamic Movement of Uzbekistan: 'Ramadan Message and Announcing in it its Bay'ah to the Caliph of the Muslims Abū Bakr al-Baghdādī,'" *Jihadology,* July 31, 2015, http://jihadology.net/2015/07/31/jund-allah-studios-presents-a-new-video-message-from-the-islamic-movement-of-uzbekistan-rama%E1%B8%8Dan-message-and-announcing-in-it-its-bayah-to-the-caliph-of-the-muslims-abu-bakr-al-bagh; Soufan Group, "Islamic State Gains Traction in Southeast Asia," Soufan Group, August 12, 2014, http://soufangroup.com/tsg-intelbrief-islamic-state-gains-traction-in-southeast-asia.

10   Shiv Malik, Ali Younes, Spencer Ackerman, and Mustafa Khalili, "How Isis Crippled al-Qaida," *The Guardian*, June 10, 2015, http://www.theguardian.com/world/2015/jun/10/how-isis-crippled-al-qaida.

11   Aaron Y. Zelin, "Picture or It Didn't Happen: A Snapshot of the Islamic State's Official Media Output," *Perspectives on Terrorism* 9, no. 4 (2015): 88, http://www.terrorismanalysts.com/pt/index.php/pot/article/view/445/html.

12   "Syria – Announcement of the Formation of a New Rebel Coalition for Aleppo, Ansar ash-Sharia," *Live Leak*, July 2, 2015, http://www.liveleak.com/view?i=1a0_1435867919; Ben Hubbard, "Al-Qaeda Tries a New Tactic to

Keep Power: Sharing It," *New York Times,* June 9, 2015, http://www.nytimes.com/2015/06/10/world/middleeast/qaeda-yemen-syria-houthis.html?_r=0; Meir Amit Intelligence and Terrorism Information Center, "Spotlight on Global Jihad (July 2-8, 2015)," Israel Intelligence Heritage and Commemoration Center, http://www.terrorism-info.org.il/Data/articles/Art_20838/H_113_15_1417619654.pdf.

13 Bill Roggio & Thomas Joscelyn, "Russian Troops Kill Leader of Islamic Caucasus Emirate," *Long War Journal,* April 19, 2015, http://www.longwarjournal.org/archives/2015/04/russian-troops-kill-leader-of-islamic-caucasus-emirate.php.

14 Alessandria Masi, "Al-Qaeda Leader Pledges Allegiance to New Afghan Taliban Leader as ISIS Makes Gains in Afghanistan," *Ibtimes,* August 13, 2015, http://www.ibtimes.com/al-qaeda-leader-pledges-allegiance-new-afghan-taliban-leader-isis-makes-gains-2053044.

Part II

The Sum of Its Parts

The Islamic State as an Intelligence Challenge

David Siman-Tov and Yotam Hacohen

The Islamic State is a rising force in the Middle East, acting to overturn the existing political order by erasing borders, overthrowing regimes, and leading a religious war. Since from an intelligence perspective its defining characteristics, both strategic and operational, differ from those that traditionally occupy the intelligence communities in the West, it presents a significant intelligence challenge.

The intelligence on the Islamic State is not of a uniform fabric, and it is not possible to detach it from the viewpoint of the interested party of a specific intelligence facility. Therefore, the intelligence challenge must be broken down into the various levels of security activity: national intelligence required for decision makers; strategic intelligence required for military leaders; operational intelligence required for arena commanders in the campaign; and tactical intelligence required for the combat forces, in the air or on the ground.[1]

Before analyzing the Islamic State intelligence challenge, it is important to distinguish between generic intelligence viewpoints vis-à-vis strategic and operational challenges, and the unique intelligence challenge that the Islamic State constitutes in Western eyes (the countless issues that derive from the intelligence war being waged against the Islamic State will not be specified here). The Islamic State represents a substantive enemy for the United States and its allies, which are fighting it with varying degrees of intensity. Although Israel constitutes an enemy for the Islamic State, as affirmed by different Islamic State spokesmen, it is not part of the entity's active efforts. However, Israel must make stringent assumptions in everything pertaining to the threats facing it from the Islamic State. These assumptions should be reflected, first and foremost, in activity by the Israeli intelligence community to study and prepare a response to the Islamic State.

The Islamic State is a broad phenomenon with branches primarily in the Middle East and Africa. Although based in Iraq and Syria, its widespread cyber activity brings it well within the purview of the West. The question of the systemic boundaries for the intelligence discussion of this phenomenon is a strategic decision stemming from the strategic context of those involved. The choice by the United States to deal with the regional presence of the Islamic State stems from the American strategic effort to stabilize the region while confronting radical Islamism. In contrast, the Israeli perspective should deal with operational military threats that the Islamic State poses on its borders.

This article will focus on the intelligence challenge posed by the Islamic State from the perspective of the party managing the overall effort against it, i.e., the international coalition led by the United States, and focus on the ramifications for Israel. It will not deal with the rising intelligence efforts of the EU countries to confront the Islamic State, which are focused primarily on homeland security issues. Despite a certain similarity between Israel and the US regarding the intelligence challenge, the nature of the confrontation that is liable to take place between Israel and the Islamic State is completely different. Therefore, the Israeli intelligence effort should be discussed separately regarding the challenge that it presents. This differentiation stems from the understanding of the strategic and operational context of the Islamic State phenomenon from Israel's standpoint, which relates to the phenomenon as it is manifested primarily in Iraq and Syria, and secondarily in the Sinai Peninsula. In this context, there are two central aspects: Israel's geopolitical interests in the northeastern territory and the impact of the rise of the Islamic State there, as well as the need for Israel to preserve a proper defense and security regime inside its borders.

The Strategic Surprise in the Rise of the Islamic State
The meteoric rise of the Islamic State in June 2014 stunned the intelligence organizations in the United States. President Obama criticized the American intelligence community,[2] claiming that it did not correctly assess events in Syria and the inability of the Iraqi army to prevent Salafi jihadi forces from establishing themselves in the territory. Another claim maintains that intelligence organizations in the US were surprised by the founding of ISIS and the speed of its advance toward the announcement of a caliphate, and

estimated that the central threat expected in this context is the return of volunteers to their Western home countries.[3]

In response to the complaints, American intelligence organizations recalled a warning that they issued in 2012 in regard to the strengthening of Salafi jihadi forces, which the administration did not address thoroughly because it did not want to become entangled once again in Iraq.[4] There were those who explained the intelligence gap by claiming that it is not the function of intelligence to monitor the Iraqi forces, which were regarded as allied forces. This argument was accompanied by an emphasis on the reduction in intelligence gathering ability in Iraq beginning in 2011.[5] Others explained that Islamic State leaders surprised themselves by their success – a claim that relates to the chaotic nature of strategic emergence, and especially for the reality in the Middle East in recent years. However, this in itself questions the very ability of intelligence bodies to supply early warning.

Nevertheless, the major significance of the aspects described above is not intelligence-related or oversight in early warning, but rather the ongoing irrelevance of Western intelligence for the current strategic environment in the Middle East. This, first and foremost, is due to the lack of understanding of the region and environment in which the Islamic State grew, as well as a lack of use of chaotic-emergence assessment models. The discussion solely around the issue of surprise misses a central function of intelligence – assistance in formulating relevant policy regarding unfolding developments in the arena.

The Islamic State as a Part of the Ecosystem

In order to gain a strategic understanding of the Islamic State, it is necessary to understand the "ecosystem" in which it grew and its overall links with states in the region and other actors. In any discussion of the ongoing struggle against global jihad, cultural and religious issues are especially relevant. The intelligence framework on the national level is required to understand the relevant phenomena and ideology, and specific religious, historical, cultural, social, and tribal aspects. A more particular way of understanding the Islamic State is through a genealogical viewpoint, i.e., the development of the Salafist jihad phenomenon.[6] Intelligence must internalize historical meanings, which include deep theological doctrine. Indeed, the commander of special operations for the United States in the Middle East noted that the West lacks an understanding of the ideology behind the phenomenon:

"We have not defeated the ideology…and we haven't even managed to understand it."[7]

In addition, strategic intelligence on the Islamic State requires an understanding of the governmental vacuum that has emerged in northeastern Syria, as well as an understanding of the battle that the Syrian regime and Hezbollah are waging against the opposition forces since 2011-2012, together with an understanding of the significance of battle for the opposition forces themselves. In order to gauge the depth of the Islamic State phenomenon, political and geostrategic understandings must thus be integrated with a cultural and social understanding of the groups in the territory.

The self-definition of the Islamic State as a caliphate, with the theological ramifications derived therefrom in regard to what may be called "redemption here and now," makes clear that this body cannot be regarded as a state in the Western configuration, but rather as a subversive ideology that challenges the existing Western and national order and has immediate implications for the phenomenon's future development. An understanding of this religious-messianic mindset will also clarify the steps taken by the Islamic State, which in Western eyes appear at first glance to be politically and strategically irrational, and which make the entire world rise up against it. As such, the major Western intelligence conceptual assets regarding Western "rational" players and issues of deterrence are highly irrelevant in this case.

Another aspect of the intelligence challenge is the need to examine the economy of the Islamic State, which is vital for assessing its viability and locating the sources of its power. These should also serve as a source for military targets to be attacked. An additional critical aspect for intelligence handling is the extent of the organization's governance and control, manifested in areas such as education, religion, law, and infrastructures, and is based in part on instilling a feeling of fear and dread among the residents. If the West succeeds in pursuing the Islamic State's centers of gravity, perhaps it will be able to strike it in order to bring about a reduction in its power at home. As such, confronting the Islamic State will occur not only on the battlefield.

How Far will the Islamic State Spread?

The question of how far the Islamic State will spread in the future is very relevant from Israel's standpoint, since it overlaps with the question of whether and in what circumstances the war against Israel would figure among the Islamic State's priorities. The answer to this question is influenced in part by the actions of all actors, especially the international coalition and the Russian effort.

The conduct of the Islamic State until now indicates that it will spread to places where there is a sympathetic ethnic infrastructure, as well as to places in which it identifies a governance vacuum. More than offering an assessment of its plans – which its own leaders might not know themselves – such mapping will help in formulating strategy that, if sound and comprehensive, could have a negative impact on the Islamic State in its efforts to expand.

The Islamic State as a New Operational Intelligence Challenge

The State of Israel has much experience in dealing with paramilitary organizations, and it has developed advanced abilities against the challenges that these impose upon Western armies. The most significant operational challenges that have arisen vis-à-vis Israel in recent years arose from ongoing friction, which makes it possible for both sides to learn and prepare themselves for future confrontation. To compensate for their inferiority, the major challenge that Israel's rivals have created from this friction is "static disappearance." The Israeli response to this challenge is embodied, inter alia, in the creation of a "target bank" for future confrontations. In contrast, the Islamic State has adopted a different alternative: "dynamic disappearance," which is based on movement, i.e., conquering territories or relinquishing them when required by circumstances.

The operational intelligence response that Israel has devised as part of the battles it conducts with paramilitary organizations lies in a combination of continuous intelligence preparation and intelligence control (such as ability to "hold territory") in real time. The most significant challenge in dealing operatively and operationally with the Islamic State is the need to develop a target bank of a phenomenon that is still not active on Israel's northern border. A partial response to this is monitoring the Islamic State's logistical deployment in Israel's direction, if this occurs.

In order to enable the development of a relevant approach to dealing with the Islamic State, intelligence is required – as with any other rival – to identify centers of gravity or logic by which it operates, and if damaged, will impact on its overall performance. In order to reach a relevant operational understanding, one must identify the links between the various provinces of the Islamic State, the manner in which its military array is structured and operates, where command centers are located and the relationship between them, the structure of the chain of command and religious leadership, and the extent of control by the Islamic State in the various regions. Operational intelligence on the Islamic State is required to investigate its logistical abilities, examine the extent of its fitness, the ways in which it raises funds and recruits manpower, and weaponry. This is in order to indicate the weak points in these processes, which could disrupt its activity if damaged.

The Cyber World as Intelligence Space for Collection and Influence

A particular central direction of intelligence activity in dealing with the Islamic State is cyberspace, the media, and social networks. One of the Islamic State's major assets is its ability to exploit these areas to recruit supporters and fighters, as well as using them as a platform for transmitting messages of deterrence and intimidation. Intelligence on cyberspace is required as a primary collection target for the branches of the Islamic State and the pool of recruits, in addition to a central target for disruption and transmission of messages that contradict the propaganda messages by the Islamic State, such as messages of psychological warfare for deepening conflicts and splits between commanders and sub-groups. Cyberspace also constitutes a space in which confrontation with the Islamic State can be created, which will enable familiarity with the entity and enhance the ability to learn about it.

Conclusion

The intelligence community discourse on the phenomenon of the Islamic State initially dealt with the issue of warning – did the American intelligence community warn about this phenomenon or not. This article contends that the critical question is not warning as a separate issue, but rather what intelligence should be developed in the West and in Israel in order to support the decision making process and the shaping of relevant policy vis-à-vis the rising challenge of the Islamic State.

In tandem, it is important to note that that Israeli intelligence requires warning about the Islamic State on various levels: (a) strategic – will Israel become a priority for the Islamic State? When? In which directions will the Islamic State spread? What are the risks for moderate regimes in the region? (b) operational – what are the concrete intentions of the Islamic State against Israel: Harassment? Development of a prolonged permanent threat? Are there operational preparations and deployments by the Islamic

State toward Israel, and if so, does it see Israel as part of the international coalition or a target in and of itself? (c) tactical – is a terror attack by the Islamic State planned against Israel, and if so, what form will it assume?

The fighting currently directed at the Islamic State has great potential for developing intelligence on its patterns of action; it also constitutes a central challenge: the State of Israel is liable to encounter a quick, adaptive rival that knows how to operate in an environment of heavy firepower and a wealth of intelligence, and conduct complex and cruel operations. Therefore, intelligence is required to prepare the system for a possible surprise, primarily out of a need to formulate an operational response vis-à-vis a phenomenon that Israel has yet to experience on the battlefield. Additional functions required by intelligence after the war begins are developing an in-depth understanding of the Islamic State phenomenon as an ideological and military and civilian establishment; an understanding of the directions in which it can spread that depend on its potential rivals; and the impact of action by the international coalition on these directions.

Intelligence on the Islamic State phenomenon must be more integrative than ever before. It must include cooperation between a country's various intelligence entities and personnel (research and gathering), as well as cooperation with foreign intelligence organizations. The intelligence communities dealing with the Islamic State challenge must establish joint teams for developing knowledge of strategic and operational issues.

The unprecedented challenge posed by the Islamic State is addressed without the experience that has accompanied the State of Israel's activity against other strategic and operational challenges for decades. This singular entity called the Islamic State, which operates with advanced methods, including the internet, and possesses the capability to adapt rapidly to modern developments, requires the Israeli intelligence community to adopt similar qualities of quickness and rapid adaptation to the changing intelligence challenge.

Notes

1   This terminology appears in Itai Brun's *Intelligence Research: Ascertaining Reality in an Era of Upheavals and Change* (Israel Intelligence Heritage and Commemoration Center – IICC, 2015), pp. 48-49.

2   Ephraim Kam, "The Islamic State Surprise: The Intelligence Perspective," *Strategic Assessment* 18, no. 3 (2015): 21-31.

3   Peter Baker and Eric Schmitt, "Many Missteps in Assessment of ISIS Threat," *New York Times*, September 29, 2014, http://www.nytimes.com/2014/09/30/world/middleeast/obama-fault-is-shared-in-misjudging-of-isis-threat.html.

4   Paul Lewis, "ISIS Not Comparable to al-Qaida pre-9/11, US Intelligence Officials Say," *The Guardian*, September 3, 2014, http://www.theguardian.com/world/2014/sep/03/isis-militants-al-qaida-911-intelligence-officials.

5   Ibid.

6   Ephraim Kam, "The Rise of the Islamic State Organization," *Strategic Assessment* 17, no. 3 (2014): 42-43.

7   Graeme Wood, "What ISIS Really Wants," *The Atlantic*, March 2015, http://www.theatlantic.com/magazine/archive/2015/03/what-isis-really-wants/384980/.

The Military Power of the Islamic State

Gabi Siboni

Of the various video clips that the Islamic State regularly uploads on the internet, two in particular provide insights about its force buildup while demonstrating the two major components of the training it seeks to instill in its fighters. The first shows children undergoing endurance training as their instructors beat them with various items. In one segment of this video, the group is shown learning how to charge while coming under fire.[1] The second video shows a group of children dressed in camouflage battle fatigues being indoctrinated as jihadi fighters at the Farouk Institute training camp in the city of al-Raqqa.[2] An analysis of a document issued by the Islamic State's education bureau in September 2014[3] makes clear the depth of the entity's penetration in schools, where it has radically changed the curricula to focus on motivation, fighting spirit, and zeal for self-sacrifice.

It is difficult to assess the Islamic State's military strength without first understanding the impact of its indoctrination and propaganda, and as a result, the power of the fighting spirit among its combatants. Moreover, it seems that it deems military training of secondary importance as compared to the effort that it puts into cultivating the combatants' desire to fight. This essay presents the military and operational capabilities of the Islamic State while examining the components of its force buildup: doctrine, armaments, manpower, organization, command and control, and training.[4] At the same time, it is important to consider soft force components – motivation and fighting spirit – which, though difficult to quantify, could have a decisive effect on the organization's military strength.

Doctrine

In the absence of authentic documents that lay out the Islamic State's doctrine on military operations, analysis of the group's operational approach is possible by observing the operational methods of its forces. This may also offer secondary evidence of the Islamic State's comprehensive strategy. Operational actions are designed on the basis of the Islamic State's so-called shock doctrine,[5] which consists of three stages described in *The Management of Savagery*, the formative strategic manual of jihadist movements.[6] The first stage focuses on the establishment of an area of savagery: the organization conquers an area with ruthless viciousness, thus inflicting shock and fear among the population. During the second stage, the organization manages to provide the region and terrorized population with a certain measure of security. In the third stage, the organization places the conquered area under a full governing authority, following the Salafist interpretation of Islamic law (*sharia*).

In accordance with this manual, the Islamic State's operational approach is grounded in three principles. First is the use of unyielding cruelty toward the enemy, so as to set an example for future opponents. Second is extensive psychological warfare implemented through a variety of tools available to it, especially the internet, rumors, and fifth columns amid enemy populations; these lead to the terrorization of civilians and defense forces, which fundamentally affects their resilience. The third principle stresses the mobility and flexibility of its actions, which allow for the rapid, as-needed mobilization of forces and reinforcements. The Islamic State operates through small battle groups moving around in commercial vehicles that enjoy easy mobility and are armed with machine guns, as well as anti-tank and anti-aircraft weapons.

When attacking and conquering nearby targets, the Islamic State uses mortar bomb fire backed by snipers and machine guns in advance of the fighters' entry.[7] When targets are further away, it makes extensive use of suicide attacks to demoralize the opposition and thus prepare the ground for the advance of its forces. In defensive battles over urban areas, the Islamic State uses fortifications to steer the enemy into crowded spaces, where it feels that it enjoys an advantage. By contrast, its fighters seem to have a hard time coping with forces that rely on long distance snipers.[8]

In the case of organized attacks on densely populated areas or large cities, the Islamic State also uses special units to penetrate frontline defenses before the main force arrives and thereby cast terror over the region through suicide attacks, IEDs, snipers, and so on. These forces are selected from within cadres of highly motivated and thus highly effective extremists, who are ready to sacrifice their lives.[9]

Armaments

The Islamic State uses whatever weapons it can obtain. There are many sources of weapons, but most arms are loot seized from the Iraqi and Syrian armies, with some coming from rebel organizations in Syria.[10] A study carried out by a London research institute[11] indicates that the Islamic State also uses American weapons and ammunition, apparently included in a Saudi Arabian arms assistance package. It possesses a large variety of rockets, mortar bombs, anti-tank weapons – including the advanced Kornet – and sophisticated anti-aircraft weapons capable of damaging the helicopters and low flying aircraft of the coalition forces in areas of fighting.[12]

The Islamic State also has heavier weapons, such as armored vehicles, several dozen Russian T55 tanks seized as loot, and even a few Scud missiles and MiG 21s, though it is not clear whether the latter are in operational condition. It uses more advanced weapons as well; videos reveal that it relies on UAVs to gather intelligence.[13] One of the most worrisome issues, however, is its desire to seize strategic weapons, such as chemical weapons; based on several reports, it has already employed chemical weapons in combat.[14]

The Islamic State is also active in cyberspace. So far, its activity in this domain has been focused on two objectives: an extensive use of social media to engage in psychological warfare and to recruit manpower and resources. Lately, there is ever more evidence of the entity's effort to carry out cyber attacks, including on national infrastructure.[15] Although this activity is still in its infancy, once the required resources have been recruited, the Islamic State will presumably not hesitate to act extensively against its enemies in this domain as well.

Manpower

Reports on the number of Islamic State's combatants vary. According to US intelligence sources, in February 2015 they amounted to approximately 20,000; in Syria alone, there are some 3,400 fighters from the West.[16] In late 2014, one CIA source set the number at 31,000 – 10,000 more than the previous count.[17] Estimates of the increase in the Islamic State's ranks run parallel to the estimated number of casualties in the organization, which claims that over 10,000 Islamic State fighters have been killed[18] since the onset of coalition attacks.[19] Experience suggests that many of those killed were not fighters but civilians, some of whom were almost certainly not involved in the fighting.

Fighters are recruited from many places, with most coming from the local population in Syria and Iraq. The total number of foreigners is estimated at 12,000, most of whom hail from various European nations, North America, Australia, North Africa, and the Arab Middle East.[20] Foreign fighters represent a significant portion of the Islamic State's potential suicide attackers – so much so that many of them believe that they are enlisting in order to die.[21] Other fighters are recruited on the basis of their knowledge and fields of expertise, therefore not only for their ability to fight, but also for their intelligence and ability to engage in psychological warfare and offer logistical and technological assistance. However, it is very difficult to assess the reliability of these numbers and determine precisely who is a fighter. The Islamic State is not monolithic, which makes it difficult to discover the contractual obligation of those assigned to fighting units, which could offer evidence of its military ORBAT.

Organization and Command and Control

The Islamic State is organized along district lines. Each district is relatively autonomous, as are the military forces within it. The forces are organized in a way that grants them maximal flexibility, with a notable absence of rigid, fixed frameworks. This looseness allows them to realize their doctrine, which requires mobility and rapid reinforcement. Most of the Islamic State's manpower lies in urban areas and along transportation routes, allowing it to move rapidly in integrated battle groups – infantry, tanks, rapid deployment, anti-tank, anti-aircraft, ordnance, and logistics – wherever needed. As coalition attacks have increased in number, the Islamic State has dispersed its larger bases, and now makes use of small, mobile battle groups. In the absence of designated communication means, it also makes use of social platforms such as Twitter and WhatsApp.[22]

The command and control structures are similarly decentralized to enable the same flexibility and mobility. Commanders thus take local initiatives with no need for a multilayered, complex command hierarchy.[23] In fact, the Islamic State has inverted the entire structure of command and control so that it operates from the bottom up. A hierarchical division of command

and control dependent on strategic, systemic, and tactical commanders no longer exists; instead, the decision making process has been flattened to allow junior commanders greater freedom of action so that they can swiftly respond to operational opportunities.[24]

Training

A significant portion of fighters were trained in military frameworks prior to joining the Islamic State; in many cases – and ironically – this training was funded by the United States.[25] As for the rookies, their training takes place in special camps through programs lasting several weeks. One source that interviewed Islamic State fighters disclosed that the camps offer different types of training that last from two to four weeks. Most of these programs, however, incorporate the Islamic State's ideology, i.e., indoctrination for the sake of expanding the Islamic faith along with basic military training.[26] Although the fighters seem to be of average ability, the training they receive is extremely strenuous and has a lasting impact on their operational capabilities. The Islamic State places great emphasis on military training for local youth, both through its influence on schools and their curricula, which it fashions to its own ends, and through training camps for school-aged children.

Conclusion

Despite the damage inflicted by the coalition, the Islamic State continues to gather strength in terms of both manpower and weaponry. One source of its growing power is its decentralized command structure, which is crucial to enhancing its operational capabilities, tenacity, and survivability. Nonetheless, Islamic State forces have been defeated in certain local incidents after encountering organized, determined enemies. Such was the case in a conflict with the Kurdish Peshmerga in Iraq, a group that also relies on decentralized fighting methods.[27] On that occasion, the Islamic State troops were exposed as being average to below average in terms of operational capability.

The Islamic State's success at expanding its ranks despite the heavy losses it has suffered at the hands of the coalition reveals the extent to which attacks carried out with no clear strategy make it difficult to attain real results. The Islamic State has a highly efficient military structure that is inflicting damage on the Iraqi and Syrian armies. Its operational capabilities are not stellar, but the high level of its fighting spirit and the readiness with which its followers embrace self sacrifice have allowed it to expand its control over the region.

In the meantime, its enemies are collapsing. In Iraq, however, the Islamic State has retreated a bit since the regime's forces have regrouped, thanks to Iranian and US aid. It is important that this retreat guide the policy of the coalition, and especially that of the United States, and encourage it to formulate a relevant and effective strategy.

One possible strategy is to see the threat of the Islamic State as a chronic illness that cannot be fully cured that the world must learn to live with while adhering to a certain regimen of medications. Less metaphorically speaking, this means seeing the conflict as lasting. At this point in time, it is obviously impossible to defeat the Islamic State in full, so no attempt to do so should be made. The objective of all action must be to contain it within smaller and smaller areas, where its influence is tolerable for the international community, and to continue long term attacks. The Islamic State has yet to face professional military forces that possess the skills of integrated battle groups. However, experience shows that even regular forces sometimes find it difficult to confront a resolute enemy that uses guerrilla tactics.

At the same time, it seems that the Islamic State is in the process of institutionalization. Its desire to control the region that it has conquered requires closer control of commanders and battle groups. Its transition to more regular military constellations and hierarchic command and control processes will develop in a natural and unidirectional way. This process, however, is bound to take its toll on the Islamic State, given that it will make it easier for conventional military forces to operate against it.

Notes

1　See the video of March 2015 at https://www.youtube.com/watch?v=f_0dOyUS0Cw.

2　AP, "In an ISIS Training Camp, Children Told: 'Behead the Doll,'" *al-Arabiya News*, July 18, 2015, http://english.alarabiya.net/en/perspective/features/2015/07/18/In-an-ISIS-training-camp-children-told-behead-the-doll-.html.

3　Yehonatan Dahoah-Halevy, "The Strategy of ISIS's Education Bureau," Jerusalem Center for Public and State Affairs, March 2, 2015.

4　This essay addresses the entity of the Islamic State established in areas of Iraq and Syria, rather than its proxies or districts.

5　Steve Niva, "The ISIS Shock Doctrine," *The Immanent Frame*, February 20, 2015, http://blogs.ssrc.org/tif/2015/02/20/the-isis-shock-doctrine.

6　Abu Bakr Naji, *The Management of Savagery: The Most Critical Stage through Which the Umma Will Pass*, trans. by William McCants, Institute for Strategic Studies at Harvard University, May 23, 2006, https://azelin.files.wordpress.com/2010/08/

abu-bakr-naji-the-management-of-savagery-the-most-critical-stage-through-which-the-umma-will-pass.pdf.

7   Alaa al-Lami, "ISIS' Fighting Doctrine: Sorting Fact from Fiction," *al-Akhbar*, October 31, 2014, http://english.al-akhbar.com/node/22280.

8   Ibid.

9   The Butcher, "'Inghemasiyoun': Secret to ISIS Success: Shock Troops Who Fight to the Death," *Pundit from Another Planet*, July 8, 2015, http://punditfromanotherplanet.com/2015/07/08/inghemasiyoun-secret-to-isis-success-shock-troops-who-fight-to-the-death.

10   "Does ISIS Keep its Same Military Strength?" *Levant News*, March 27, 2015, the-levant.com/tag/does-isis-keep-its-same-military-strength.

11   "Islamic State Weapons in Iraq and Syria: Analysis of Weapons and Ammunition Captured from Islamic State Forces in Iraq and Syria," Conflict Armament Research, London, September 2014, http://www.conflictarm.com/wp-content/uploads/2014/09/Dispatch_IS_Iraq_Syria_Weapons.pdf.

12   Kirk Semple and Eric Schmitt, "Missiles of ISIS May Pose Peril for Aircrews in Iraq," *New York Times*, October 26, 2014, http://www.nytimes.com/2014/10/27/world/middleeast/missiles-of-isis-may-pose-peril-for-aircrews.html?_r=0.

13   "Islamic State Weapons in Iraq and Syria."

14   "Islamic State Used Chemical Weapons against Peshmerga, Kurds Say," *The Guardian*, March 14, 2015, http://www.theguardian.com/world/2015/mar/14/islamic-state-isis-used-chemical-weapons-peshmerga-kurds.

15   Tobias Feakin, "ISIS Pushes for Offensive Cyber Capability," *The Strategist*, June 1, 2015, http://www.aspistrategist.org.au/isis-pushes-for-offensive-cyber-capability.

16   Kevin Strouse, "We Don't Actually Know How Big ISIS Is – And Neither Does ISIS," *Overt Action*, March 3, 2015, http://www.overtaction.org/2015/03/we-dont-actually-know-how-big-isis-is-and-neither-does-isis.

17   Denver Nicks, "CIA Says ISIS Ranks May Have Tripled," *Time*, September 12, 2014, http://time.com/3340662/cia-isis-isil.

18   In the absence of an estimate of the number of wounded, experience with this sort of fighting suggests double the number of dead.

19   Laura Smith-Spark and Noisette Martel, "U.S. Official: 10,000-plus ISIS Fighters Killed in 9-Month Campaign," *CNN*, June 4, 2015, http://edition.cnn.com/2015/06/03/middleeast/isis-conflict.

20   L.L. "Foreign Fighters In Iraq and Syria," *Radio Free Europe*, updated on January 29, 2015, http://www.rferl.org/contentinfographics/foreign-fighters-syria-iraq-is-isis-isil-infographic/26584940.html.

21   See note 9.

22   Metin Gurcan, "How to Defeat Islamic State's War Machine," *al-Monitor*, October 14, 2014.

23   Ibid.

24 Dog Leaks, "The ISIS and its Military Tactics," *Invisible Dog* No. 35, November 2014, http://www.invisible-dog.com/isis_tactics_eng.html.

25 Souad Mekhennet, "The Terrorists Fighting Us Now? We Just Finished Training Them," *Washington Post*, August 18, 2014, https://www.washingtonpost.com/posteverything/wp/2014/08/18/the-terrorists-fighting-us-now-we-just-finished-training-them/.

26 Hassan Hassan, "The Secret World of Isis Training Camps – Ruled by Sacred Texts and the Sword," *The Guardian,* January 25, 2015, http://www.theguardian.com/world/2015/jan/25/inside-isis-training-camps.

27 Metin Gurcan, "Don't Expect Peshmerga to Beat Islamic State," *al-Monitor*, September 1, 2014, http://www.al-monitor.com/pulse/originals/2014/09/turkey-syria-iraq-kurdistan-isis-military-pesmerga.html#.

The Islamic State:
Rich Organization, Poor State

Shmuel Even and Carmit Valensi

This essay deals with economic aspects of the Islamic State. It presents estimates of its sources of income and expenditures in view of the organization's effort to found an actual state, and surveys the financial warfare waged against it by the international coalition.

Economic Aspects of the Development of the Islamic State

The Islamic State started out in Iraq in 2003 as the Islamic State in Iraq and Syria (ISIS), an association of Sunni Salafist jihadist groups that used terrorism against the Western coalition fighting in Iraq. In 2004, the organization joined the global al-Qaeda movement, but by 2006 was financially independent. It financed its activities in Iraq with oil smuggling and other illegal activities, as well as with donations from Sunni entities in the Persian Gulf.[1] ISIS's sound economic state, as compared to that of al-Qaeda, was one of the factors that led to its ascendancy and expansion throughout the Middle East.

Over the years, differences of opinion emerged between the al-Qaeda leadership and its Iraqi proxy. These peaked in 2013 following ISIS's drive to expand its activities into Syria. In February 2014, al-Qaeda's leaders, who a year earlier had formed Jabhat al-Nusra – the official al-Qaeda proxy in Syria – decided to sever all connections with ISIS. In June 2014, ISIS announced the establishment of an independent Islamic caliphate in the areas under its control in Iraq and Syria, to be known as the Islamic State. Assessments of the total population under its rule vary, depending on definitions of the area that it controls. The highest estimate is 8 million, while the lowest, which refers to the population under the Islamic State's direct control, is 5 million.[2] To put this in perspective, the entire population of Iraq stands at some 33 million, and that of Syria at around 18 million.

In addition to Syria and Iraq, the Islamic State has proxies in Egypt, Libya, Nigeria, and elsewhere, as well as activists and supporters all over the world. The proxies, which can hardly be termed as such since true proxies would be a drain on resources, are small, local organizations whose connection to the Islamic State is manifest primarily through ideological loyalty.

The uniqueness of the Islamic State, called the richest terrorist organization in the world, lies in its economic independence. Thus, for example, unlike al-Qaeda or Hezbollah, it is capable of generating a significant income flow from various sources and financing its organizational activities without depending on external funds. The resources at its disposal allow it to spread at a rapid pace, and in turn, seize control over further resources.

Islamic State Income

In the past two years, the Islamic State has managed to gain control over various economic assets, including oil wells and gas fields, cement and phosphate industries, farmlands, and food storehouses in both Iraq and Syria.[3] It now also controls money that it stole from Iraqi banks and weapons and equipment that it looted from the Iraqi and Syrian armies, as well as vehicles and buildings. In addition, it levies various taxes and collects extortion and ransom money. It also receives donations from individuals and Islamic associations in the Middle East and Europe.[4] Moreover, it reportedly traffics in women, drugs, antiques, and even human organs.[5]

The Islamic State's total income and the breakdown among the various sources of income fluctuate greatly. According to a May 2015 report, a professional source in the US administration estimated that the organization's annual income exceeds $2 billion.[6] According to a claim made in August 2014 by French Foreign Minister Laurent Fabius, the Islamic State controls several billion dollars. In this instance, Fabius was referring to the organization's fundraising abroad, while noting that Western and Middle East countries must agree on steps to limit the organization's financial resources.[7]

Energy

As of September 2014, the Islamic State controlled oil fields yielding about 120,000 barrels per day, with a daily income of $3-6 million.[8] This is a small amount compared to Iraq, for example (the amount of Iraq's total daily output in 2014 was 3.3 million barrels per day[9]), but for the Islamic State this is a significant income. Factions in Syria, including Bashar al-Assad's regime, have been forced to buy oil from the Islamic State on a daily basis, despite the ongoing war. The Islamic State also controls some 45 percent of Syria's gas reserves (though it lacks the ability to produce gas, at least for now), as well as four Syrian power stations with a total potential output of 2,300 MW.[10]

The US-led coalition against the Islamic State, including its economic sources, began operations in the final quarter of 2014. One noteworthy result has been a drop in the Islamic State's oil revenue. The coalition attacked oil production installations as well as a refinery under the Islamic State's control. Since August 2014, global oil prices have also fallen by over 50 percent, which lowerd the already low price at which the Islamic State can sell its oil. Consequently, its revenue has decreased sharply – to $1 million a day – and it will continue to decline as the coalition offensives succeed.[11]

The gap between the large oil resources in southern Iraq and those in northern Iraq will continue to be one reason for the conflict between the Islamic State and the Baghdad regime, which at present controls chiefly the Shiite region in the south. By contrast, the amount of oil in Syria is relatively small and is located primarily in the Deir ez-Zor district, in the eastern part of the country.

Taxes and Extortion

The Islamic State supplements its income through taxes and extortion, channels that unlike loot, a finite resource, and oil revenue, which is affected by the international coalition's aerial activity, ensure a steady flow of revenue. Here too, however, the potential for extortion is limited by the population's ability to hand over money when economic conditions are difficult.

One of the chief taxes collected by the Islamic State is income tax. Iraqi government officials who reside in the area under Islamic State control must pay up to half of their income; this generated some $300 million in 2014. Companies pay up to 20 percent on contracts and income.[12] According to some reports, taxes are imposed on the transit of goods, and people must pay "service and protection fees" (doubled for families whose children have not enlisted in the Islamic State's military). Families seeking to emigrate through Turkey must pay a per capita ransom of $8,000.[13] Extortion and ransom moneys include the *jizya* (an Islamic poll tax for religious minorities that is akin to protection money) imposed on minorities such as Christians, as well as payments extracted from the families of hostages held by the Islamic State for ransom.

According to one estimate, the total amount of taxes and extortion collected by the Islamic State in 2014 came to some $600 million. The amount stolen from Iraqi banks has been assessed at $500 million,[14] a one-time windfall within the current borders of conquest.

Water

Despite the attention lavished on the oil resources controlled by the Islamic State, control over water supplies plays a larger role in its expansion. The Islamic State and its population are located between the Tigris and Euphrates, the rivers critical to both Syria and Iraq for water, industry, oil production, farming, and electricity.

Control over water enables the Islamic State to continue fighting the regime in Baghdad and its supporters while enslaving people in the territories that it has conquered. In the last two years, it has seized strategic dams close to the rivers' sources, and cut off water to government-controlled areas, including the Shiite cities of Karbala and Najaf. The Islamic State has also flooded areas to gain military advantage. In Syria, for example, the Islamic State conquered the Tabqa Dam and Assad Lake on the Euphrates that provide electricity to Aleppo, for which it now collects fees.[15]

Expenditures of the Islamic State

The Islamic State's main expenses are salaries and current activity. It employs tens of thousands of activists in Syria and Iraq.[16] It seems that the Islamic State is exploiting the economic devastation of the local population in order, whether or not by force, to expand its circle of activists and supporters through economic incentives.

The largest expenditure is salaries, which is estimated to be $5-10 million per month. Until early 2015 Islamic State offered fighters in Syria a monthly salary of $200-300, with bonuses for each of their children and funding for wives (more than offered by other organizations in Syria).[17] Commanders earn more depending on their positions. Over the course of 2015, however, the Islamic State salary offers fell to half these sums.

Each of the other components of its expenditure seem to be lower because the Islamic State supports itself by looting military and civilian equipment and seizing land and infrastructures. The Islamic State's total expenditure has been calculated at several hundred million dollars per annum. This is significantly lower than its income.

Establishing the Islamic State's Economy

The realization of a vision to establish an independent Islamic caliphate responsible for the population under its control is an extraordinary challenge for a terrorist organization in the midst of a concerted fight against the international community. Nonetheless, progress toward this vision is evident in the Islamic State's activities, which include the establishment of an interior ministry and a finance ministry, a police force, welfare authorities, schools, universities (as well as curricula), and even bakeries.[18] The Islamic State would like to govern every place that it conquers, and thus takes the trouble to provide the local population with services such as water, roads, and a legal system.[19]

Using an exact interpretation of *sharia*, the Islamic State brutally imposes its rule on the populations of its conquered territories. This might eventually have a negative impact on the economy in conquered areas, for instance by leading to lower employment among women,[20] a decrease in investments, foreign trade, and so on. In addition, the taxes it collects are more a form of extortion than a social contract of the kind used to found a genuine state. Interestingly, the Islamic State uses the term "charity" rather than "tax" in order to grant a legitimate Islamic quality to its collection system.[21]

In November 2014, the Islamic State introduced its own currency and minted a series of coins: copper *fulos* in values of 10 and 20 (6 and 12 US cents, respectively), the silver *drahm* in values of 1, 5, and 10 (approximately equivalent to $1, $5, and $10); and the 1 and 5 *dinar* gold coin (1 gold dinar being worth about $160).[22] In August 2015, it went public with the process of minting these silver and gold coins, which seem to already be in use in Islamic State-controlled areas of Syria and Iraq.[23]

The income of the Islamic State is currently much higher than what it needs to fund its immediate organizational needs but insufficient to finance the expenditures required to support the daily needs of a state with millions of residents and a state's institutions. However, the Iraqi government, which does not tolerate any violation of its sovereignty within its official borders, finances governing mechanisms that fall under Islamic State control in Iraq, which is what enables them to function.[24] The Islamic State collects taxes on salaries paid by the Iraqi government.

Economic Warfare by the International Coalition against the Islamic State

The Islamic State faces an international coalition that is waging both military and economic warfare. The coalition's economic warfare strategy is based on several main efforts:

a. Firepower against economic assets, such as oil facilities, controlled by the Islamic State.

b. Increased supervision of the transfer of resources and money to and from Islamic State-controlled areas, with Turkish and Kurdish help.

c. Damage to the financial system through internal disruption; identification of and harm to financial personnel; and isolation of the Islamic State within Iraq and elsewhere. One way of doing this is by denying the Islamic State permission to use financial institutions to manage and transfer money in Iraq, Syria, Turkey, Jordan, and elsewhere. Another is by harming the Islamic State's fundraising efforts, especially among foreign donors. The coalition tries to expose the external financial and acquisitions networks used by the Islamic State. As long as coalition attacks continue on the areas controlled by it, the Islamic State will have to rely on these external networks to import resources and equipment.[25]

In applying these methods, the international coalition is careful not to cause humanitarian or ecological damage while attacking Islamic State-controlled targets. This is the greatest constraint on the coalition's efforts against the economy of the Islamic State.

Conclusion

The Islamic State has more than enough assets to finance its military activity and even impose some governance on the areas that it controls. But the organization's transition to an established, functioning state over time will require an income of much greater scope. If the Islamic State manages to seize control of the oil in southern Iraq and engage in its trade (and the coalition does not prevent this), it would earn a huge leap forward in its economic capabilities. By contrast, if it stops expanding or even contracts, or if it loses assets or the ability to exploit loot, its economic capabilities will suffer significantly. The Islamic State's control of the dams vital to all of Iraq is a huge strategic advantage that allows it to have a fundamental, concrete, and psychological impact both on the areas it controls and beyond. This is a risk to the regime in Baghdad and to those who remain loyal to it.

Given the importance of the economic and financial element to the functioning of the Islamic State, the international coalition should continue to improve efforts to inflict substantive economic damage on the Islamic State and thus clip its financial wings, but under the very important constraint of reducing, as much as possible, any harm to the local population.

Notes

1   Jean-Charles Brisard and Damien Martinez, "Islamic State: The Economy-Based Terrorist Funding," Thomson Reuters, October 2014, https://risk.thomsonreuters.com/sites/default/files/GRC01815.pdf.

2   James Fromson and Steven Simon, "ISIS: The Dubious Paradise of Apocalypse Now," *Survival: Global Politics and Strategy,* May 11, 2015, https://www.iiss.org/en/publications/survival/sections/2015-1e95/survival--global-politics-and-strategy-june-july-2015-b48d/57-3-02-fromson-and-simon-02f.

3   Brisard and Martinez, "Islamic State: The Economy-Based Terrorist Funding."

4   Nour Malas and Maria Abi-Habib, "Islamic State Economy Runs on Extortion, Oil Piracy in Syria, Iraq," *Wall Street Journal,* August 28, 2014, http://www.wsj.com/articles/islamic-state-fills-coffers-from-illicit-economy-in-syria-iraq-1409175458.

5   "For Sale: Heart and Liver, Made in ISIS," *PZM,* December 21, 2014, http://www.mako.co.il/pzm-magazine/Article-c9735393eac6a41006.htm.

6   John Hall, "Are ISIS Earning MORE than $2billion a Year? New Study of Terror Group's Income Suggests Previous Estimates are far too Low," *Mail Online,* March 20, 2015, http://www.dailymail.co.uk/news/article-3003919/Are-ISIS-earning-2billion-year-New-study-terror-group-s-income-suggests-previous-estimates-far-low.html.

7   "ISIS has Several Billion Dollars in Donations from Qatar," *Calcalist,* August 23, 2014, http://www.calcalist.co.il/articles/0,7340,L-3639007,00.html.

8   Yoav Zeitun, "Senior Source in Israeli MI: 'Only eight of the 8200 document signatories were involved in classified conversations," *Ynet,* September 17, 2014, http://www.ynet.co.il/articles/0,7340,L-4572229,00.html; *al-Arabiya News,* "Experts: ISIS Makes Up to $3 Million Daily in Oil Sales," *al-Arabiya,* August 28, 2014, http://english.alarabiya.net/en/perspective/analysis/2014/08/28/Experts-ISIS-makes-up-to-3-million-daily-in-oil-sales.html.

9   "BP Statistical Review of World Energy, June 2015," bp-statistical-review-of-world-energy-2015-full-report.

10 Zeitun, "Senior Source in Israeli MI: 'Only eight of the 8200 document signatories were involved in classified conversations.'"

11 Michal R. Gordon and Eric Schmitt, "U.S. Steps Up Its Attacks on ISIS-Controlled Oil Fields in Syria," *New York Times*, November 12, 2015, http://www.nytimes.com/2015/11/13/us/politics/us-steps-up-its-attacks-on-isis-controlled-oil-fields-in-syria.html.

12 Sarah Almuktar, "ISIS Finances are Strong," *New York Times*, May 19, 2015, http://www.nytimes.com/interactive/2015/05/19/world/middleeast/isis-finances.html.

13 "For Sale: Heart and Liver, Made in ISIS."

14 Almuktar, "ISIS Finances Are Strong."

15 Hadas Maman, "Water as Weapons," *MiddleNews*, June 14, 2015.

16 Zeitun, "Senior Source in Israeli MI: 'Only eight of the 8200 document signatories were involved in classified conversations'"; "CIA Reveals ISIS Ranks have Tripled to More than 30,000 Fighters – Including 2,000 Westerners," September 12, 2014, http://www.dailymail.co.uk/news/article-2753004/CIA-believes-ranks-ISIS-fighters-swollen-TRIPLE-number-previously-thought-31-500-fighters-2-000-Westerners.html.

17 Lina Khatib, "The Human Dimension of Life Under the Islamic State," Carnegie Middle East Center, March 4, 2015, http://carnegie-mec.org/2015/03/04/human-dimension-of-life-under-islamic-state.

18 Charles C. Caris, Samual Reynolds, "ISIS Governance in Syria," *Middle East Security Report* 22, Institute for the Study of War, July 2014.

19 Hannah Fairfield, Tim Wallace, and Derek Watkins, "How ISIS Expands," *New York Times*, May 21, 2015.

20 ISIS calls on women to stay at home, as stated in an official document entitled "The Town Document in Raqqa": "Stay in your courtyards, women, unless you must go out. This is how the mothers of the believers, the Prophet's friends, acted," June 13, 2014, http://en.abna24.com/service/iraq/archive/2014/06/13/615736/story.html.

21 Sarah Birke, "How ISIS Rules," *NYR Daily*, February 5, 2015, http://www.nybooks.com/blogs/nyrblog/2014/dec/09/how-isis-rules/.

22 "ISIS Introduces New Coin: The Islamic Dinar" *Haaretz*, November 14, 2014, http://www.haaretz.co.il/news/world/middle-east/1.2485948.

23 Ro Yeger, "Worth their Weight in Gold: ISIS Reveals New Coins to Replace 'Satanic Conception of Banks,'" *Jerusalem Post*, August 30, 2015, http://www.jpost.com/Middle-East/ISIS-Threat/Worth-their-weight-in-gold-ISIS-reveals-new-coins-to-replace-satanic-conception-of-banks-413689.

24 The income of the government in Baghdad in 2014 was estimated to be several billion US dollars, or $217 billion in terms of buying power (CIA, *The World Fact Book, Iraq*, July 2015). In 2015, there was a sharp drop in the income of the Iraqi state because of falling oil prices.

25 Daniel Glaser, Assistant Secretary for Terrorist Financing, Department of the Treasury, in ASPEN conference: "Iraq/Syria: Worse Now Than Before?," July 23, 2015, https://www.youtube.com/watch?v=vN7uePaY9nE&feature=youtu.be.

The Islamic State:
Governance and Civilian Consolidation

Carmit Valensi

In 2004, Abu Bakr Naji, a philosopher and strategist of the al-Qaeda movement, published a book entitled *The Management of Savagery*, in which he presented an organized plan for disseminating jihadist ideas throughout the world and founding an Islamic caliphate. The book's title was a reference to a chaotic "interim situation" between the decline of one ruler and the rise of another.[1] One decade later, whether or not through Naji's direct influence, the idea began to materialize under the direction of the Islamic State, which sprouted from a branch of al-Qaeda in Iraq. In fact, the stages of the establishment of the Islamic State recall the course charted in *Management of Savagery*, especially in terms of the nature of Islamic State governance in the currently chaotic regions of Syria and Iraq.

The announcement in June 2014 of the founding of an Islamic caliphate by the organization's leader, Abu Bakr al-Baghdadi, turned the Islamic State from yet another violent Salafi jihadist terrorist organization into an entity responsible for the daily lives of millions of residents of the territories it conquered in Syria and Iraq. Since then, the Islamic State has integrated itself into the civilian population and cultivated signs of governance. In other words, it has come to manage a civilian system and maintain control over a population in a given territory in a manner similar to that of a state.

Governance by violent organizations is not a new phenomenon; examples date back to as early as the eighteenth century (e.g., with slave leader Toussaint Louverture during the civil war in Haiti). Later examples can be found in Colombia, Indonesia, Nigeria, Sri Lanka, and more recently, with Hezbollah in Lebanon and Hamas in the Gaza Strip.

The Islamic State's Forms of Governance

The Islamic State's nation-building process is based on three concepts that feed on each other: idea, utility, and coercion. These are translated into practice and into institutions that aim to further its consolidation.

On the ideological level, the Islamic State operates through a range of mechanisms that help spread its ideology and implement *sharia*. In the summer of 2013 courts of religious law were established in northern Syria, and approximately one year later in Iraq, to adjudicate disputes between residents as well as between residents and Islamic State operatives. Interestingly, like other governing organizations, the Islamic State places a high priority on establishing courts, and started doing so at an early stage of its civilian establishment.[2] Like its other enforcement mechanisms, the court system has been designed to demonstrate the organization's power, reinforce its status as a ruling entity among civilians, and prove its effectiveness in managing civilian life.

Another key way in which the Islamic State aims to entrench its religious ideology is through the establishment of schools. In Iraq, it seized control of the University of Mosul. In Syria (Aleppo and al-Raqqa) it set up elementary and high schools for the local population as well as for the families of foreign volunteers (whose instruction takes place in English).[3] The educational system is based on an independent curriculum focused on religious studies; it insists on separate classrooms for women and men, and forbids the study of "Western" disciplines (philosophy, psychology, history, and music) or any other subjects inconsistent with its perception of the values of Islam.[4] Along with these measures, the Islamic State tries to erase civilians' former identities – for example, in destroying archives, destroying the antiquities of other religions and civilizations, and even issuing passports and minting gold coins in the name of the Islamic caliphate.[5]

On the utilitarian level, the Islamic State offers the population material rewards in the form of cash grants, services, and humanitarian aid, such as food and water, clothing, fuel, electricity, and medical and sanitation services. Public relations offices occasionally publish video clips that aim to instill the message that routine daily life and commerce continue undisturbed in the city. The clips show Islamic State operatives cleaning and repairing streets, maintaining power lines and irrigation canals, and operating a food market, a soup kitchen for the needy, an orphanage, and even a hotel.[6]

This aspect of governance is designed to confirm legitimacy and win support from the population. It demonstrates the Islamic State's ability to provide order and security, as well as basic goods and services that allow people to lead normal daily lives, which previously were possible only to some degree, if at all, due to the ineptness of the local state regimes and the chaos overcoming the area.

Finally, the means of consolidation most closely identified with the Islamic State are coercion, fear, and violence. In addition to its regular police force (*al-shurta al-Islamiya*), it operates a morality police corps (*al-hasba*), whose job is to enforce Islamic religious law and acceptable codes of behavior. It has also devised a method for collecting taxes from the population, which it refers to as "charity." In Syria, for example, residents of the Islamic State are required to pay a monthly tax of 1,500 Syrian lira (about $8.30). Anyone who does not pay this fee risks beatings, kidnapping, and even execution.[7]

Stages in Civilian Consolidation

The features of the Islamic State's civilian consolidation and nation-building processes, as they occurred in al-Raqqa in Syria and Mosul in Iraq, resemble those of other organizations, and are likely to indicate future Islamic State strategy, in territories already conquered and areas it may conquer in the future.

In most cases, armed organizations do not establish governance in the initial stages of their activity, but only after a developmental period that culminates with control over a given territory. Before February 2014, when it was still operating as an al-Qaeda branch in Iraq, the Islamic State concentrated on military operations. However, since then (in part even as early as late 2013), it has established civilian institutions as part of its vision of an Islamic caliphate, but also for the purpose of obtaining power, support, and stability, while preserving its organizational relevance and legitimacy.

The Islamic State's consolidation strategy is based on a dynamic of juggling the three concepts mentioned above: idea, utility, and coercion. Accordingly, the first stage consists of a military takeover (coercion). Once it has a grip on the territory, it shifts to utility, and develops basic social services, while "buying" the residents' trust through benefits and rewards. In terms of ideology, one of the Islamic State's first acts is to erect billboards around the city that proclaim the importance of religion, jihad, and *sharia*.

Next, the Islamic State takes over existing institutions and redefines them under its identity (usually by hanging its flag from their buildings). The first institutions it usually takes over are courts (as occurred in northern Syria),[8] which is not technically difficult, requires few resources, and generally does not rouse public disapproval. At a later stage, it broadens its ideological message by creating coercive religious mechanisms, while establishing educational systems. The level of complexity demanded by the creation of educational institutions is higher, since these require professionals and experts. At the same time, the organization makes it easier for people to adjust to the new situation by offering them humanitarian aid (again a utilitarian measure). Only at a subsequent stage, after its consolidation in the territory, does the Islamic State add more complicated services, such as electricity and water.

After its utilitarian and ideological consolidation, it steps up coercive mechanisms and threats directed at the population. Violent enforcement agencies are created only at this advanced stage, since excessive intimidation runs the risk of losing popular support. This explains why the Islamic State's morality police, which is perceived as threatening and inflexible, was established in Syria (Aleppo and al-Raqqa) only in the spring of 2015, after other governance mechanisms were already in place.[9]

One strategy of the Islamic State is to use local leaders and tribal heads to fill bureaucratic positions and operate various institutions. It hires them as technocrats in their area of expertise, be it health care, education, management, or accounting. This allows the Islamic State to enhance its legitimacy by co-opting potential opponents, minimizing the resources needed to train new personnel, and creating dependency and affinity between organizations and people.

The Significance of the Islamic State's Civilian Establishment

As with other violent organizations, the consolidation of the Islamic State's civilian governance does not necessarily indicate a process of total institutionalization that will conclude with the abandonment of a military struggle. Rather, it means that it manages civilian activity as it continues to engage in military activity. For the Islamic State, the interface between civilian and military identities fosters a source of strength and a broader support base than those of other violent organizations that do not govern. Consequently, this is liable to make dealing with the Islamic State more difficult. At the same time, a closer look reveals that despite the growing strength of the Islamic State, strain and weak points are appearing due to tension between the two identities.

The first weak point concerns the Islamic State's ability to win concrete support and legitimacy from the public, given the tension between its cruel, violent, and intimidating image and its self-portrayal as a social movement beneficial to citizens and their welfare. The fear it casts over the population may undermine its efforts to integrate the population into a "state" and reduce the use of services and facilities that it offers. Popular support for the Islamic State is therefore likely to remain superficial and fear-based, and consequently be temporary and unstable.

Second, although civilian establishment is likely to increase support for the Islamic State, it comes at a price that it may not be able to pay in the long term. Governance requires capabilities, experience, professionals, and administrative personnel, as well as a large reserve of resources and money to enable the Islamic State to achieve its ambitious vision. Despite its income, estimated in March 2015 at $2 billion per year,[10] it appears that the Islamic State is hard pressed to maintain governance on an ongoing and stable basis. Its difficulties stem from a shortage of professional and trained personnel to operate infrastructure efficiently and according to an overall plan. Thus, for example, its incompetent use of the Tabqa Dam in Syria caused a significant drop in the water level of the nearby Assad River, which cut the supply of water in the area of Aleppo and al-Raqqa.

Finally, a weak point typical of any violent organization undergoing institutionalization and establishing a social or political wing is the emergence of military targets for its opponent. From an organization that initially operated with a low signature and relied on patterns of disappearance and concealment on the battlefield has emerged an Islamic State with an "address," concrete institutions, and exposed officeholders that can serve as targets of attack. Thus, after the first air raids by the international coalition, which included two attacks on the Islamic State's civilian facilities at al-Raqqa, Islamic State operatives blended into the population by reducing their presence in government institutions during the day (at roadblocks and administrative offices, for example), and renewed their activity only after dark.[11]

In conclusion, the Islamic State's ambition to govern is an expression of its strength and its power of attraction. At the same time, it may well prove to be its Achilles' heel. In the long term, the capabilities and resources needed by the Islamic State to manage a country will have to grow in direct proportion to its expansion.

The violent military dimension at the core of the nature and deeds of the Islamic State converges with ideological and utilitarian dimensions that grant it the appearance of a government. Recognition of this and the tensions generated by it in the various theaters in which the Islamic State operates is a key to formulating effective ways to deal with it. Hence, an effective solution cannot be confined to a military operation, for it will also require civilian and political efforts. As long as there is no sustainable alternative to the political governance for the populations living in the Islamic State territories, the Islamic State is liable to continue to attract people who do not necessarily identify with its ideological and religious idea. In the long term, supporting and guiding local parties in creating a just civil infrastructure and fair political representation are likely to provide a solution for the population, and thus detract from the attraction of the Islamic State.

Notes

1   Abu Bakr Naji, *The Management of Savagery: The Most Critical Stage through which the Umma Will Pass* (Cambridge, MA: Harvard University, 2006), https://azelin.files.wordpress.com/2010/08/abu-bakr-naji-the-management-of-savagery-the-most-critical-stage-through-which-the-umma-will-pass.pdf.

2   As happened, for example, in the case of the Tamil Tigers (LTTE) in Sri Lanka, the Sudan People's Liberation Movement (SPLM), and the Rally for Congolese Democracy (RCD) in the Congo.

3   "ISIS Opens English-Language Schools in Syria's Raqqa: Report," *al-Arabiya News*, February 24, 2015, http://english.alarabiya.net/en/perspective/features/2015/02/24/ISIS-opens-English-language-schools-in-Syria-s-Raqqa-report-.html.

4   Aymenn Jawad Al-Tamimi, "Aspects of Islamic State (IS) Administration in Ninawa Province," January 17, 2015, http://www.aymennjawad.org/15946/aspects-of-islamic-state-is-administration-in.

5   "ISIS Issues Passports to Attract Supporters around the World," *al-Aarabiya*, August 17, 2014, http://goo.gl/2CKuOa.

6   "ISIS New Propaganda Video – John Cantlie Report From Mosul Iraq," *YouTube*, January 4, 2015, https://www.youtube.com/watch?v=RN3ktXbLzlY.

7   Sarah Almuktar, "ISIS Finances Are Strong," *New York Times*, May 19, 2015, http://www.nytimes.com/interactive/2015/05/19/world/middleeast/isis-finances.html.

8   Charles C. Caris and Samuel Reynolds, "ISIS Governance in Syria," *Middle East Security Report*, Institute for the Study of War, July 2014, http://www.understandingwar.org/sites/default/files/ISIS_Governance.pdf.

9   Ibid.

10   John Hall, "Are ISIS Earning MORE than $2billion a Year? New Study of Terror Group's Income Suggests Previous Estimates Are Far Too Low," *Mail Online*, March 20, 2015, http://www.dailymail.co.uk/news/article-3003919/Are-ISIS-earning-2billion-year-New-study-terror-group-s-income-suggests-previous-estimates-far-low.html.

11   Sarah Birke, "How ISIS Rules?," *NYR Daily*, February 5, 2015, http://www.nybooks.com/blogs/nyrblog/2014/dec/09/how-isis-rules/.

Fighting against the Islamic State:
The Legal Challenges

Keren Aviram

The appearance of the Islamic State on the global stage, marked in particular by the atrocities that it committed in Iraq and Syria, has led states and international organizations to recognize it as a threat in both the Middle East and beyond, and to take action on various levels to cope with the problem. The United States has conducted military strikes against the Islamic State in Iraq since August 2014. Various states, including Australia, the United Kingdom, Canada, and France, have since joined it to establish a coalition of over 60 countries in order to engage in operations in Iraq and aid Iraqi security forces. In September 2014, alongside Jordan, Qatar, Bahrain, and Saudi Arabia, the US began launching attacks against the Islamic State in Syria as well. This article offers a brief overview of the legal aspects of three core issues in the fight against the Islamic State: the legality of attacks on the organization in Iraq and Syria; the role of the International Criminal Court (ICC); and the problem of foreign fighters.

The Legality of Military Strikes against the Islamic State in Iraq and Syria

The international campaign against the Islamic State, which is known as "Operation Inherent Resolve,"[1] raises questions pertaining to the legal basis for employing military force against it. As clarified below, there is relatively broad consensus on the legality of military action in Iraq. On the other hand, the strikes in Syria have led to disagreements over the legal rationale of using force in that country.[2]

Article 2 (4) of the UN Charter stipulates the basic rule of *jus ad bellum* ("use of force") and prohibits "the threat or use of force against the territorial integrity or political independence of any state, or in any other manner inconsistent with the Purposes of the United Nations." The Charter's general ban on force, however, includes two clear exceptions to the rule: authorization by the Security Council pursuant to Articles 39 and 42, and self-defense (individual or collective) pursuant to Article 51. An additional exception, rooted in customary international law, is consent by a state to allow military actions on its territory. Disagreement exists, however, if additional exceptions, such as the use of force to prevent a severe humanitarian crisis (humanitarian intervention) can also be justified.

The Security Council has not authorized military strikes either in Iraq or Syria due to the international political dynamics among its members. Had such authorization been given, any further legal discussion regarding the legality of the military strikes would have been rendered moot, and the international legitimacy of the campaign would have been strengthened significantly.

The Military Campaign in Iraq

The primary legal basis for military action against the Islamic State in Iraq lies in Iraq's consent. A letter from the Iraqi Foreign Minister to the UN Secretary-General of June 2014[3] emphasized the security threat posed by Islamic State activity in Iraq, as well as the country's request to the international community for aid though military training, advanced technology, and weapons. An additional letter from the Iraqi Foreign Minister to the Security Council in September 2014[4] reported that the Islamic State established safe havens on Iraq's borders, where it trains for, plans, finances, and launches terrorist attacks on Iraqi territory, thereby endangering Iraqi citizens. It also emphasized that the government of Iraq, in accordance with international law and with due regard for complete national sovereignty, has requested the United States to lead international efforts to strike Islamic State sites and strongholds with its express consent. The Iraqi government's consent grants a solid legal basis for military actions in Iraq by the United States and the coalition of nations, as long as these meet with the concrete consent of Iraq in timing and scope.[5]

The Military Campaign in Syria

In contrast to the case in Iraq, the legal situation in Syria is more problematic. So far the Syrian government has not consented to military actions by foreign nations on its territory, even though it benefits from strikes against the Islamic State, which is operating to overthrow the Syrian regime. One can argue that the Syrian regime has tacitly agreed to the strikes, as it cautiously avoids intervening or disrupting them. However, any justification of this type is controversial, especially when it attempts to offer legal justification for military actions in the sovereign territory of another state.

Another justification may lie in self-defense, as per Article 51 of the UN Charter. A position that prohibits self-defense against attacks initiated by a non-state organization was manifested in the advisory opinion issued by the International Court of Justice (ICJ) in 2004 with regard to Israel's security fence. Nonetheless, it seems that states reject this position, which is dubious, especially in a situation in which a non-state organization controls territory and essentially functions as if it was a state. Many states interpret the right of self-defense broadly and permit the use of military force against a non-state entity in another country's territory if that country is "unwilling or unable" to prevent the use of its territory for acts of terror.

A central condition for self-defense by a state is an "armed attack" of sufficient intensity against it. There seems to be no doubt that in the case of Iraq, which has absorbed and continues to absorb murderous onslaughts by the Islamic State, the intensity is sufficient to legitimize individual self-defense and allow Iraq to launch strikes in Syria. When it comes to other states, however, the question is whether the actions of the Islamic State within Syria amount to an "armed attack" of required intensity against them, or, alternatively, justify their need to thwart an imminent "armed attack" under the framework of "anticipatory self-defense." Indeed, there are arguments for using an exception that enables the use of force in the territory of a foreign state to "rescue nationals abroad." However, this is a limited exception and one whose very existence and scope are in doubt. Despite these legal difficulties certain countries have justified their military activity in Syria against the Islamic State, inter alia, based on individual self-defense including anticipatory self-defense.[6]

The United States and the international community can try to justify their military operations under the notion of "collective self-defense," because they have acted on Iraq's request for assistance in fighting the Islamic State, i.e., one or more nations used force after being asked by the country attacked for assistance in defending itself. It seems that this is the principal legal justification used by the United States. In a letter dispatched to the UN

Secretary-General in September 2014, US Ambassador to the UN Samantha Power noted Iraq's explicit request that the US lead international efforts against the Islamic State, while justifying US military activity in Syria with the argument that the Assad regime has shown that it cannot and will not confront the Islamic State effectively itself.[7]

Nonetheless, the legal complexity of the matter may well have discouraged many countries from joining the coalition's endeavors in Syria.

The International Criminal Court (ICC)

The widespread crimes committed by the Islamic State in Iraq and Syria have increased the number of calls for intervention by the International Criminal Court. In April 2015, the Court's Prosecutor published a statement noting the crimes of unspeakable cruelty allegedly committed by the Islamic State – including mass executions, rape, torture, and persecution of ethnic and religious minority groups. These atrocities allegedly committed by the Islamic State constitute serious crimes of concern to the international community and threaten the peace, security, and well-being of the region and the world.[8] Yet despite this statement, the Prosecutor concluded that the Court has no "territorial jurisdiction" with regard to crimes committed in Iraq and Syria, because these two states are not party to the Rome Statute, which is the statute of the ICC. However, the Court may nevertheless exercise "personal jurisdiction" over perpetrators who are nationals of a state party, even without territorial jurisdiction. The information gathered by the office of the Prosecutor does indeed point to thousands of foreign fighters from member states such as Jordan, France, the United Kingdom, Germany, Belgium, the Netherlands, and Australia who have joined the Islamic State. The Prosecutor, however, noted that the Court's policy focuses on those "most responsible" for serious crimes, and that as of April 2015, the Islamic State was led militarily and politically by operatives who are nationals of Iraq and Syria. It was on this premise that the Prosecutor concluded that "the jurisdictional basis for opening a preliminary investigation into the situation is too narrow at this stage."

Despite this position, there are other ways to grant the Court jurisdiction over crimes committed by the Islamic State. The Security Council can refer situations to the Court even if they do not meet the ordinary conditions of jurisdiction, as occurred in the cases of Darfur[9] and Libya.[10] Despite the fact that political constraints in the Security Council, specifically, opposition by

Russia and China, prevent the adoption of such a resolution in the case of Syria, efforts can be intensified to adopt such a resolution at least with regard to Iraq. In addition, Iraq itself could join the Court's statute, which would thus grant the Court jurisdiction to investigate crimes conducted on its territory. In September 2015, there were reports on efforts by the former Prosecutor of the Court, Luis Moreno Ocampo, to grant the Court jurisdiction over the Yazidi community in Iraq.[11] Ocampo claimed that "ongoing genocide" was being committed against the Yazidi minority, and that the capture of foreign Islamic State leaders from a country which is signatory to the Rome Statute would provide necessary ground to open a criminal investigation. An easier way to grant jurisdiction to the Court over the Yazidi minority would be through an ad hoc declaration by Iraq directed specifically at the crimes committed against the Yazidis in the Sinjar region since August 2014 (when the attacks against them began). The Court has even expressed its willingness to investigate crimes by organizations affiliated with the Islamic State operating in Libya, a country in which the Court holds jurisdiction due to a referral from the Security Council in 2011.[12]

Foreign Fighters

The growing phenomenon of citizens from various countries enlisting for combat in Iraq and Syria (hereafter, "foreign fighters") has become one of the central concerns of the international community, especially among European nations. Estimates indicate more than 20,000 foreign fighters in Iraq and Syria, with about one fifth of them citizens of European nations. Foreign fighters, particularly those with significant combat experience, pose many dangers to their countries of origin after their return home, including the potential to provide ideological inspiration for further acts of terror.

Coping with the foreign fighter phenomenon is a direct continuation of the fight against world terror. Over the years, the UN has adopted conventions against terrorism, and several Security Council resolutions have been adopted on the topic. In 2014, the Security Council passed two central and binding resolutions on foreign fighters pursuant to Chapter 7 of the UN Charter. Resolution 2170,[13] passed in August 2014, continues the system of obligations of previous resolutions, and obligates countries to take action against the financing of terror, with special emphasis on oil fields, which provide economic revenue for operating terrorist organizations. The Security Council has expressed its readiness to include in the list of UN sanctions those recruiting fighters, participating in the activities of the Islamic State, and/or financing or organizing the movement of foreign fighters. In addition, it called upon states to take measures to prevent foreign fighters from joining terrorist organizations and bring them to justice.

The term "foreign terrorist fighters" was defined for the first time in Resolution 2178[14] of September 2014: "foreign terrorist fighters, namely individuals who travel to a State other than their States of residence or nationality for the purpose of the perpetration, planning, or preparation of, or participation in, terrorist acts or the providing or receiving of terrorist training, including in connection with armed conflict." The resolution mandates that the movement of foreign terrorist fighters along with the collection of funds for financing their activities, organization, or recruitment be defined as criminal offenses in domestic laws and regulations. In addition, the resolution obligates states to prevent foreign terrorist fighters from entering or passing through their territory and calls upon them to require airlines operating in their territories to provide advance passenger information to the appropriate national authorities, while calling for international cooperation on this matter.

On the state level, various measures have been employed to fulfill such international commitments. In Israel, for example, the Islamic State has been designated as a prohibited association,[15] and several citizens have been tried for traveling to and joining its ranks. Other states have adopted measures such as confiscating the passports of foreign fighters or stripping them of their citizenship. Still others have focused on programs to reintegrate them into the community.[16] Yet their positive aspects notwithstanding, Security Council resolutions and state legislation have received more than a little criticism, primarily out of fear that they will be exploited and lead to wide ranging violations of human rights.

Conclusion

The fight against the Islamic State presents significant legal challenges. The difficulty of justifying the use of force to deal with new threats in the international arena in the past decade demonstrates the importance of interpreting and adapting the law to a changing reality. The framework for the use of force and the right to self-defense was drafted in an era of wars between sovereign states. It no longer fully applies to the realities of today and most likely the foreseeable future, when prolonged and often indecisive armed conflicts against terror organizations based in and operating from failed states accelerate humanitarian problems and pose a continuous threat to the security of multiple nations. As long as the fighting in Syria continues and additional states conduct military actions within the country against the Islamic State under the notion of self-defense, the interpretation of the right to self-defense in international law may evolve, including the central concept of "armed attack," and actually assist in the defeat of the Islamic State.

Another issue regards the International Criminal Court. In order to overcome the lack of territorial jurisdiction, states must increase intelligence efforts and assist the Court to exercise personal jurisdiction over senior leaders of the Islamic State, who are nationals of states party to the Court's statute. Bringing these senior figures to trial can assist in presenting a united front by the international community against the Islamic State and also in providing a role for international criminal law as a tool in the fight against crimes committed by organizations of Salafi jihadist Islam.

Nevertheless, the most effective solution seems to lie in the political international sphere, especially in the Security Council and its willingness to disentangle legal knots. The international effort to defeat the Islamic State while complying with international law and human rights requires the navigation of international politics with the goal of maximizing action to achieve this objective. This applies to military action permitted by the Security Council, the imposition of economic sanctions on Islamic State operatives or states that assist them, referral to the International Criminal Court, growing international cooperation with regard to sharing data, and the adoption of measures against terrorism.

Notes

1 United States Central Command, October 15, 2014, http://www.centcom.mil/en/news/articles/iraq-and-syria-ops-against-isil-designated-as-operation-inherent-resolve.

2 For additional details, see Louise Arimatsu and Michael N. Schmitt, "Attacking 'Islamic State' and the Khorasan Group: Surveying the International Law Landscape," *Columbia Journal of Transnational Law Bulletin* 53 (2014): 1-29.

3 Letter dated June 25, 2014 from the Permanent Representative of Iraq to the United Nations addressed to the Secretary-General, U.N. Doc. S/2014/440, June 25, 2014, http://www.securitycouncilreport.org/atf/cf/%7B65BFCF9B-6D27-4E9C-8CD3-CF6E4FF96FF9%7D/s_2014_440.pdf.

4 Letter dated September 20, 2014 from the Permanent Representative of Iraq to the United Nations addressed to the President of the Security Council, U.N.

Doc. S/2014/691, September 20, 2014, http://www.securitycouncilreport.org/atf/cf/%7B65BFCF9B-6D27-4E9C-8CD3-CF6E4FF96FF9%7D/s_2014_691.pdf.

5   See for example Britain's position with regard to the military actions against the Islamic State in Iraq, September 25, 2014, https://www.gov.uk/government/publications/military-action-in-iraq-against-isil-government-legal-position/summary-of-the-government-legal-position-on-military-action-in-iraq-against-isil.

6   See for example the speech by President Barack Obama on September 10, 2014, which includes a variety of statements on military intervention in Iraq against the Islamic State and the feasibility of similar activity in Syria, inter alia, based on collective self-defense (aid to Iraq), individual self-defense (the defense of American citizens), and anticipatory self-defense (the growing threat beyond the nations of the region, including the United States), https://www.whitehouse.gov/the-press-office/2014/09/10/statement-president-isil-1. See also Britain's legal claim for self-defense in its attack on Islamic State operatives in Syria: "David Cameron: Britain Mounted Fatal Air Strikes in Syria," *The Telegraph*, September 8, 2015, http://www.telegraph.co.uk/news/uknews/terrorism-in-the-uk/11848600/David-Cameron-Britain-mounted-fatal-air-strike-in-Syria-live.html. Following the deadly terror attacks in Paris on November 13, 2015, French Foreign Minister Laurent Fabius said that France's decision to launch retaliatory airstrikes on the Islamic State stronghold of Raqqa in Syria was an act of "self-defense." See Ben Doherty, "France Launches 'Massive' Airstrike on ISIS Stronghold of Raqqa," *The Guardian*, November 6, 2015, http://www.theguardian.com/world/2015/nov/16/france-launches-massive-airstrike-on-isis-stronghold-in-syria-after-paris-attack.

7   Letter dated September 23, 2014 from the Permanent Representative of the United States of America to the United Nations and addressed to the Secretary-General, U.N. Doc. S/2014/695, September 23, 2014, http://www.securitycouncilreport.org/atf/cf/%7B65BFCF9B-6D27-4E9C-8CD3-CF6E4FF96FF9%7D/s_2014_695.pdf.

8   Statement of the Prosecutor of the International Criminal Court, Fatou Bensouda, on the alleged crimes committed by ISIS, April 8, 2015, http://www.icc-cpi.int/en_menus/icc/press%20and%20media/press%20releases/Pages/otp-stat-08-04-2015-1.aspx.

9   Security Council Resolution 1593, U.N. Doc. S/RES/1593, March 31, 2005, http://www.icc-cpi.int/NR/rdonlyres/85FEBD1A-29F8-4EC4-9566-48EDF55CC587/283244/N0529273.pdf.

10 Security Council Resolution 1970, U.N. Doc. S/RES/1970, February 26, 2011, http://www.icc-cpi.int/NR/rdonlyres/081A9013-B03D-4859-9D61-5D0B0F2F5EFA/0/1970Eng.pdf.

11 "Former ICC Prosecutor Recognizes Yezidi Genocide," *RUDAW*, September 2, 2015, http://rudaw.net/english/kurdistan/020920151. See also "Former ICC Prosecutor Pushes for Yazidi Genocide Case," *Reuters*, September 2, 2015, http://www.reuters.com/article/2015/09/02/us-mideast-crisis-yazidis-icc-idUSKCN0R21NQ20150902#GvFsbJIbTEQDTSbF.97.

12 Statement to the United Nations Security Council on the Situation in Libya, pursuant to UNSCR 1970 (2011), International Criminal Court Website, May 12, 2015, http://www.icc-cpi.int/en_menus/icc/press%20and%20media/press%20releases/Pages/otp-stat-12-05-2015.aspx .

13 Security Council Resolution 2170, U.N. Doc. S/RES/2170, August 15, 2014, http://www.un.org/en/ga/search/view_doc.asp?symbol=S/RES/2170 (2014).

14 Security Council Resolution 2178, U.N. Doc. S/RES/2178, September 24, 2014, http://www.un.org/en/sc/ctc/docs/2015/SCR%202178_2014_EN.pdf. See also "Policy Brief, Responding to Foreign Terrorist Fighters: A Risk-Based Playbook for States and the International Community," Global Center on Cooperative Security, November 2014, http://www.globalcenter.org/publications/responding-to-foreign-terrorist-fighters-a-risk-based-playbook-for-states-and-the-international-community/.

15 On September 3, 2014, Israel's Minister of Defense, Moshe (Bogie) Ya'alon, declared the Islamic State a prohibited association; see Digest of Publications 6872, September 7, 2014, p. 7922, http://index.justice.gov.il/Units/Reshomot/publications/Pages/OfficialGazette.aspx.

16 For additional details, see "Treatment of Foreign Fighters in Selected Jurisdictions: Country Surveys," Library of Congress (Law Library), http://www.loc.gov/law/help/foreign-fighters/country-surveys.php.

The Islamic State's Use of Social Media: Terrorism's Siren Song in the Digital Age

Adam Hoffman

One of the most remarkable aspects of the Islamic State is its extensive use of social media and its presence on social media. The organization's meteoric rise to global awareness in the summer of 2014 was accompanied not only by its conquest of vast territories in Iraq and Syria, but also by an impressive and well-planned, multilingual campaign on social media. This campaign, which included video clips, images, stylish magazines, Islamic chants (*nasheeds*), and widespread activity on Twitter, transformed the terms ISIS (the Islamic State of Iraq and Syria, the organization's original name) and Islamic State from the labels of a small and brutal jihadist organization established after the American invasion of Iraq in 2003 to a brand synonymous with global terrorism and Salafi Islam, familiar to every household in the West and the Arab world. Indeed, it was through its extensive and sophisticated activity on social media and the production of Hollywood-quality, horrific video clips that the Islamic State and its leader, Abu Bakr al-Baghdadi, became the new face of Islamic terrorism in the twenty-first century.

The Islamic State is not the first terrorist organization to exploit the internet and other technological tools of the Information Age. Al-Qaeda, founded by Osama Bin Laden in the late 1980s, already made extensive use of the internet,[1] while al-Shabaab, a Somali organization, began using Twitter in English as early as 2011.[2] Yet the use of these platforms never constituted a key feature of either organization's media strategy.

According to a comprehensive study by the British Quilliam Foundation, Islamic State propaganda has radically changed the nature of Salafi jihad media activity by abandoning the principle of operational security, typical of earlier terrorist organizations, for dynamism. The essential change lies in the fact that the Islamic State now generates propaganda that can tailor and tell a story that will touch or horrify, depending on the particular audience.[3] This use of social media has enabled the Islamic State to present its narrative independently of traditional media (print, television, and radio), and to design the image it would like to see reflected in global public opinion. While in 1998 Osama Bin Laden had to announce the establishment of the World Islamic Front for Jihad Against the Jews and the Crusaders in the Pan-Arab newspaper *al-Quds al-Araby* and rely on al-Jazeera to broadcast his speeches, in the first decade of the twenty-first century, the Islamic State has been able to use social media, an open communications channel accessible to all, to produce and distribute hundreds of propaganda films and other media products to a vast audience without the restrictions and censorship imposed on traditional media. Indeed, the Islamic State's massive presence on social networks as well as its use of official production departments demonstrates that it is taking far greater advantage of these technological opportunities than any other non-state actor operating in cyberspace.

The Islamic State's Modus Operandi on Social Media

Several key media offices are responsible for producing and distributing the Islamic State's propaganda content. The al-Furqan and al-I'tisaam agencies produce Arab language films, the al-Hayat Media Center is in charge of films and publications for a Western audience, and al-Ajnad issues *nasheeds*. The Islamic State also runs a radio station named al-Bayan, which broadcasts propaganda in the territories of the Islamic caliphate, and a news agency that reports relevant news on Twitter. In addition to these important agencies, each province (*wilaya*) within the Islamic State has its own local media office to film and distribute videos and "photographed reports" about current events in its area.

According to a study published in August 2015, the local media agencies in the provinces are responsible for 78 percent of the Islamic State's media output.[4] The decentralized structure of key media agencies, combined with local media offices, account for the high volume and frequency of the Islamic State's publications: the study found that the various agencies generate an average of 18 media products a day.[5] This structure allows the Islamic State to create an impression of continual activity on a global scale (or at least one that extends beyond its core territories, i.e., Iraq and Syria), and to demonstrate to its supporters that its forces are making steady progress toward building a caliphate and waging war on its enemies.

The principal innovation in the Islamic State's media strategy, as compared to that of earlier terrorist organizations, lies in its exploitation of social networks for spreading propaganda. Indeed, these networks, especially Twitter, constitute its main channels of communication. According to a comprehensive Brookings study of March 2015, supporters of the Islamic State operate at least 46,000 active Twitter accounts at any given moment;[6] senior American officials estimate that the organization generates 90,000 tweets per day.[7]

In addition to their massive public presence on Twitter, Islamic State supporters use "innocent" hashtags (content categories that correspond to a given subject), that is, ones unrelated to the organization or any other terrorist activity, in order to maximize the exposure to the Islamic State's messages in the general discourse on social media. They have thus used hashtags associated with the World Cup in 2014, as well as the referendum in Scotland, to distribute their videos and tweets among the general public.[8] This "hashtag hijacking" causes users who are not necessarily Islamic State supporters to transmit its propaganda, which is thus relayed to a Twitter audience of millions. Such use of Twitter, which takes optimal advantage of social media's decentralized structure and relies on the Islamic State's online supporters to distribute and promote its official propaganda, is unprecedented in the history of terrorist organizations.[9]

The Islamic State's reliance on the decentralization of the internet is not incidental, but rather part of a deliberate strategy to spread its messages and maintain its online presence in the long term. An official e-book issued by the Islamic State likened its decentralized presence on social media to its physical activity:

> The Islamic State's Online world is similar to its practical real life world, in that everything is decentralised....The Islamic State's content (videos, ebooks, social media accounts) are scattered all around the internet. Just like the different provinces of the Islamic State are scattered in different locations. Each province has its own responsibility in creating its own videos and social media accounts to share its successes. By decentralising everything from the core leadership, even if a province fails

online or offline, the leadership and overall Khilafah (Caliphate) leadership project is still safe and can grow elsewhere.[10]

The Islamic State's decentralized activity on social media thus enables it to continue spreading its message and complicates counter efforts to block its propaganda.

The Effects of the Islamic State's Social Media Activity

The main result of the Islamic State's widespread activity on social media is its rising influence throughout the world and its successful self-marketing as a global brand. This brand presents the ideology behind the caliphate as the "pure" Islamic utopia that necessitates cruel warfare against its enemies, but ensures social justice, proper administration, and a righteous and authentic religious and moral life for its faithful. While Western audiences are for the most part familiar with the brutality depicted in the horrific films produced by the Islamic State, the idea of utopia that the organization is selling on social media is extremely attractive to new recruits. Its seductive power is evident in the vast number of foreign combatants (over 25,000 according to an official UN report) who have joined the Islamic State – the largest documented number of foreign fighters ever to join a conflict anywhere.[11]

Social media's latent potential for spreading propaganda and recruiting operatives has led a few researchers to dub it the "radical mosque" of the current decade – a favored site for recruiting volunteers and spreading the ideology of various jihadist organizations.[12] While the number of foreign combatants joining Islamic States forces is the most alarming statistic for Western and Israeli security services, the attraction is not limited to young men seeking to become soldiers. In contrast to al-Qaeda and other jihadist organizations, which presented a model of elitist struggle and therefore appealed to a very specific segment of the population, the Islamic State presents itself as a comprehensive cultural project and a home for Muslims around the world. As specified in Arabic in one particular propaganda film, its goal is "to arouse the Islamic *umma* [the global community of believers]."[13] The Islamic State thus calls on Muslims from all over the world "to make *hijra* ["migration," the term used for the transformative journey made by the Prophet Muhammad from Mecca to Medina in 622] to its territory,"[14] and uses social media as a main channel to spread its message and attract recruits from diverse backgrounds. Thus, for example, one finds three women from the UK leaving their husbands and traveling to Syria with their children to join the Islamic caliphate, or a young American couple from a small town in Mississippi – a high school honors student and a psychology major – trying to reach Syria for the same purpose.[15] These and many other cases reveal how the siren call of the Islamic State has sounded its ideology far beyond the battlefields in Iraq and Syria in order to draw into its world people who, despite lacking a Salafist jihadi background, are exposed to the Islamic State's propaganda via social media and lured into supporting it, both ideologically and in practice.

The Need for a Competing Narrative
Understanding the nature of the Islamic State's decentralized activity on social media can help in the formulation of effective solutions for dealing with this phenomenon. Naturally, many countries are disturbed by the Islamic State's widespread use of social media. Robert Hannigan, director of Government Communications Headquarters (GCHQ), a British intelligence organization dealing with electronic intelligence, has described the internet and social networks as "the command and control networks of choice for terrorists and criminals."[16] Other politicians have demanded that the accounts of Islamic State supporters on Twitter and other social networks be closed.

Technological solutions of this type, however, are either very difficult or impossible to implement, due to the decentralized nature of the flow of information through social media channels and a limited control over its content. Whenever an IT company manages to close the account of an Islamic State supporter, a new one surfaces a few minutes later under a different name. Moreover, once social media companies began closing thousands of accounts linked to the Islamic State, supporters began using hashtags to transmit new announcements and propaganda to the general public via Twitter. Unlike personal accounts, which can be blocked and suspended, content hashtags are very difficult to delete. In short, simply closing the accounts of Islamic State supporters is of limited value and merely a partial solution to the Islamic State's exploitation of social media.

In addition to using technological means to combat this phenomenon, a competing narrative based on Muslim and Middle East voices – the Islamic State's main target audience – must be presented on social media. Recent initiatives appear to be moving in this direction. In July 2015, for example, a new center in charge of digital communications against the

Islamic State, the *Sawab* (Arabic for the "correct" or "proper" path) Center, was established as a joint venture between the United States and the United Arab Emirates.[17] The Quilliam Foundation has also launched a social media campaign entitled "Not Another Brother," in order to emphasize the human cost that the enlistment of young Muslims to the Islamic State inflicts on the Muslim community in the UK.[18] The highlight of the campaign is a video clip featuring a British recruit to the Islamic State imprisoned in Syria, who expresses remorse at having joined the organization and urges others to avoid making the same mistake.[19]

In addition to these important online initiatives, which present alternative Muslim voices and expose the atrocities of the Islamic State, the military campaign against its physical existence and expansion must continue. Islamic State propaganda sells continual victory and never-ending warfare against a broad array of enemies to its supporters and the general public. Steady defeats on the battlefield, however, will undermine the attractiveness of this message, and make it difficult to recruit new members. A combined effort on social media and the "real world" is the best way to influence potential recruits and combat the Islamic State's siren call, which has been sounded for more than a year on social networks.

Notes

1   Jarret M. Brachman, "High-Tech Terror: Al-Qaeda's Use of New Technology," *Fletcher Forum for World Affairs* 30 (2006): 149.

2   Alex Altman, "Why Terrorists Love Twitter," *Time*, September 11, 2014, http://time. com/3319278/isis-isil-twitter/; Will Oremus, "Twitter of Terror," *Slate*, December 21, 2011, http://www.slate.com/articles/technology/technocracy/2011/12/al_shabaab_ twitter_a_somali_militant_group_unveils_a_new_social_media_strategy_for_ terrorists_.html.

3   Charlie Winter, "The Virtual Caliphate: Understanding Islamic State's Propaganda Strategy," Quilliam, 2015, p. 4, http://www.quilliamfoundation.org/wp/wp-content/ uploads/publications/free/the-virtual-caliphate-understanding-islamic-states-propaganda-strategy.pdf.

4   Aaron Y. Zelin, "Picture Or It Didn't Happen: A Snapshot of the Islamic State's Official Media Output," *Perspectives on Terrorism* 9, no. 4 (2015): 88, http://www. terrorismanalysts.com/pt/index.php/pot/article/view/445/html.

5   Ibid.

6   J. M. Berger and Jonathan Morgan, "The ISIS Twitter Census," *Analysis Paper* No. 20, Brookings, March 2015, p. 7.

7   Eric Schmitt, "U.S. Intensifies Effort to Blunt ISIS' Message," *New York Times*, February 16, 2015, http://www.nytimes.com/2015/02/17/world/middleeast/us-intensifies-effort-to-blunt-isis-message.html?_r=0.

8   Heather Marie Vitale and James M. Keagle, "A Time to Tweet, as Well as a Time to Kill: ISIS's Projection of Power in Iraq and Syria," *Defense Horizons* 77, no. 1 (2014), http://ndupress.ndu.edu/Portals/68/Documents/defensehorizon/DH-77.pdf.

9   Yannick Veilleux-Lepage, "Retweeting the Caliphate: The Role of Soft-Sympathizers in the Islamic State's Social Media Strategy," Conference paper, presented at the 6th International Symposium on Terrorism and Transnational Crime, Antalya, Turkey, December 4-7, 2014, http://goo.gl/Cb7MdH.

10 *The Islamic State,* e-book, 2015, p. 80.

11 Edith M. Lederer, "UN Report: More than 25,000 Foreigners Fight with Terrorists," *AP*, April 2, 2015, http://bigstory.ap.org/article/cec52a0dbfab4c00b89bc543badf6c20/un-report-more-25000-foreigners-fight-terrorists.

12 Winter, "The Virtual Caliphate," p. 7.

13 al-Furqan Media, "Upon the Prophetic Methodology," July 2014.

14 al-Hayat Media, *Dabiq* 3, September 2014.

15 Hassan Hassan, "Three Sisters, Nine Children, One Dangerous Journey to the Heart of Isis. What is the Lure of the Caliphate?" *The Guardian*, June 21, 2015, http://www.theguardian.com/world/2015/jun/21/three-sisters-nine-children-what-is-the-lure-of-the-isis-caliphate; Richard Fausset, "Young Mississippi Couple Linked to ISIS, Perplexing All," *New York Times*, August 14, 2015, http://www.nytimes.com/2015/08/15/us/disbelief-in-mississippi-at-how-far-isis-message-can-travel.html?hp&action=click&pgtype=Homepage&module=first-column-region&region=top-news&WT.nav=top-news.

16 Robert Hannigan, "The Web is a Terrorist's Command-and-Control Network of Choice," *Financial Times*, November 3, 2014, http://www.ft.com/intl/cms/s/2/c89b6c58-6342-11e4-8a63-00144feabdc0.html#axzz3QhKyjb33.

17 Asma Ajroudi, "U.S., UAE Take on ISIS in 'Information War,'" *al-Arabiya*, July 8, 2015, http://english.alarabiya.net/en/media/digital/2015/07/08/-Sawab-UAE-U-S-launch-anti-ISIS-digital-communication-center-.html; "US, UAE Launch Anti-IS Online Messaging Center in Abu Dhabi," *Daily Star*, July 8, 2015, http://www.dailystar.com.lb/News/Middle-East/2015/Jul-08/305796-us-uae-launch-anti-is-online-messaging-center-in-abu-dhabi.ashx.

18 Mark Sweney, "Anti-ISIS YouTube Video Aims to Counter Terror Group's Social Media Campaigns," *The Guardian*, August 4, 2015, http://www.theguardian.com/media/2015/aug/04/anti-isis-youtube-video-notanotherbrother.

19 "NotAnotherBrother," *YouTube*, August 3, 2015, https://www.youtube.com/watch?v=IjIQ0ctzyZE&list=PLyCnHE3hqgntzaUH-S_36IfNZowpzUF8e&index=1.

A Hitchhiker's Guide to the Islamic State Galaxy

Orit Perlov

The current primary arena of the Islamic State's intensive activity is in the Arab world, particularly the Fertile Crescent, where it seized large swaths of territory in Syria and Iraq. One of the most important – if not the most important – perspectives from which to examine the phenomenon of the Islamic State is that of the civilians who come into direct or nearly direct contact with it.

This article traces the voices emerging from Arab countries on various subjects related to the Islamic State: What is its ideology? What is their strategy for recruitment? What are its fundraising methods? What is its target audience? And, most significantly, how and for what purposes does it make use of social networks?

The analyses and conclusions presented below are the products of conversations with leaders of public opinion on social media between 2014 and 2015 in Iraq, Syria, Lebanon, Jordan, Egypt, and Libya. The intention here is not to analyze how the Islamic State views itself, but rather to come to a better understanding of its image and its perception among the public, as expressed in public discourse within Arab society. Thus, preparation of this article did not make use of any social media accounts of the Islamic State's military or media wings, the forums (open or closed) of its activists, or the "ISIS fanboys" accounts and its online supporters.

Profiling the Islamic State: The Idea, the Goal, the Method, and the Means

The key to undermining the Islamic State's long term sustainability is understanding the essence of the phenomenon. The Islamic State's primary goal is to establish a caliphate for all Muslims. What began as an al-Qaeda splinter group in Iraq has turned into the "Islamic State in Iraq and Syria," or simply the "Islamic State," to which new *wilayat* (provinces) are gradually annexed, both in the original regions and beyond.

Underlying this goal of the Islamic State is the concept that serves as the ideological foundation of the phenomenon as a whole. More specifically, in addition to the establishment of a geographically contiguous caliphate that reflects the ideology of the Islamic State, the citizens of this state must accept an interpretation of Salafist Sunni doctrine that goes back to the Prophet Muhammad. The first goal on the road to the caliphate is to redirect Sunni Muslims who have "strayed from the path" to "the straight path." The Islamic State views these people as "infidels" who are unwilling to accept true Islam. The second goal is to win the struggle first against the Shiites, known by members of the Islamic State as *rafida*, that is, "opponents" or "rejecters," then against the Alawites (Nusayris), and lastly against the Christians, Turkmen, Yazidis, Kurds, Druze, and finally, the Jews.

From the perspective of the Islamic State, these goals must be broken down into several levels. On the geopolitical level, the first course of action is to eliminate the nation states. According to Islamic State philosophy, these are artificial, imperialist Western constructs crafted in the nineteenth century to destroy the tribal, religious, and historical identity of the Middle East. By doing away with these borders, the Islamic State can create the geographical contiguity needed to establish a strong and just caliphate. The weakening of Middle East regimes and the governance capability of various states and the failure of political Islam since 2011 have provided the Islamic State with an opportunity to advance its particular aims and garner public support.

On the organizational level, the Islamic State maintains hierarchical decision making mechanisms that provide it with substantial fluidity and mobility. It relies on a dual mode of operation: a centralized senior leadership on the one hand, and fighters and field leadership plus a media wing that works in a dynamic and decentralized manner, on the other hand. The caliph and his deputies set policy and strategy, but grant freedom of action to the field leadership when it comes to tactics, timing, and alliances created on the ground in real time. As a result, any damage inflicted on the Islamic State will have limited impact on the performance capabilities of its leadership from the middle echelon downward.

On the personal level, the Islamic State relies on an effective traditional mechanism, namely, an oath of allegiance (*al-bay'ah*) to the caliph in Islam.

The *bay'ah* does not require being under the geographical rule of the caliph or being part of the caliphate structure. The moment subjects recognize the rule of the caliph, the caliph recognizes them; the enemies of the caliph are the enemies of his subjects, who will sacrifice everything, including their lives, in the struggle against these enemies. By swearing the *bay'ah*, people state that they recognize the caliph as their ruler, and therefore he should recognize them as his subjects, and that the caliph's enemy is their enemy, and their enemies are the caliph's enemies.[1] For example, if the United States were to attack the Islamic State in Iraq, a US citizen who has sworn allegiance to the caliph and lives in the United States would be obligated, with no advanced coordination, to take action against targets in the US. This obligation is applicable worldwide in the case of any attack by the enemy. Even if the Islamic State is not party to the planning behind such an operation, it will not mind, distance itself from the act, or deny involvement, and most likely will claim responsibility.

On the economic level, the Islamic State finances itself in a number of ways, including through ransom payments for abductions, arms smuggling, the extortion of protection money, seizure of financial institutions, and exploitation of natural resources. Donations solicited at "house gatherings" (*diwaniyat*), parlor meetings of sorts, mentioned frequently on social media, are also an important source of funding. During these events, held primarily in Kuwait, Saudi Arabia, the Maghreb, Pakistan, and Afghanistan, the teachings of learned and well-known religious figures in Salafist Islam are used to persuade others to contribute to the Islamic State. Fighters and public relations experts travel to contribute in person to the meetings, with videos produced by each brigade to publicize its importance and its manpower; many of these videos include words of praise and thanks for individual benefactors. The unit with the most impressive presentation receives funding and support. This method was popular in the first phase of the organization's existence, before it reached its current form, and declined somewhat following the international coalition's declaration of war and their attempt to impose sanctions on its sources of funding.

The Islamic State as a Contagious "Disease"

The elements described above comprise the Islamic State's expressed worldview, especially since the announced establishment of the caliphate. The common platform used to realize these elements is social media. This is, in fact, the major feature that distinguishes the Islamic State from any predecessors and current rivals and thus requires separate discussion. In addition to their ability to circulate information and propaganda with the help of social media tools, Islamic State fighters can coordinate and document their exploits by using self-created applications and production companies. The Islamic State in fact has one of the broadest and most effective information dissemination systems in the Middle East. It has also developed a public relations network that operates in 24 languages throughout Europe, Africa, and Asia, and uses sophisticated marketing to draw foreign Muslim fighters and civilians to the regions under its control.

At present, many people on the internet regard the Islamic State as a cancerous growth in the body of Sunni Islam spread by multiple carriers of its ideology (referred to on the internet as its "fan club") through social media. Contagion is quick and efficient, requiring negligible investment and simple logistics. The Islamic State compensates for its lack of advanced munitions with innovative communication technologies that offer its members reverberations that are exponentially greater than the actual size and volume of its activity.

The Islamic State is an excellent illustration of what happens when seventh century ideology meets twenty-first century technology. One reason for the mythos of the Islamic State's success and transformation into a strategic threat to the states of the Middle East and beyond lies in its combined reliance on barbarous means and the radicalization of unemployed youth in Arab countries. The Islamic State draws its scare tactics and methods of deterrence from the Salafist Wahhabi tradition, and implements them with the help of modern technological means in the name of the ideology of the school of Ibn Taymiyya and Sayyid Qutb. Examples of this dynamic can be seen in the many short videos filmed by Islamic State fighters during and after their conquest of various sites that depict them beheading people, throwing homosexuals off roofs, using children to carry out brutal acts of murder, holding mass executions with firing squads, and incarcerating victims in cages, burning them alive, chopping off their hands and feet, or stoning them.

Whereas the West seeks to distance the public from acts that inspire fear and horror, the Islamic State strives to bring these closer to them and make them accessible to anyone interested in viewing such scenes unmediated and at close range. Consequently, the burning of a pilot or the decapitation of a journalist is seen on YouTube in less than seven minutes by some 150 million viewers throughout the Middle East and beyond. Shocking videos of this sort are produced for negligible amounts of money and successfully reach broad audiences that can compete in size with those of any Hollywood action film. Such content together with the tools for disseminating it have spawned a mighty communications monster, resulting in a disproportionate relationship between the true scope of the Islamic State phenomenon on the one hand, and the image and fear that it conjures on the other. This impression, accompanied by a sense of victory, serves to attract masses of Muslim youth and immigrants in the West.

Methods of Delivery behind the Use of Social Media

The resonance that the Islamic State has achieved on the internet serves a number of its objectives, first and foremost, the recruitment of manpower.[2] The internet, however, also serves other ends: it encourages radicalization of the target audience in Arab and Western countries,[3] helps with fundraising,[4] generates fear at a minimal cost and with few logistical needs, effects mass mobilization, enables the creation of a visually prestigious brand through the production of broader and higher quality audio and video tracks, helps coordinate the movement of forces in the field, and finally, grants "eternal life" to its ideas and ideology (since the fighters of the Islamic State themselves can die). Every attempt made thus far to fight the Islamic State on the internet has simply strengthened its power.

The Islamic State has used a variety of social networks to achieve its ends. Although the organization has been blocked on Facebook, Diaspora, and Friendica, it has remained active on Twitter. They have official Twitter accounts that are specialized, diversified, and multilingual. They also have an army just for hashtag engagement and re-tweets, with a focus on messaging and branding concepts that are more sophisticated than what many digital agencies offer. Twitter offers the best degree of anonymity, the fastest and largest reach, and since it is based upon crowdsourcing information, it is perfect for both disseminating propaganda and fundraising. In addition, it has a large, well trained "online army" responsible for discussing religious subjects as well as hashtagging, branding, and focusing discussions. Prior to the internet's counter-campaign led by Twitter, Google, and YouTube, the Islamic State succeeded in achieving an average of 10,000 tweets and hashtag references[5] on a daily basis. Although the number has fallen thanks to these counter-measures, the Islamic State's media apparatus is still able to invade the timeline and trend listings and has created special tools to do just that.

Social Media as Recruitment Centers

The assessment of any digital campaign begins and ends with its target audience, and the Islamic State is no different. Analysis of its conduct indicates that its target audience outside of Iraq and Syria consists of four primary groups: (a) jihad-minded individuals; (b) frustrated Islamists who can be prodded toward violent radicalization (former supporters and members of the Muslim Brotherhood); (c) the citizens of whatever region or town the Islamic State intends to attack, as a form of psychological warfare that aims to break their spirit and limit the resistance they might face; and (d) the "lone wolves": men who suffer from arrested development, wishing to fulfill fantasies of warfare, conquests, and gun battles, probably fueled by many hours of playing violent video games.

The Islamic State's media department, particularly its military propaganda and recruitment wing, has made extensive use of GoPro technology to design realistic simulations of war games in real time. This indicates that the prime target audience of the organization's recruitment of external manpower does not actually consist of fighters of the first category – Islamist jihadi types – as one might expect, but rather fighters of the fourth category, those seeking kicks and action.

The Islamic State makes pointed use of the internet not only for recruitment purposes but also for the coordination and logistics of its forces. One way it does so is through various web applications. The primary one used by Islamic State fighters is Zello, a coded application that transforms cellular telephones into tactical two-way radios and thus makes it possible to provide all fighters with a sophisticated yet logistically simple coordination apparatus. With their "Dawn of Glad Tidings" application, which was launched in April, 2014 and lately killed by Google Play, the Islamic State has effectively managed to replace the drums of war with the tweets of war. Users who download the app register on it with their Twitter accounts, which gives the app creators permission to use their users' timelines to disseminate their messaging. The app thus gives the Islamic State the power to tweet from the accounts of all their registered users when it so desires, allowing it to flood the timeline with the same tweet, which could include a link, a hashtag, and/or an image, while keeping in mind to space those "tweet waves" in order to avoid triggering Twitter's spam detection algorithms. It allows the Islamic State to have unparalleled reach, which it can use for any of its three goals or target audiences. For example, the day the Islamic State invaded Mosul, it tweeted 40,000 tweets about it, making it seem like an endless legion to anyone monitoring them.

This app may seem invincible, but its main strength is also actually its weakness. Once the identification process became easier and Twitter, Google, and YouTube declared war on the Islamic State, thousands of accounts were suspended and the broadcast time for videos on YouTube was reduced from fifteen to approximately seven minutes before their removal from the sites.

Conclusion

This article has looked at the critical role played by new technological tools in the service of the Islamic State, from its establishment until the present. Such means are actually leading to a new and advanced form of terrorism that relies on a support and communications system that generates maximum fear at a minimum cost and minimum logistics, and thus creates a new language and a new world of images and perceptions. The Islamic State has branded and positioned itself as a successful product (at present) despite its setbacks in the confrontation with international coalition forces, its lack of advanced weaponry, and its loss of more territory each day. All this has made it more difficult for the Islamic State to substantiate the idea of the caliphate that it promotes. The immediate need is to formulate an overall policy and strategy for dealing with the phenomenon of the Islamic State, that is, to consider the reasons behind the emergence of the "disease" within Sunni Islam (e.g., the corruption of regimes; the ineffectiveness of public systems; sectarian discrimination; human rights violations; the absence of liberties; and unemployment among young adults) and treat them as elements of the modern battlefield: the tools (smartphones, tablets, laptop computers), the arena (the various types of social media), and the "doctrine of warfare" used by the Islamic State to facilitate its existence and continue "spreading the disease."

Notes

1   Mahmoud Salem, "Egypt's Border with Libya, Sudan Ripe for Islamic State Expansion," *al-Monitor*, September 22, 2104, http://www.al-monitor.com/pulse/

iw/originals/2014/09/egypt-sudan-libya-border-lack-control-terrorist-expansion. html.

2   Aaron Y. Zelin, "Foreign Jihadists in Syria: Tracking Recruitment Networks," *PolicyWatch* 2186, December 19, 2013,https://www.washingtoninstitute.org/ policy-analysis/view/foreign-jihadists-in-syria-tracking-recruitment-networks.

3   J. M. Berger and Bill Strathearn, "Who Matters Online: Measuring Influence, Evaluating Content and Countering Violent Extremism in Online Social Networks," *Developments in Radicalisation and Political Violence*, March 2013, http://icsr. info/wp-content/uploads/2013/03/ICSR_Berger-and-Strathearn.pdf.

4   Ibid.

5   See ActiveHashtags, https://twitter.com/ActiveHashtags.

Part III

From Where It Sprang, and the Nearby Environment

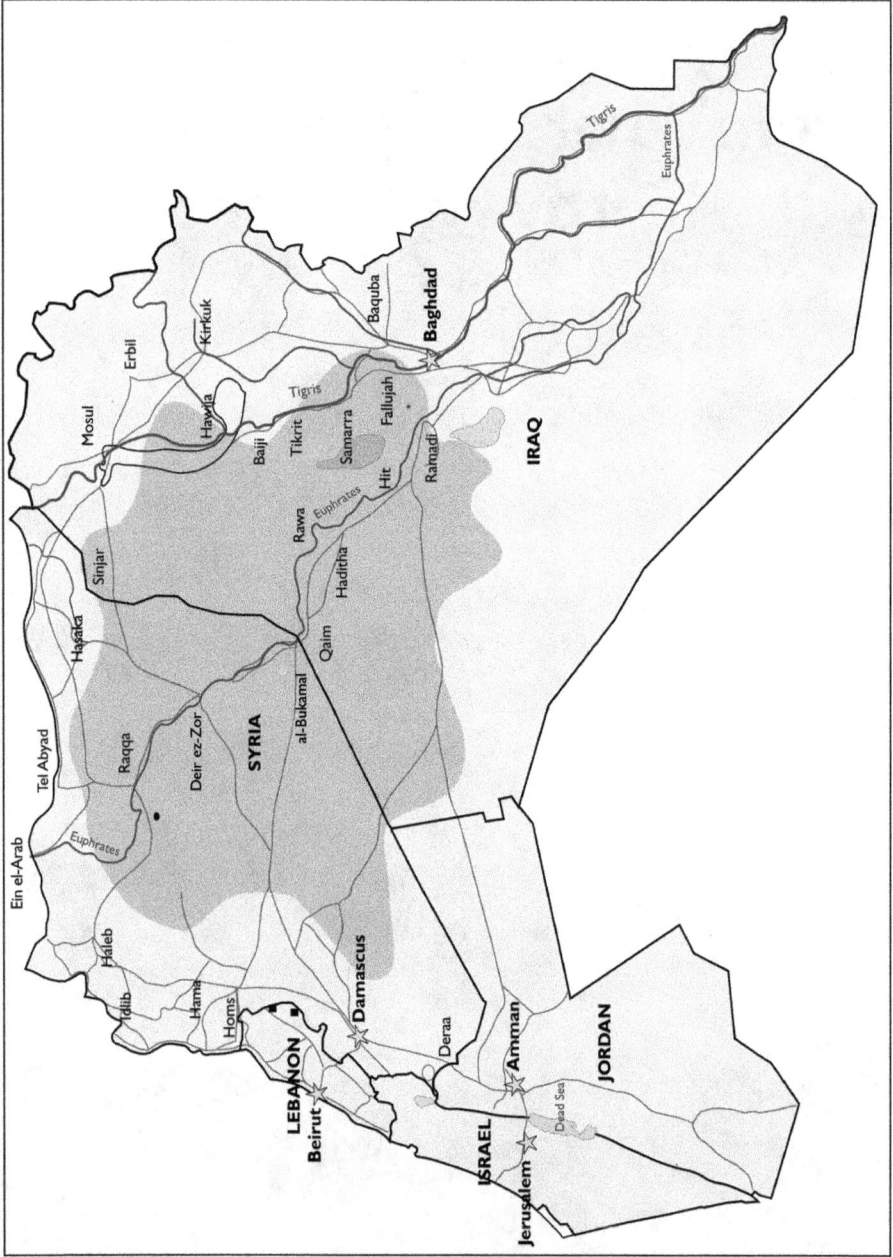

Figure 1. Areas attacked and controlled by the Islamic State (September 2015)

The Islamic State and the Iraqi State:
A Guide to the Perplexed

Ronen Zeidel

Background

August 2015 was oppressively hot in Iraq, with temperatures in Baghdad rising to 51°C (124°F). The heat wave sparked widespread popular protests, directed primarily against the Minister of Energy, who is responsible for the faltering supply of electricity, and indirectly against the political leadership and its corruption. The police did not suppress the demonstrations; in fact, they distributed bottles of water to the demonstrators. Significantly, the spirit of protest extended to all sections of the Iraqi public, including politicians, public figures, and the Shiite militias. Even Prime Minister Haider al-Abadi joined the protest, and thanks to the support he received from the leading Shiite religious figure in Iraq, Ali al-Sistani, managed to escape the threat of being overthrown.[1]

At the time, it seemed as if the battlefront against the Islamic State received only minor attention in news broadcasts; the attack on Mosul appeared remote, certainly under the prevailing summer conditions; and a routine was established reminiscent of the daily reports about the Iran-Iraq War. This routine, of course, can be misleading.

This article describes the situation in Iraq, and indicates the principal trends on the two sides – the Iraqi state and the Islamic State – in the short and medium terms.

The State of Iraq

Faced with the most serious threat to its existence, the state of Iraq has managed to assemble a substantial force, including its regular security forces (army, internal security, police), well established popular militias (al-Hashd a-Shaabi), regional security forces in the Sunni governorates, and Sunni tribal organizations. Since the summer of 2015, the United States has tried to renew the activity of the Sahwa groups – Sunni semi-military tribal forces that operated mainly in western Iraq. Kurdish Peshmerga forces operating in northern Iraq are expected to be senior partners in the campaign to take control of Mosul.

It is still premature to say that the state of Iraq is doomed. The impressive rate of volunteers for the militias indicates internal power and extensive patriotic and ethnic enthusiasm. No less important, the Iraqi state enjoys a number of prominent advantages over its enemy, the Islamic State: in the military sphere, it has an enormous edge in manpower, arms, and ammunition, as well as exclusive control of the air. The Iraqi government also enjoys active international and regional support. In other aspects as well, the Iraqi state is far more of a state than its rival: it is a highly centralized state, with the capital Baghdad of great significance. The Islamic State in Iraq is forced to use Iraqi currency printed in Baghdad. Furthermore, the residents of Baghdad, who are under the control of the Iraqi government, enjoy a supply of electricity eight hours a day, while the city of Mosul, occupied by the Islamic State, was hooked up to electricity only in the spring of 2015, through the Mosul dam under Kurdish control: until then, it was cut off from the central electricity grid. Even today, it has a supply of electricity only two hours a day.

The state of Iraq's main weakness, which prevents a breakthrough in its struggle with the Islamic State, is the abysmal lack of coordination between the elements of its various forces, and between them and the regional players – Iran, Turkey, the Kurds, Jordan, Syria, and Saudi Arabia – and the international coalition headed by the United States. As a result, simple operations take more time than expected, and the various forces are incapable of dealing with the Islamic State on more than one front at a time.

In addition, every achievement by the Islamic State, such as the re-conquest of the city of Ramadi in western Iraq in May 2015, undermines the Iraqi state system's self-confidence and disrupts its plans. The reoccupation of Ramadi prompted sharp criticism of the Iraqi forces by US Secretary of Defense Ashton Carter.[2] It is possible that it was this American pressure that led to the sudden decision to switch the effort from an offensive to liberate Mosul, which was delayed repeatedly, to an offensive in western Iraq. This offensive highlighted the lack of coordination between the various Iraqi forces, especially between the army and the al-Abadi government and the Shiite militias, which enjoy Iranian backing and support al-Abadi's rival, Nouri al-Maliki. For example, while the Iraqi army and government were calling for the recapture of Ramadi as the highest priority target in the western Iraqi governorate, the militias demanded that the city of Fallujah be captured first.[3]

The main battlefield of the Iraqi state is in the area between Fallujah and Ramadi in western Iraq. For Iraq, control of this area will protect Baghdad on its vulnerable western flank, and prevent the arrival of Islamic State forces in the direction of the holy Shiite cities in the south of the country.[4] The Iraqi forces lay siege to Fallujah and Ramadi in July 2015. Fallujah, which fell into the hands of the Islamic State already in February 2014, is expected to be a more difficult objective for conquest.

The second main battleground is the Salah al-Din governorate north of Baghdad. After the city of Tikrit was recaptured in April 2015, the Iraqi forces continued northward toward the town of Baiji, near the site of the country's largest oil depot. The forces penetrated into the village, but were unable to completely suppress the Islamic State forces there. The oil depot, which was rendered unusable, was surrounded, but was not captured from the Islamic State.[5] In October 2015, the Iraqi forces recaptured the refinery and claim to have liberated most of the town of Baiji.

In order to advance its forces near Mosul, the Iraqi state needs further northerly progress, which has meanwhile ground to a halt. An initial batch of Iraqi forces was advanced with Kurdish and American cooperation toward the area of Hawija, east of Mosul, now still under the control of the Islamic State. Fighting in this area erupted in October and it is believed to be the precursor of a future operation on Mosul.

Another effort by the government forces is to strengthen control of the desert area between the city of Samarra north of Baghdad and the western governorate of al-Anbar. Several important air bases are in this area, and the American advisors are also located there.[6] At the same time, it is doubtful whether the government will be successful in this effort; the region consists mostly of desolate desert, and the nearby border crossing, Abu Kamal, is controlled by the Islamic State.

The Islamic State

The re-conquest of Ramadi in May 2015 (in parallel to the conquest of Palmyra in Syria) was the first significant territorial accomplishment by the Islamic State since the summer of 2014. The organization does not pose an immediate threat to Baghdad, as it once did. It has lost control of the eastern Diyala governorate and Tikrit, and has retreated from the territory it captured in the Kurdish north. Its main achievements are therefore the fact of its survival and its ability to organize for new conquests.

The "project" of Abu Bakr al-Baghdadi is based on the simultaneous goals of establishment of a state with institutions and jihad. In places held by the Islamic State, its control mechanisms have improved, with alternatives and challenges eliminated. In Mosul (the capital of the Islamic caliphate), Tal Afar, Fallujah, Hawija, Sharqat, and other cities, a rigorous Islamic regime has been instituted, together with enforcement measures. The public systems, such as the municipality and the educational system, continue to function and provide the public with services in all of these places. Note that the Islamic State does not operate these professional mechanisms; it merely oversees their functioning. And in contrast to the prevailing opinion, the Islamic State is not a terrorist organization that has been retrained in order to manage a country; it is an entity that continues to operate the public institutions while using terrorism against a submissive population.

Most of the Islamic State's efforts are in the military sphere, and divide into two types of missions: offensive and defensive. Prominent offensive operations included the prolonged siege of the city of Haditha, west of Ramadi.[7] The city is in the heart of an area completely controlled by the Islamic State, but nevertheless has not yet fallen into its hands. This situation supports the already proven assessment that the Islamic State has difficulty in conducting sieges. The capture of Haditha will strengthen the Islamic State's control of the western part of the al-Anbar governorate, and create a homogenous area there. Such a conquest will also provide the Islamic State with a major source of money and weapons; the city's location on the highway stretching from Syria into the depth of Iraqi territory will likewise render this conquest significant.

As part of its defensive operations, the Islamic State is preparing for an attack on Mosul, and its forces are trying to prevent the advance of the Iraqi forces in the Baiji area and to protect Fallujah and Ramadi, where the siege against them is tightening. In addition, Islamic State operatives are continuing to sow fear and destruction in other places in Iraq, especially in Baghdad.

Fighting against a number of armies on several fronts, the Islamic State suffers from many weaknesses. It must cope with difficult challenges of control, manage a country, and wage war at the same time. It suffers from shortages of manpower, income, and recently also weapons and ammunitions.[8] All these problems are likely to worsen, and require the Islamic State to make difficult decisions and take practical measures.

The Islamic State does not possess a single contiguous territory. It has a number of governmental centers, including empty spaces where the organization has a certain presence and nothing more. Indeed, a military analysis of the fighting highlights that the Islamic State in Iraq is not a single unit. There is no link between the control centers in Mosul in the north and those in the al-Anbar governorate to the south. Communication between these two regions can take place only through Syria. Moreover, the Islamic State in Iraq is connected to areas under its control in Syria. Another weakness of the Islamic State is that despite the mobility of the field vehicles it possesses, it is very dependent on the network of roads. This renders its convoys vulnerable, and makes it difficult for the Islamic State to exercise effective control of territories in which there is no road system.

Finally, the Islamic State might well be disturbed at the possibility of a change in Turkey's policy toward it. If it is thinking strategically, the Islamic State should be aware that Turkey is its second most important strategic asset, after Syria. A real change in Turkey's stance toward it will harm the Islamic State's main channel for foreign volunteers joining the organization, greatly restrict its sources of income from trade and its supply of weapons, and is liable to pose a dangerous military threat to the territories controlled by the Islamic State in Iraq and Syria. The permission granted by Turkey in the summer of 2015 to American warplanes to operate from the Incirlik base against Islamic State targets is a bad omen for the group.

Future Efforts

Ab al-Lahab ("blazing August") made it necessary to suspend operations on the various fronts. The attack on Mosul has been delayed, and Iraqi Minister of Defense Khaled al-Obeidi hinted at this when he said on August 15, 2015, "The Iraqi army is aiming for victory at al-Anbar and Baiji," but did not mention Mosul.[9] It appears that the Iraqi government is concentrating on regaining control of the cities of Fallujah and Ramadi, while the Islamic State is concentrating on the conquest of Haditha. The new offensive of the Iraqi state in the fall of 2015 occurred successfully on two fronts, the west (Ramadi) and the north (Baiji). Significantly, the United States, the Iraqi army, and Abadi prevailed in their decision to take Ramadi first and not Fallujah, as the militias suggested. The recent successes hasten the preparations to advance on Mosul.

As of now, the many weaknesses of the forces on both sides cancel each other out, thereby creating the impression of a standoff. For the Iraqi government, the key to success is better coordination between the elements of the coalition in the various theaters of the struggle against the Islamic State. This is ostensibly a simple task, but in practice, the dispute between the security forces and the militias is a reflection of the dispute between the government and the ethnic Shiite forces – between al-Abadi (who is behind the security forces) and al-Maliki (favored by the militias), and between the Shiites (the militias) and the Sunnis, and even between the United States, which has called for reducing the presence of the militias in the field, and Iran. Successful coordination between these parties, as occurred in the capture of Tikrit and the killing of Abu Muslim al-Turkmani, is apparently an exception that does not prove the rule. In addition, the Iraqi forces suffer from an almost total absence of field intelligence.

The role of the United States in the battles should be much greater. The option of using the Incirlik air force base in Turkey should significantly increase the number of missions. Apache helicopters in the area can increase assistance to the fighting forces. The United States has already supplied four F-16 warplanes to Iraq, and continues to train Iraqi pilots to fly them. Warplanes of this type, however, are needed less than combat helicopters. The United States would also do well to supply defense equipment against suicide terrorists and roadside bombs, such as robots for dismantling bombs and anti-tank missiles for use against truck bombs. In addition, the US should continue training Sunni tribal militias, especially in areas under the absolute control of the Islamic State, in other words, western al-Anbar and the area around Mosul. The Shammar, al-Jubour, and al-Ovaidi tribes – very large Sunni tribes living and operating in a region under the control of the Islamic State or near it – are fighting against it, and are in great need of American aid. The United States should continue strengthening Prime Minister al-Abadi and the Iraq security forces against the militias and Iran, and avoid unnecessary criticism through the media. The United States focus would best be on the battles, while taking into consideration what is liable to happen in Iraq when they are over: a possible strengthening of the militias and what amounts to their takeover of the Iraqi state.

The Islamic State is a dogmatic Salafi jihad entity. As a Sunni group, it attaches enormous importance to the principle of the "unity of God" (*tawhid*) and the war on polytheism (*shirk*); it is not suited to compromise, especially not compromise with bitter ideological enemies – first and foremost the Shiites. Jihad, in the sense of active warfare to spread the ideology and expand the state, is fundamental in its theory. Its achievements in Iraq do not satisfy it, and in the future, it is likely to attempt to conquer Baghdad or invade and damage the Shiite holy cities of Karbala and Najaf.

The Islamic State has not yet attempted to bypass the settled region along Iraq's two rivers by way of the southwestern desert. The reason for this may be logistical, but it cannot be ruled out that it will try such a maneuver in the future. Success in such an attempt will bring it to the area of the border with Saudi Arabia. To be sure, not much is known about the decision making processes among the Islamic State leadership. Nonetheless, assuming this is its intention and the Islamic State continues to adhere to the policy formulated by al-Baghdadi, it is likely that the future of Iraq will be decided by military, not political, means. Even if the Islamic State is defeated in Iraq, however, and is forced to withdraw from all the territories it has conquered in the country, its presence in Syria will continue to threaten Iraq. Establishing a real and concrete border between Iraq and Syria will be an essential step in this state of affairs.

Notes

1   Mustafa Habib, "The Hero of Baghdad's Protests: Senior Iraqi Cleric 'Saves' the Government – and Iraq from Iran?" *Niqash*, August 12, 2015, http://www.niqash.org/en/articles/politics/5077.

2   Barbara Starr, "Carter: Iraqis Showed no 'Will to Fight' in Ramadi," *CNN*, May 24, 2015, http://edition.cnn.com/2015/05/24/politics/ashton-carter-isis-ramadi/.

3   Karim 'Abd Zair, "The Militias Lay Siege to Fallujah from Three Directions and Daesh is attacking al-Khalidiya," *al-Zaman*, July 10, 2015.

4   Muhammad al-Salihi, "The Units are Preparing to Break the Siege on Haditha and Enter Fallujah," *al-Zaman*, July 7, 2015.

5   'Ali al-Musawi, "The Joint Forces Take Baiji and Prepare for the Taking of Sharqat and Enter Mosul," *al-Zaman*, June 29, 2015.

6   Ronen Zeidel, "Fighting in Iraq: The Military Aspect," *Tel Aviv Notes* 9, no. 13, July 23, 2015, http://www.dayan.org/tel-aviv-notes-vol-9-no-13-july-23-2015#_ftn7.

7   See note 4.

8   Muhammad al-Salihi *al-Zaman*, June 16, 2015.

9   Muhammad al-Salihi, *al-Zaman*, August 17, 2015.

The Islamic State Kingdom in Syria

Eyal Zisser

Five years of civil war and bloodshed have led to the collapse of the Syrian state and the shattering of its social mosaic. The Islamic State (ISIS) burst forth from the ruins – first of Iraq, then of Syria – to assume power and fill the vacuum left behind by crumbling states. In eastern Syria, which it occupied in the summer of 2014, the Islamic State serves as an effective alternative to the Syrian state institutions that have since disappeared. The entity aims to seize western areas of the country if and when the Syrian regime collapses – an outcome that is virtually assured, as it appears as though none of the rebel groups active in western Syria have the power to stop this from happening.

Such a development has far reaching implications for Syria, because unlike the other rebel elements active in the country, the Islamic State is not a local group seeking simply to rule the country. Rather, it hopes to turn Syria into a Salafist Islamic entity. It is, in fact, an entity with an all-Islamic worldview and identity, interested in far more than geographical expanses in Syria and Iraq. Alternatively, it is at the very least an Iraqi project whose foundations lie in the Sunni Muslim base in Iraq that gave rise to its leader, Abu Bakr al-Baghdadi, and his closest advisors and assistants.

In any case, however, it is clear that the Islamic State still sees itself as a warring, expanding jihadist outfit; in areas under its control, it proclaims the war of jihad and a campaign of conquest. Ironically, for the millions of Syrians finding themselves under Islamic State rule, this is a reprieve – albeit temporary and illusory – from the horrors of the bloodshed possessing their country. The population, mostly traditional Sunni Muslim, though occasionally still tribal in structure, accepts with ease if not enthusiasm the practicality of the Islamic State as well its mechanisms, which seek to turn the Syrian-Iraqi clock back more than a thousand years to the earlier years of Islam.

The Summer of 2014: ISIS Seizes Control of Eastern Syria

In June 2014, ISIS surged from the depths of the Syrian-Iraqi desert and seized large portions of northwestern Iraq, including Mosul. In tandem with its success there, ISIS fighters also managed to wrest control of most of eastern Syria (the Jazeera region), starting with Abu Kamal on the Syrian-Iraqi border, through al-Raqqa, a city that became the seat of their rule in eastern Syria, to the outskirts of Aleppo in the west. Their military successes paved the way for al-Baghdadi's announcement on June 29, 2014 of the founding of an Islamic caliphate under his leadership,[1] henceforth known as the Islamic State.

Ever since the seizure of eastern Syria in the summer of 2014, the Islamic State has tried to expand its circle of influence and control in four principal directions:

a. In eastern Syria, it has tried to entrench its control of the Jazeera region (eastern Syria, the provinces of Deir ez-Zor, Haskha, and al-Raqqa) while trying to eliminate enclaves such as Tabeka (which it conquered in the summer of 2014), and Haskha and Deir az-Zor (which became a steady target for its attacks), which were still controlled by the Assad regime in the region. At the same time, the Islamic State tried, unsuccessfully, to unseat the Kurds from their enclaves in the north, such as Kubani (Ein al-Arb).

b. In northern Syria, in the summer of 2014 and the spring of 2015, the Islamic State succeeded in entrenching itself in the rural areas north and east of Aleppo, though its attempts to reach the city itself were rebuffed by various rebel groups.

c. In central Syria, ISIS fighters unsuccessfully tried to make their way toward Homs, though in May 2015 they managed to conquer the city of Tadmur, the entrance point into the heart of Syria from the eastern desert.

d. In the spring of 2015, Islamic State fighters managed to gain control of some suburbs of Damascus in southern Syria, while advancing to the eastern foothills of the Druze Mountains. In addition, they managed to gain the loyalty of some of the rebel groups operating on the Syrian-Lebanese border in the mountain range of Qalamoun and the Syrian Golan Heights.[2]

The Syrian Portion of the Islamic State Kingdom

The part of Syria under Islamic State control is a portion of the Islamic caliphate that extends to the northwestern part of Iraq. The caliphate is headed by the Ibrahim caliph, Abu Bakr al-Baghdadi (full name: Ibrahim Awad Ibrahim Ali al-Badri al-Samrani). Several councils operate at his side and constitute the core of the Islamic State.[3] Abu Bakr al-Baghdadi has two deputies who are responsible for managing the various provinces (*wilayat*) of the country. The deputy in charge of the provinces in Syria is Abdullah al-Anbari, also known as Abu Ali al-Ambari, who served as an intelligence officer in the Iraqi army during Saddam Hussein's rule. The province (*wilaya*) governors are thus subordinate to religious law and his authority.[4]

Each province is divided into counties (*qita'*), which in turn are subdivided into cities and rural areas. Every province is headed by an emir and has local institutions charged with managing the province's routine needs: law and law enforcement, religious matters, including the enforcement of religious laws, and the provision of services to residents (managed by the ministry of service – *diwan al-hidamat*, or the institute for public services – *mu'asasat al-hidamat al a'ama*). These are subordinate to the province governor but coordinate issues and maintain contact with the councils and ministries at the level of the Islamic State leadership.[5]

Islamic State Provinces in Syria

Islamic State provinces are for the most part congruent with already existent administrative divisions in Iraq and Syria. The Syrian provinces of the Islamic State consist of: al-Raqqa, whose capital is al-Raqqa; Aleppo; Idlib, the province of Damascus; al-Badiya, the desert province and the official name of Homs province; Hama; the coast province, the official name of Latakiya province; al-Khayr ("the good"), the new name given to Deir ez-Zor province; and al-Baraka ("the blessing"), the name given to Haskha province. In late August 2014, the Islamic State founded the Euphrates province (*wilayat al-Frat*), which includes the Syrian city of Abu Kanal and the Iraqi city of al-Qa'im. The establishment of this new province was meant to symbolize the breakdown of Sykes-Picot borders, i.e., the Iraq-Syria border imposed by the West. All the same, some provinces, such as Idlib, the coast, and Damascus, are still not under Islamic State control.[6]

It seems that the Islamic State, the Syrian regime, the Kurds, Turkey, and even certain rebel groups such as Jabhat al-Nusra share a quiet understanding on the free flow of goods and people through the various areas of Syria, especially when it comes to the sale of oil and petroleum products and the maintenance of infrastructure facilities, such as dams and power stations controlled by the Islamic State. This maintenance is carried out jointly by the Islamic State and the Syrian government, which continues to pay the salaries of government workers in the areas controlled by the Assad regime.[7]

Two other aspects of the Islamic State's governance of eastern Syria are worth mentioning: first, its attitude to the Arab tribes that constitute a significant power in this area; second, its attitude toward minorities. The tribes were certainly an important source of power and support for ISIS when it first made its way in Iraq. In Syria the Islamic State worked to win various tribal coalitions over to its cause. On the other hand, the Islamic State's relations with Arab tribes are tense and hostile, as many refuse to subjugate themselves to its authority and surrender the autonomy they have been enjoying since the onset of the civil war in Syria. Their insubordination has forced the Islamic State to act with lethal violence in order to impose its will.[8]

When it comes to minorities, the Islamic State accepts the existence of "protected people" or *dhimmis* – a concept applicable to the various Christian sects in the region – and allows them to lead their lives wherever they reside. Thus in February 2014, for example, the Islamic State agreed to provide Islamic protection (*ahad aman*) to the Christian residents of al-Raqqa in Syria, which allowed them to continue living as usual in the city, but imposed on them the *jizya* per-capita tax, which they must pay twice every year. The agreement also banned them from publicly celebrating Christian rituals or exhibiting religious symbols. In reality the Islamic State's treatment of the Christian population is marked by continued harassment and persecution, implying that its real goal is to expel Christians from areas under its control or even to force them to convert to Islam. Given this state of affairs, it is hardly surprising that most of the Christian population has left eastern Syria.[9]

Unlike Iraq, where the Islamic State treated the Yazidi population horrendously, slaughtering its men while selling its women on slave blocks in the cities of the Islamic State,[10] eastern Syria contains few people who are neither Sunni Muslims nor Christians. Yet in Syria too, the Islamic State is acting savagely toward anyone who is not Sunni, including Alawites and Shiites who have fallen into its hands.

Conclusion

The importance of the presence of the Islamic State in eastern Syria lies in the fact that it was the first rebel organization fighting the Syrian regime that managed to position itself as a realistic alternative to Assad both militarily and politically, and to establish an administrative entity that sustains, even if only partially, systems of governance and a range of economic, social, and legal services.

The Islamic State has in practice established a state-like system whose objective, motives, and ideological foundations are fueled by jihad war and expansionism. Its new conquests are thus meant to achieve not only its ideological goal but also – and especially – its practical goal of maintaining the momentum it had gained through its conquests and continued maintenance of the state that it runs using a range of conquests and the manpower joining its ranks in the wake of each new conquest. In this sense, there is a surprising resemblance between the Islamic State and the tribal nations that the region has known since the beginning of Islam or even earlier, and between the current Islamic State and the one instituted by the Prophet Muhammad in the Arabian Peninsula.

The story of the Islamic State in eastern Syria is one of success. An organization that once lacked a real presence, support, or infrastructure has managed to sweep out of the desert and seize control of vast tracts of land in eastern Syria within the course of a few years. It is now looking to seize control of western Syria as well. However, it is not the Islamic State that toppled the Syrian state, as it did in Iraq. Rather, it is the collapse of the Syrian state that enabled the Islamic State to conquer eastern Syria with relative ease. The power of the Islamic State actually lies in the weakness of its enemies – local forces that cannot gather the strength to stand up to it and in many cases opt to join its ranks. Nonetheless, wherever the Islamic State has encountered firm opposition, as it has from the concentrations of Shiites in southern Iraq or the Kurds in northern Syria and Iraq, it has halted, at least for now.

Finally, eastern Syria, which has been controlled by the Islamic State since the summer of 2014, was seized and dominated easily. Still, one should not assume that this relative success in the region augurs what might happen should all of Syria fall into its hands. The western parts of the country are densely populated by mixed populations of minority groups as well as wealthy urban Sunnis, mostly secular and harboring moderate worldviews.

In conclusion, the Islamic State is neither a decree of destiny nor a natural disaster that must be accepted passively. Notwithstanding its ability to adapt to the changing regional reality, to confront complex challenges and a range of enemies while exploiting their weaknesses, and especially to fill the vacuums left by the collapse of Iraq and Syria, the Islamic State has weaknesses of its own. Indeed, wherever it has encountered fierce resistance it has withdrawn. In the long term, the radicalization and lack of pragmatism that currently constitute its sources of strength are liable to become key weaknesses that will generate broad coalitions that would otherwise never cooperate against it. In addition, the Islamic State may encounter friction with Israel on the Syrian front sooner than expected. Israel must therefore find a way of joining the broad coalition that is currently operating against the Islamic State.

Notes

1   On ISIS's military achievements in the summer of 2014, see "How ISIS Stormed Iraq: A Chronology of the Militant Offensive," June 16, 2014, http://english.alarabiya. net/en/perspective/features/2014/06/16/How-ISIS-stormed-Iraq-A-chronology-of-the-militant-offensive-.html. For more on al-Baghdadi's announcement on the establishment of a caliphate, see Hannah Strange, "Islamic State Leader Abu Bakr al-Baghdadi Addresses Muslims in Mosul," *The Telegraph*, July 5, 2014.

2   On ISIS's military successes starting in the summer of 2014, see "The Fall of Tadmur, Ramadi and the Border Crossings Impose ISIS organization as a Main Player," *Khalifa*, May 22, 2015, http://www.khilafah.com/the-fall-of-tadmur-ramadi-and-the-border-crossings-impose-isis-organization-as-a-main-player.

3   For more about the organization of ISIS, see "ISIS: Portrait of a Terrorist Organization," Meir Amit Intelligence and Terrorism Information Center, November 26, 2014, http://www.terrorism-info.org.il/he/article/20733; see also Charles C. Caris and Samuel Reynolds, "ISIS Governance in Syria," *Middle East Security Report* 22, July 2014, www.understandingwar.org/report/isis-governance-syria.

4   See Charles Lister, "Islamic State Senior Leadership: Who's Who," Brookings Institution, http://www.brookings.edu/~/media/Research/Files/Reports/2014/11/profiling-islamic-state-lister/en_whos_who.pdf?la=en.

5   See "ISIS: Portrait of a Terrorist Organization," pp. 65-66, 70-71.

6   For more on Islamic State provinces in Syria, see "The Provinces of ISIS," *Watan*, http://www.watan.fm/syria-news, and the website associated with ISIS, https://isdaratdawlatalislam.wordpress.com.

7   See Orlando Crowcroft, "Isis: Inside the Struggling Islamic State Economy in Iraq and Syria," *International Business Times*, April 11, 2015, http://www.ibtimes.co.uk/isis-inside-struggling-islamic-state-economy-iraq-syria-1495726.

8   See, for example, "Mass Grave of 230 Tribespeople Found in Syria's Deir Ezzor: Monitoring Group," *al-Akhbar*, December 18, 2014, http://english.al-akhbar.com/node/22938.

9   On the *ahad aman* document, see http://baretly.net/index.php?topic=33284.0.

10   See "Isis Slave Markets Sell Girls for 'As Little as a Pack of Cigarettes,' UN Envoy Says," *The Guardian*, June 8, 2015, http://www.theguardian.com/world/2015/jun/09/isis-slave-markets-sell-girls-for-as-little-as-a-pack-of-cigarettes-un-envoy-says.

Kurdistan, the Islamic State, and Paradigm Shifts in the Middle East

Ofra Bengio

At the turn of the millennium, paradigm shifts in the Middle East changed the rules of the game and thus the political balance of power among the various forces in the region.

One hundred years ago, the map of the Middle East was drafted by external powers – the United Kingdom and France. Today, the designers of the regional map are local actors. While nation states were the accepted political framework in the twentieth century, non-state elements have joined them – perhaps overtaken them – in the twenty-first century. While nationalism and pan-Arab ideology were the dominant factors in the twentieth century, ethnic identity and Islamic religion determine the political agenda today. Whereas organized armies dictated political and military moves in the past, their role to a large extent has now been taken over by irregular armies, militias, and terrorist organizations.[1]

The Kurds as a Barrier to the Islamic State

The struggle between the Kurds and the Islamic State, which erupted openly in the summer of 2014, constitutes a test case of these changes. These two actors currently shaping the political map are not states, but local players. Both rely on irregular military forces that are becoming increasingly regular, and both represent trends that undermine the legitimacy of existing states. In the case of the Kurds, the trend is ethno-national; in the case of the Islamic State, it is Islamic Salafi. Developments in Kurdistan in the Fertile Crescent mirror those in al-Dawla al-Islamiyya fi al-ʿIraq wal-Sham (ISIS), which adopted the name "Islamic State" in June 2014. Both players have been nourished by the crisis in Iraq and Syria and have challenged these states by taking forceful control of regions beset by political vacuums and establishing autonomous governments. Both have striven to erase the borders between Syria and Iraq while aspiring to reach the sea and thus achieve economic and political independence.

In many respects, however, the two groups are antithetical and exhibit many clear differences, among them, ideology, political orientation, and overall objectives. The Islamic State is anti-Western, anti-democratic, Salafi, and an advocate of jihad, while both parts of Kurdistan are fighting the Islamic State, maintaining their distance from a politicized Islam, and developing the foundations of democracy.

The Kurds were once regarded as a group that placed regional stability in jeopardy. A 1948 CIA document, for example, warned against the Kurdish threat to Turkey, Iran, and Iraq.[2] Today, however, it is the Kurds who represent stability, tolerance, and relative moderation, especially if compared to the Islamic State, notorious for its extremism and unprecedented brutality that recalls the destructive campaigns waged by the Mongols in the thirteenth century. Another interesting factor is the emergence of an operational Kurdish sub-system in Turkey, Iran, Iraq, and Syria – the four countries that are home to the areas of Kurdistan – with tools and systems that interface and affect one another in each of these regions. All this complicates the picture and makes it far more difficult for those four countries to decide what to do about the Kurdish question.

What is the nature of relations between the Kurds and the Islamic State? In the immediate aftermath of the conquest of Mosul by the Islamic State and the conquest of the Kirkuk area by Kurdish Pershmerga forces in June 2014, it seemed that the two groups would be able to achieve some kind of modus vivendi. Two months later, however, the Kurds were taken by complete surprise when they became the chief target of an Islamic State offensive and their capital, Erbil, was nearly toppled.[3] The reasons behind the attack on the Sunni Kurdish area were strategic economic motives; the Islamic State sought to gain control over the oil resources of Kirkuk, and to control a strategic road between Iraq and Syria in the Sinjar area. Similar considerations led to its subsequent attempts to occupy the Kurdish area in Syria, where the Kurds had established three autonomous cantons in the summer of 2012. Concurrently, the Kurds and the Islamic State have been engaged in a struggle over control of the oil wells in Hasakah in the Kurdish areas of Syria.[4]

The enmity between the two has become especially bitter due to the success of Kurdish fighters in bringing the Islamic State's momentum to a halt on their territory – in contrast to developments elsewhere. Their success in this respect is particularly noteworthy given the failures of the Syrian and Iraqi armies, which have thus far proven utterly helpless in fighting the Islamic State. It is enough to recall the fall of Mosul, in which the Iraqi army outnumbered the forces of the Islamic State by 15 to 1.[5] An even more extraordinary claim asserts that hundreds of Islamic State soldiers defeated 75,000 Iraqi soldiers.[6]

On Balance: Gains and Losses among the Kurds

As they are fighting over the same territory and resources, a key question is whether the Islamic State is boosting nationalism among the Kurds, as well as their drive toward autonomy. What, in fact, have the Kurds gained and lost from the rise of the Islamic State?

On the positive side, the Kurds have earned credit for their strategy and benefited from improved international awareness and public relations. Their most significant gain lies in Iraq, where they have had little trouble occupying oil-rich territory whose control is disputed by the central government in Baghdad. Their most important conquest has been Kirkuk, which they refer to as the "Jerusalem of the Kurds."[7] It is highly unlikely that they would have dared such a move had the Islamic State not engaged in an offensive campaign that threatened Kirkuk and thus justified and granted urgency to the Kurdish takeover. These developments also strengthened Kurdish national identity in other regions of Greater Kurdistan and increased their will to fight the Islamic State. As at other times and places since the onset of the new era in the Middle East, so too here the war was an important factor in building national solidarity among Kurds while weakening national identity in Syria and Iraq – a process that grants legitimacy to dissolution of these nation states.[8]

The image of the Kurds in the international arena, as well as their links to the outside world, was upgraded significantly following the emergence of the Islamic State. The actions by the Islamic State have cast the Kurds in a far more positive light and highlighted their importance to the West as a stabilizing element in the Middle East. Erbil has hosted an increasing number of European leaders, the most important of whom was French President François Hollande, who visited the city in September 2014.[9] Since their exposure in the international arena, the Kurds have begun receiving economic and military assistance. The most significant to date has been in the form of aerial attacks aimed at halting the advance of the Islamic State, a move that has further aggravated the hostility between the Islamic State and the Kurds.

On the negative side, the conflict with the Islamic State has exposed the Kurds' military weakness, which while not necessarily reflecting their fighting ability, highlights their severe shortage of weapons and sophisticated military equipment. While the Islamic State has modern, heavy American weapons that it seized as spoils of war from the Iraqi army in Mosul in June 2014 and Ramadi in May 2015, the Kurds of Iraq rely almost entirely on light, outdated weapons. The number of modern, heavy weapons reaching them is a tiny fraction of those reaching Baghdad. It is ironic indeed that although the Iraqi army has become a bottomless pit and proven its abject failure at confronting the Islamic State, most American military aid is still flowing to Baghdad. Even the small amount being sent to the Kurds is channeled through Baghdad, which delays and sometimes prevents the supply from reaching the Kurds. The other negative consequence of the rise of the Islamic State is extreme economic damage, which is most severe in the Kurdish region of Iraq due to the need to absorb over 1.5 million refugees. Iraqi Kurdistan Prime Minister Nechirvan Idris Barzani has claimed that the region's population had grown by 28 percent as a result of this influx, and that a sum of $1.4 billion is needed to address this situation.[10] Similarly, the long borders of over 1,000 kilometers with the Islamic State, and the need to protect them, divert attention from the project of state building in Kurdistan.

In Iraq, the emergence of the Islamic State has led to a bloody and complicated triangle that reflects the country's tangled reality. All three sides of this triangle – the Islamic State, Kurdistan, and the Baghdad government, with all its Shiite militias – are engaged in simultaneous warfare or power struggles. Outgoing Iraqi Prime Minister Nouri al-Maliki declared that the al-Hashd al-Sha'bi militia had become the third most important group after the Iraqi army and police force.[11] As for the general goals of each of these three sides, the Kurdish entity is limiting its territorial ambition to the area under its present control, while both the Baghdad government, which is controlled primarily by Shiite Arabs and has a close affinity with Tehran, and the Islamic State seek to overtake all of Iraq. At a time that the Kurdish entity is in effect trying to break away from Iraq, the other elements are trying to preserve the territorial integrity of the country under their exclusive rule.

What further complicates this triangular relationship is the involvement of foreign parties, which are tugging at the sides of the triangle, sometimes in opposite directions. The three main external actors have been the United States, Iran, and Turkey, each of which is simultaneously aiding two of the internal parties: the US and Iran are helping both the Kurds and the Baghdad government, while Turkey is offering minor aid to the Kurds in Iraq while secretly offering assistance to the Islamic State.

The Kurds in Syria are likewise waging a desperate struggle against the Islamic State. In the summer of 2012, only a year after the uprising in Syria, the Kurds managed to establish an autonomous entity, which they called Rojava (literally, West Kurdistan).[12] Considering their situation, the Kurds' achievements in Syria and their steadfast resistance to the Islamic State are extraordinary: their population in Syria is a silent minority that until now has received almost no international recognition; topographically and geographically, the three areas they inhabit consist primarily of plains with no territorial contiguity, a situation that makes defense difficult; and most importantly, their weapons are far lighter and less numerous than those of the Islamic State. Their principal fighting organization is the Yekîneyên Parastina Gel (YPG), which is closely bound to the Partiya Karkerên Kurdistanê (PKK) in Turkey. This explains their tight links to the Kurds in Turkey as well as Turkey's major involvement in events on the southern border. The picture created is that these fighters are even more resilient and have greater spirit than the Peshmerga in Iraqi Kurdistan, thanks in part to the participation of Kurdish women in the struggle in Syria and their courage. These capabilities were reflected during the struggle in Kobani (`Ayn al-`Arab) – under siege by Islamic State forces from September 2014 until January 2015, and eventually liberated – and during the Kurdish offensive at Tal Abyad and other strategic locations. The YPG is trying to connect the territory between the three Kurdish cantons and also to reach the Mediterranean Sea.

The principal obstacle to these maneuvers is the presence of the Islamic State, which has been silently backed by Turkey. Although Turkey has developed strategic ties with the Kurdish region in Iraq, it regards Kurdish autonomy in Syria as a strategic risk of the highest importance since it fears that the border between the Kurds in Syria and their brethren in Turkey will be erased. The Turkish Kurds, who emerged stronger after the June 2015 elections in Turkey, are regarded in Ankara as a concrete threat working toward the formation of a Greater Kurdistan that will include parts of Turkey. The skirmishes that erupted in the aftermath of the June elections between the Turkish army and the PKK have put further pressure on the Kurds of Syria.

The Russian engagement in the fighting in Syria since late September 2015 added further complications to the already entangled situation of the Kurds, especially in Syria but in Iraq as well. The Kurds in these two regions have been receiving support from the US-led coalition since 2014. Thus, while Russia's sudden involvement may cause friction between Moscow and the US-led coalition, it may also put the Kurds in a dilemma with regard to the choice of foreign support against the Islamic State. So far they have managed to remain above the Russian-United States rivalry but it remains an open question if they can retain this position in the longer run.

Israeli Hesitancy, and Policy Shrouded in Uncertainty

These developments confront Israel with some difficult decisions. First, from a practical standpoint, Israel must determine whether it is worthwhile to give aid to the Kurds at a time when it is regularly accused of attempting to dismantle existing countries. Next, it must consider what it will gain by standing beside the Kurds at a moment when such an act is liable to alienate Turkey. Finally, Israel must decide whether it is wise to side publicly with the Kurds, as former President Shimon Peres, Prime Minister Benjamin Netanyahu, and former Minister of Foreign Affairs Avigdor Liberman have done.[13] Their declarations, which followed each other in short order in June 2014, were made in the context of the sudden rise of the Islamic State and the desire of policymakers to back the Kurdish stand against it.

The Kurds too are faced with more than a few dilemmas. On the popular front, they harbor sympathy for Israel, desire to develop ties with it, and even deem it as a model for imitation. Yet despite hoping to obtain aid of some kind from Israel, Kurdish leaders totally object to any public acknowledgment of such a connection, since they fear a response from the surrounding countries, above all Iran and Turkey.

Although there are no definitive answers to these questions, a few general conclusions may be drawn. Like the Western world as a whole, Israel has a significant interest in the Kurds emerging victorious in their struggle against Salafi Jihad Islam. The fact that they are pro-Western, moderate, and relatively secular, and have proven organizational-institutional capabilities, is an important strategic asset, given the forces of destruction in the region. Moreover, the Kurds have also proven themselves much friendlier to Israel than other peoples in the region, owing to their sense of sharing a fate with another small people whose right to their own country is not recognized. Strategically speaking, if in the past the Kurds served as Israel's "eye" on events in Iraq, then today they can play a similar strategic role with respect to Iran for Israel and the West.

In practice, there is much room for cooperation, mainly with the Kurdish area in Iraq. In addition to the realm of security and commerce, a new potential channel has been opened: the purchase of oil from the Kurdish area in Iraq, an arrangement thus far avoided by outside countries due to opposition from the Baghdad government and one that is likely to lead to the tacit formation of an undeclared triangle between Israel, the Kurdish area of Iraq, and Turkey, through which this oil flows. Israel would do well to extend as much humanitarian aid as possible to the Kurds of Syria, a measure that is unlikely to upset relations with Turkey, which itself is providing shelter to masses of fleeing Kurds. Another important conclusion to be drawn here is that – at least for the Kurds – the best way to conduct relations at this stage is behind the scenes.

In sum, the geopolitical map of the Fertile Crescent is in a state of flux and is being shaped by complex and sometimes destructive processes, some of which are by now so deeply rooted that they appear to have passed the point of no return and will probably make it difficult for Iraq and Syria ever to go back to being the united countries that they were in the twentieth century. The Kurds continue to move slowly toward independence in Iraq and autonomy in Syria. As for the Islamic State, it is premature to dismiss it; even if it is defeated, one may reasonably assume that it will be replaced by Salafi groups under one name or another that will wage a battle to restore the Sunnis to their ancient glory. And for "Shiistan" in Iraq to survive, it will have to accept – whether it desires it or not – the Iranian umbrella, which has been significantly strengthened by the nuclear deal signed in July 2015. From this perspective, the United States will be less relevant in reshaping the regional map. As an American researcher stated in an article summarizing his country's situation in Iraq, "We are lost in Iraq because Iraq…is itself lost."[14] If this is true about Iraq, it is even more relevant to Syria. Given the situation, it is advisable that Israel seek options and paths for positive, powerful forces in the region, even if the West is slow to recognize them.

Notes

1   This article is an expanded and revised version of an article that appeared in *Tzomet HaMizrach HaTichon* (Middle East Crossroads) of the Moshe Dayan Center for Middle East and African Studies.

2   "The Kurdish Minority Problem," declassified CIA Report, http://www.foia.cia. gov/sites/default/files/document_conversions/89801/DOC_0000258376.pdf.

3   The Islamic State forces were only 40 kilometers away from Erbil. See "Kurdish Forces, ISIS Clash Near Arbil," *al-Arabiya*, August 6, 2014, http://english.alarabiya. net/en/News/middle-east/2014/08/06/U-N-condemns-ISIS-attacks-in-Iraq.html.

4   Sam Dagher, "Control of Syrian Oil Fuels War Between Kurds and Islamic State," *Wall Street Journal*, November 23, 2014, http://www.wsj.com/articles/control-of-syrian-oil-fuels-war-between-kurds-and-islamic-state-1416799982.

5   Michael Knights, "Battle for Mosul: Critical test Ahead for Iraq," *BBC*, June 11, 2014, http://www.bbc.com/news/world-middle-east-27789770.

6   Ghazi Hars, "The Fall of Mosul: Anatomy of a City's Collapse," *Rudaw*, June 10, 2015, http://rudaw.net/english/middleeast/iraq/100620153.

7   Sheren Khalel and Matthew Vickery, "The Kurds Are at Demographic War with ISIS in Kirkuk," *Haaretz*, February 26, 2015, http://www.haaretz.com/news/world/. premium-1.644202.

8   For a comprehensive discussion of these developments, see Mohammed M. A. Ahmed and Michael Gunter, eds., *The Kurdish Spring: Geopolitical Changes and the Kurds* (Mazda Publishers: Costa Mesa, California, 2013).

9   "Hollande Pledges More Military Help to Erbil and Baghdad in Iraq Visit," *Middle East Eye*, September 12, 2014, http://www.middleeasteye.net/news/hollande-pledges-more-military-help-erbil-and-baghdad-iraq-visit-186242625#sthash.P3RWoASi. dpuf.

10 "KRG Prime Minister: Refugees Have Changed the Demographics of Kurdistan Region," *Basnews*, February 12, 2015, http://www.basnews.com/en/news/2015/02/12/ krg-prime-minister-refugees-have-changed-the-demographics-of-kurdistan-region/.

11 Abdelhak Mamoun, "al-Hashd al-Sha'bi Became Third Military Force after Army and Police, says Maliki," *Iraqi News*, April 14, 2015, http://www.iraqinews.com/ features/al-hashd-al-shabi-became-third-military-force-army-police-says-maliki/.

12 See Michael Gunter, *Out of Nowhere: The Kurds of Syria in Peace and War* (London: C. Hurst & Co, 2014), pp. 103-17.

13 For the complex relations between Israel and the Kurds, see Ofra Bengio, "Surprising Ties between the Kurds and Israel," *Middle East Quarterly* (Summer 2014); and Ofra Bengio, "Why the Kurds Will Become the Second Non-Arab State in the Middle East," *Tablet*, August 14, 2014.

14 Steven A. Cook, "Lost in Iraq," Council on Foreign Relations, May 26, 2015.

Lebanon and the Rise of the Islamic State

Benedetta Berti

Situated at the very heart of *bilad as-sham* – often translated as "the Levant" or "Greater Syria" – Lebanon is clearly part of the Islamic State's ideological, political, and territorial state-building project. Indeed, with the announcement of the caliphate in 2014, the group declared itself to be the only legitimate political system, thereby rejecting pre-existing states and their borders in the Levant and insisting that all Muslims are obliged to accept the religious and political authority of "Caliph Ibrahim" (referring to Abu Bakr al-Baghdadi).[1] The Islamic State sees Lebanon as part of its caliphate project, with the group's long term ambitions with respect to the small Mediterranean nation inherent in its battle cry, *aqiya wa tatamadad* – "lasting and expanding." Lebanon's particular geostrategic significance is not lost on the Islamic State, nor is the importance of Lebanon's main armed group, Hezbollah, in its support of the Bashar al-Assad regime in Syria.

In this context, it is not surprising to note the growing impact of the self-proclaimed Islamic State on Lebanon's security, social cohesion, and political stability, adding to the already dire economic, political, and social effects of the Syrian civil war.

The Islamic State and Domestic Security: Strengthening the Salafi Jihadist Camp?

The Islamic State represents a security challenge for Lebanon, exacerbating the general rise in activism by domestic Salafi jihadist groups unleashed by the Syrian civil war.

Closely monitored and repressed during the so-called "Syrian tutelage" of Lebanon between the end of the civil war in 1989 and 2005, both Islamist groups in general as well as Salafi organizations more specifically expanded their domestic role and visibility following Lebanon's "Independence Intifada" and the Syrian withdrawal from Lebanon. After 2005, these groups benefited from what was generally a more accommodating attitude displayed by the anti-Syrian March 14 coalition and its leading party, the Sunni Tayyar al-Mustaqbal (Future Movement).[2] In the same period, Salafi jihadist groups with ideological and/or operational links to al-Qaeda – including Asbat al-Ansar, Jund al-Sham, and Fatah al-Islam – also increased their activism, operating primarily in the areas around Lebanon's second largest city, Tripoli, and the Nahr al-Bared Palestinian refugee camp in the north, and in Sidon and the Ain al-Hilweh camp in the south.[3] The conflict between the small Salafi jihadist camp and the Lebanese state eventually escalated in May 2007, leading to a bloody confrontation between Fatah al-Islam and the Lebanese Army, which claimed over 400 lives.[4] Thereafter, even though sporadic clashes between Sunni Salafist factions and pro-Hezbollah Alawite residents in northern Lebanon continued, the overall threat posed by radical Salafist groups subsided.

The Syrian civil war reinvigorated the Salafist camp in general, including its more radical and violent manifestations, and exacerbated an existing sectarian-political cleavage between the Sunni and Shiite communities in Lebanon, now split between anti- and pro-Assad supporters. This trend has led to growing clashes between these opposite camps, with violent exchanges localized primarily in the historically troubled areas around the northeast border city of Tripoli.

Fueled by rage over Assad's bloody response to the Syrian uprising and angered by Hezbollah's alliance with and assistance to the Assad regime, inter-sectarian clashes have been followed by direct attacks against Hezbollah, including rocket attacks against the Dahiye neighborhood, Hezbollah's stronghold in southern Beirut; suicide bombings against Shiite, Hezbollah, and Iranian targets; and operations targeting the Lebanese Armed Forces.[5] The main actors behind these attacks have been the al-Qaeda-affiliated Abdullah Azzam Brigades – responsible also for the high profile bombing of the Iranian Embassy in Beirut in November 2013[6] – and the al-Nusra Front in Lebanon claiming responsibility for a series of sectarian attacks, including a bloody suicide bombing in the Alawite Jabal Mohsen neighborhood in Tripoli in January 2015.[7] The Islamic State itself claimed responsibility for a January 2014 car bombing attack against Hezbollah's political office in the Beirut neighborhood of Haret Hreik and for a major terror attack in Dahiye in November 2015, and many other attacks were allegedly foiled.[8]

Yet despite reportedly discussing the appointment of an emir and the stepped-up domestic activities in Lebanon, the Islamic State's rise in Lebanon– along with that of the broader Salafi jihadist camp[9] – remains contained and closely monitored by the Lebanese security and intelligence apparatus. In this sense an important recent success of the Lebanese security sector against emerging Salafi jihadist forces has been the arrest of fugitive radical Salafist cleric Ahmad al-Assir, accused not only of engaging in a bloody confrontation with the Lebanese army, but also responsible for inciting sectarian strife and violence within Lebanon.[10] Hezbollah has also been closely watching the "takfiri threat," as described by Secretary General Nasrallah, taking the rise of hostile groups in Lebanon extremely seriously. In response, Hezbollah has boosted its own internal and community security, increased cooperation with the Lebanese Armed Forces, and lobbied at the political level to address the rise of Salafi jihadist forces in Lebanon as a top national security problem.

At the same time, there is a real concern over the growing political influence of Salafism within the Sunni community. Although not powerful or significant enough to challenge the political dominance of the Future Movement, these groups have been gaining more followers within Lebanon as a reaction to the Syrian civil war and Hezbollah's role fighting alongside Assad.

The Lebanese-Syrian Border and the Battle for Arsal

A related way through which the jihadist camp and the Islamic State in particular threatens Lebanon is more closely connected to the war raging in Syria and its direct spillover to Lebanon and the border areas. Indeed, the assessment over the danger posed by jihadist elements rose substantially after the August 2014 dramatic cross-border attack of the Lebanese border town of Arsal by al-Nusra and the Islamic State fighters, in response to the arrest by the Lebanese Armed Forces of a pro-Islamic State rebel commander who had turned not long before. In the Arsal confrontation, the jihadists directly attacked the Lebanese Army and police forces, kidnapping over 30 members of the Lebanese security sector – 25 of whom remain in captivity to this day.[11]

Following the armed confrontation on Lebanese soil, the Lebanese Armed Forces, in tacit coordination with Hezbollah, increased their presence and engagement on the ground, directly confronting the Islamic State and al-Nusra-affiliated groups operating in the border region.[12] Rebel groups had themselves sought refuge in the mountainous border area between Lebanon and Syria after engaging with the Syrian regime and Hezbollah in a long battle for the strategic Qalamoun region. Their eventual retreat from late 2013 resulted in the porous and barren lands surrounding Arsal becoming an operational base for roughly 3000-4000 fighters, mostly militants belonging to al-Nusra and, since mid-to-late 2014, the Islamic State. While these groups initially seemed able to coordinate and even achieve ad hoc cooperation, eventually inter-group rivalry and inner fighting emerged.[13] Despite the Islamic State presence on the ground, however, al-Nusra remained the most significant armed faction in the area, with the group better able to broker alliances with other factions, attract support from within Lebanese border towns, and access resources.[14]

Yet regardless of group affiliation, the presence of the Islamic State and al-Nusra fighters not only represents a direct security threat but also risks destabilizing inter-sectarian relations as well as relationships between local residents and Syrian refugees residing in the Bekaa governorate.[15] It is therefore not surprising to note that the uneasy predicament at the border has continued to impact on Lebanon. This is especially the case since early in the summer of 2015, when Hezbollah further stepped up its campaign against the takfiri threat by conducting, in coordination with the Syrian army, extensive military operations to destroy the last remnants of anti-regime opposition in the broader Qalamoun region. The confrontation extended further following the Islamic State attack against Hezbollah posts on June 9, 2015 around the town of Ras Baalbek just north of Arsal, expanding the battlefield on both sides of the border.[16] The Lebanese Army has also been tackling the takfiri threat, with the international community recognizing this role in the larger confrontation against the Islamic State and supporting it with increased military aid and military equipment.[17]

Lebanon and the Islamic State

Lebanon is definitely one of the regional actors that has been most affected by the events of the Syrian civil war and its broader implications. The post-

2014 rise of the Islamic State of Iraq and Sham (ISIS) and its transformation into the Islamic State also spells trouble for Lebanon.

Domestically, the country has seen a modest but still worrisome rise in activism of Salafi jihadist groups, reacting to the Syrian civil war and Hezbollah's support for the Bashar al-Assad regime and emboldened by the rise of the Islamic State project. This has led to a string of domestic terrorist operations targeting Hezbollah, the Shiite community at large, and the Lebanese security sector. Although these groups are small and fail to hold significant political clout within Lebanon's Sunni community, they nonetheless reflect a larger sense of frustration and powerlessness over the status quo. As such, concerns over the potential of more individuals becoming radicalized and joining the ranks of the Salafi jihadist camp are not unfounded. In the long term, this trend can also worsen an already delicate and frail sectarian-political balance within Lebanon.

In addition, the direct spillover of the Syrian civil war and the presence of the Islamic State and al-Nusra militants along the Syrian-Lebanon border represent a further source of instability, as reflected not only by the ongoing hostage crisis – itself the product of a jihadist attack on Lebanon – but also by the repeated and continued clashes between Hezbollah and the Lebanese Armed Forces on the one hand, and the Islamic State and al-Nusra on the other.

Notes

1   The video announcing the creation of the caliphate "This is the Promise of Allah" (*Hadna wa'd Allah)* was released in June 2014.

2   Omayma Abdel-Latif, "Lebanon's Sunni Islamists—A Growing Force," Carnegie Endowment for International Peace, Middle East Center (Washington, DC: Carnegie Endowment for International Peace, 2008), http://carnegie-mec.org/2008/02/04/lebanon-s-sunni-islamists-growing-force.

3   Bilal Y. Saad and Magnus Ranstorp, "Securing Lebanon from the Threat of Salafist Jihadism," *Studies in Conflict and Terrorism* 30 (2007).

4   Tine Gade, "Fatah al-Islam in Lebanon: Between Global and Local Jihad," Norwegian Defence Research Establishment (FFI), 2007, http://www.ffi.no/no/rapporter/07-02727.pdf.

5   Yoram Schweitzer and Benedetta Berti, "The Bombing of the Iranian Embassy in Beirut: Hitting Two Birds with One Stone," *INSS Insight* No. 488, November 21, 2013, http://www.inss.org.il/index.aspx?id=4538&articleid=5999.

6   Martin Chulov, "Lebanon 'Captures Iranian Embassy Bombing Mastermind,'" *The Guardian,* January 1, 2014, http://www.theguardian.com/world/2014/jan/01/lebanon-captures-iranian-embassy-bombing-mastermind.

7   Nour Samaha, "Twin Suicide Bomb Attacks Rock Lebanon," *al-Jazeera,* January 11, 2015, http://www.aljazeera.com/news/middleeast/2015/01/twin-suicide-bomb-attacks-rock-lebanon-2015111113944330224.html.

8   "Qaeda-linked ISIS Claims Beirut Suicide Blast," *al-Akhbar,* January 4, 2014, http://english.al-akhbar.com/node/18116. See, for example, Anne Barnard and Mohammad Ghannam, "Lebanon Detains 17 Said to Be Islamist Militants," *New York Times,* June 20, 2014, http://www.nytimes.com/2014/06/21/world/middleeast/a-dozen-men-reportedly-islamist-militants-detained-in-beirut-hotel.html.

9   "Report: ISIL Names 'Emir' for Lebanon, Sets Up Suicide Bombers Training Camp," *Naharnet,* June 29, 2014, http://www.naharnet.com/stories/en/136872.

10 "Lebanon Arrests Fugitive Cleric Ahmad al-Assir," *al-Arabiya,* August 15, 2015, http://english.alarabiya.net/en/News/middle-east/2015/08/15/Lebanese-authorities-detain-hardline-leader-Ahmed-al-Assir.html.

11 Benedetta Berti, "Lebanon's Growing Fragility," *INSS Insight,* June 11, 2015, http://www.inss.org.il/index.aspx?id=4538&articleid=9877.

12 See Lizzie Dearden, "Lebanese Soldiers Killed during Border Battle with Islamist Militants from Syria," *The Independent,* January 24, 2015, http://www.independent.co.uk/news/world/middle-east/lebanese-soldiers-killed-during-border-battle-with-islamist-militants-from-syria-10000144.html; "22 Dead in Hezbollah Clashes with ISIS on Northeast Lebanon Border," *Daily Star,* June 9, 2015, http://www.dailystar.com.lb/News/Lebanon-News/2015/Jun-09/301207-isis-attacks-hezbollah-posts-in-north-of-arsal.ashx.

13 Radwan Mortada, "Jihadi militants in Lebanon establishing 'Islamic State of Qalamoun' near Ersal," *al-Akhbar*, January 8, 2015, http://english.al-akhbar.com/node/23129.

14 Mario Abou Zeid, "The Emerging Jihadist Threat in Lebanon," Carnegie Middle East Center, January 28, 2015, http://carnegie-mec.org/2015/01/28/emerging-jihadist-threat-in-lebanon/i0s2.

15 Nicholas Blanford, "Lebanese Christians Next in Line for Islamic State," *The Times,* September 30, 2014, http://www.thetimes.co.uk/tto/news/world/middleeast/article4221655.ece.

16 *Ad-Diyar*, June 8, 2015, http://www.addiyar.com/article/899799; "Hezbollah Repels IS Attack on Lebanon-Syria Border," *AP,* June 9, 2015, http://news.yahoo.com/hezbollah-repels-attack-lebanon-syria-border-090543560.html.

17 "US Delivers $25m Weapons to Lebanon for Fight against Islamic Extremists," *The Guardian,* February 8, 2015, http://www.theguardian.com/world/2015/feb/08/us-25m-weapons-lebanon-islamic-extremists.

Jordan and the Islamic State Challenge

Asher Susser

Since its founding in 1921, Jordan's geopolitical centrality has been both a blessing and a curse. On the one hand, as a small, poor state locked between Iraq and Israel-Palestine and between Syria and Saudi Arabia, Jordan has always been at the mercy of regional trends and ideologies over which it has had no control. Now it must face both the regional ramifications of the Arab Spring and the new phenomenon of the Islamic State, which is rocking the political order in Jordan's immediate vicinity. The country has thus far survived all these crises, however, for two fundamental reasons. The first lies in the external support it has consistently garnered due to its geopolitical centrality and the fear that its collapse would lead to chaos throughout the region. The second, no less important, is its "stateness."

Stateness can be defined as the degree to which states fulfill at least two conditions: first, they possess an effective central government that maintains exclusive control over the use of force in a given sovereign territory whose borders are recognized both domestically and internationally; and second, there is a basic agreement among the citizenry on the rules of governance and political participation, and on who legitimately belongs to the people and the nation.

As it faces the challenge of the Islamic State, Jordan suffers from several serious internal weaknesses. The Islamic opposition in the country is undergoing serious radicalization, due in part to a faltering economy that is further burdened by the influx of hundreds of thousands of refugees from Syria. At the same time, Jordan also boasts some notable strengths. The ruling elite and security establishment show a generally high degree of internal cohesion and resolve, even if criticism and dissatisfaction are occasionally sounded among the elite. There is a strong sense of national solidarity among Jordanians, and the state has an effective central government with a monopoly on the use of force in the kingdom. Jordan thus possesses a level of stateness that is inestimably higher than that of its Arab neighbors. Therefore, a current situation assessment indicates that given the balance of the country's strengths and weaknesses, the scales at present are tipped in favor of the kingdom and the stability of the regime.

The Islamic State and Jordan's Internal State of Affairs

Regional Islamic radicalization processes have a direct effect on Jordan's internal state of affairs. For decades, the Muslim Brotherhood and its political party, the Islamic Action Front, was the strongest and most organized opposition group in the kingdom. Since late 2012, however, the Muslim Brotherhood has faced the most severe crisis in its history, as its status has weakened and it has largely been supplanted by more militant Salafi jihadists, the natural allies of entities such as the Islamic State and Jabhat al-Nusra.

In the early stages of the Arab Spring, the Muslim Brotherhood stood at the forefront of social protests against the Jordanian regime. It seemed as though the status of the organization was on the rise, especially after its Egyptian and Tunisian branches seized control of their respective countries. In Syria too the organization played a central role in the unrest. Nevertheless the Muslim Brotherhood eventually lost its grip on both Egypt and Tunisia, while the popular struggle in Syria has turned into a full-fledged, blood-soaked civil war that is abhorrent to most Jordanians. Salafi jihadists rose to prominence in Syria, and Arab Spring protests were curbed in Jordan. Thus the status of the Muslim Brotherhood waned, and internal disputes within the organization grew sharper. For years, the so-called hawks, mostly Palestinian, and the so-called doves, mostly Jordanian, had expressed differences of opinion regarding the regime on the one hand, and Palestine and Hamas on the other. Compared to the Palestinians, the Jordanians took a more conciliatory approach to the regime and favored less involvement with Hamas. Subsequently, severe internal disagreements grew to the point of a split.

As the Muslim Brotherhood underwent a process of self-destruction, organizations that began to flourish in Syria and Iraq such as the Islamic State and Jabhat al-Nusra became far more attractive to a younger generation of both Jordanians and Palestinians. Many among this younger generation are unemployed and lack faith in the Jordanian economy, which has been in a persistent state of a seemingly irreversible crisis. Moreover, key leaders of Jabhat al-Nusra are Jordanians with Palestinian roots.[1]

In Ma'an, a city in southern Jordan that has been a locus of a socioeconomic crisis and anti-government sentiment for decades, popular support for Salafi jihadists has long outstripped loyalty to the Muslim Brotherhood. Ma'an has witnessed more than one public manifestation of support for the Islamic State and other groups of similar ilk. Other areas in the south, or Zarqa and Russeifa to the north of Amman (likewise centers of economic depression, but unlike Ma'an, home to large Palestinian populations) are the home of many of the thousands of Jordanian volunteers who have joined the jihadist organizations fighting in Syria.[2]

Thus, Jordan's faltering economy has driven thousands of its young citizens to a profitable jihad adventure that may not only prove lucrative but also allows them to express their sectarian identification with the struggle of their Sunni cohorts against Shiites and their Alawite allies. Estimates of Jordanian volunteers fall in the range of 2,000-5,000. The Salafi movement, however, is also making inroads in Jordan itself. One source claims that there are 6,000-7,000 Salafists in Jordan plus an additional 2,000 supporters.[3] Other sources, however, calculate 15,000 hardcore Salafists and another 10,000 supporters.[4] These are rough estimates that do not differentiate between Salafi jihadists and Salafists who do not support violence.

According to the Islamic State, Syria and Iraq are *Dar al-Tamkin* (the "enabling region," i.e., one that allows for the organization's expansion) en route to *Bilad al-Sham* (Greater Syria), an entity that will include Jordan. Nonetheless, the immediate threat to Jordan is not conquest by the Islamic State or Jabhat al-Nusra, but rather subversion within its own borders, which is organized in bases in Syria or Iraq and furthered by volunteers returning home and other activists and supporters within Jordan.

Salafi Islam is present in Jordan, even dominant in social media, and is exerting its influence in new ways. At the same time, there is a tendency to exaggerate the value and political impact of these platforms. One problem with the Arab Spring was the major confusion between the virtual and the real. In Egypt, for example, the power of social groups with a large presence in social media was greatly overestimated, while the real, non-virtual power of two opposing groups – the Muslim Brotherhood on the one hand, and the armed forces on the other – was greatly underestimated.

Like its Arab neighbors, Jordan too faces opposition from different social groups, be they tribal, Islamic, leftist, liberal, or others in the new social media. The actual power of this opposition is difficult to measure, but it could prove dangerous to the regime if and when it calls on Jordanian political powers, especially tribal, to act in non-virtual ways and express their very real frustrations through violence. This may or may not lead to a different reality, one in which security forces will find it difficult to act against the opposition or even refuse to do so because the opposition will be composed of members of the same East Bank tribes that constitute the core of the security establishment. The possibility that a subversive association between the Islamic State and local Salafist supporters will lead to such a reality is of great concern to Jordanian intelligence officials. For now this is a theoretical scenario, but as is evident from elsewhere in the Middle East, familiar realities are easily overturned.

Cracks in the Loyalty of the Elite

As neighboring states fall apart, Jordan has become awash with an unprecedented wave of refugees. Salafi jihadists with apocalyptic worldviews, such as those promoted by the Islamic State and Jabhat al-Nusra, are filling the vacuum that failed states such as Iraq and Syria have left behind. In turn, Sunni sectarian identification, acute economic distress, and a sense of looming catastrophe have made Salafist ideas more palatable throughout the kingdom.

Consequently, as the Jordanian government faces these serious challenges and is exposed to the ramifications of unprecedented regional collapse, a few cracks in the traditional loyalties of the elites and the tribes affiliated with them have become evident. Voices of dissatisfaction and critiques of King Abdullah can now be heard from the veteran East Bank elites. The economic belt-tightening and reforms of recent years have affected East Bank Jordanians more than they have their Palestinian countrymen, because government spending cuts hurt primarily those who depend on the government for their income, that is, government employees or recipients of government benefits, who are mostly from the East Bank. Since Palestinians are more involved in the private sector, they have been less affected by the situation. In the eyes of the East Bank population, which had granted the regime their unquestioned support in return for its attention to their financial security, government cuts represent a violation of their unwritten social contract with the regime.

A new element has recently joined this internal tension: the Jordanians' general lack of identification with the role played by the kingdom in the US-led coalition against the Islamic State. In their view, this is not Jordan's war. Thus "a dangerous lack of trust between state and street"[5] has developed due to Jordan's involvement in the fighting, especially the airstrikes. While many in the country understand that fighting the Islamic State and defeating the blatant barbarism it represents is for Jordan's own good, for many others, this is an American war against their Sunni brothers; from their perspective, the Islamic State and similar organizations are not barbaric terrorist groups, but courageous combatants engaged in a just war of the Sunnis against the Shiites, their historic enemies. According to these critics, Jordan would do anything to receive aid from the United States, and is thus "fully subservient to Washington" and does "not have any independent political will."[6]

The Flip Side of the Coin

Concomitantly, however, there is another side to this coin, namely, national solidarity and loyalty to the existing political order. This was dramatized in early February 2015 with the release of the video of First Lieutenant Muath al-Kasasbeh, a Jordanian pilot who had fallen into captivity, being burned to death by Islamic State militants. The entire population of Jordan, Jordanians and Palestinians alike, united behind the government with their expression of revulsion as well as their demand for vengeance and continued warfare against the Islamic State. Their rallying around the regime and the national flag amounted to an impressive show of national solidarity, so often overshadowed by internal rifts in the Jordanian collective.

In Jordan, tension between Jordanians and Palestinians is ongoing and tribal rivalries are routine. Since the 1970s, Jordanians of Palestinian descent have consistently and gradually sought to establish themselves as equals, which is more than native Jordanians have been willing to allow. Over the years, those of the East Bank have become the standard-bearers of what it means to be Jordanian – a notion based on an historic alliance between the region's tribes and the Hashemite dynasty. Despite cracks in tribal loyalty, Jordan is still their homeland. The tribal identity has merged with Jordanian identity, in which deep identification with the Jordanian kingdom is highly important. The tribes see the monarchy as the cohesive element holding the

Jordanian state and Jordanian society together, and they also understand that there are no attractive alternatives – certainly not a Palestinian-majority government or the nightmare of Islamic State rule.

Unlike other nations in the Fertile Crescent, such as Lebanon, Syria, and Iraq, all on the brink of disaster, Jordan is not a mosaic of warring sects. It is homogeneous in its sectarian composition; over 90 percent of the population are Sunni Muslim Arabs, with a tiny minority – less than 5 percent – of Christians, mostly Greek Orthodox. Much has justifiably been said about Jordanian-Palestinian tensions. Although the two groups do indeed compete in terms of identity, insufficient attention has been paid to the fact that most Jordanians and Palestinians are Sunnis. In a time of militant sectarianism, a unifying sectarian factor is more important than a divisive national one. Jordanian and Palestinian identities, no matter how real, are new and historically shallow. Their relative importance is of little consequence when compared to the historic enmity between the Sunna and the Shia, which dates back to Islam's very origins in the seventh century.

The powerful response to the murder of the Jordanian pilot led to speculation about Jordan's imminent participation in the ground war against the Islamic State.[7] But it soon became clear that the Jordanians had no intention of joining the offensive. Although some believed that a ground war against the Islamic State was critical, they did not feel as though it was their job, but rather that of the countries directly involved, i.e., Syria and Iraq.[8] The demonstration of national solidarity was an expression of the Jordanians' willingness and resolve to defend their country against Salafi jihadist threats, but this willingness did not extend to sending Jordanian troops across the border to fight the Islamic State on the behalf of others – certainly not the Shiites of Iraq, or even their allies, such as the United States.

Conclusion

Jordan faces internal challenges and economic hardships that are feeding off each other. Many young people are unemployed and see no way to attain power, prestige, and prosperity for themselves and their families. Salafism and Salafi jihadism thus have an appeal to this generation. Nonetheless, Jordan is coping relatively well with the ramifications of the Arab Spring and the challenges posed by the Islamic State thanks to its degree of stateness, internal cohesion, the resolve of its elites (their criticism of the kingdom notwithstanding), and the interests and goodwill of its allies.

It is difficult to imagine real and immediate solutions for Jordan's problems: the challenge of dealing with the Islamic State and the Salafists, the country's economic difficulties, and the Palestinian question. It appears that the Jordanians will continue to muddle through, as they have for decades, while relying on complex political maneuvers and increasingly generous help from their friends, first and foremost the United States. One day, however, this aid may no longer prove sufficient, nor is there any guarantee that it will continue to flow indefinitely.

Notes

1   Mona Alami, "The New Generation of Jordanian Jihadi Fighters," Sada – Middle East Analysis, Carnegie Endowment for International Peace:, February 18, 2014, http://carnegieendowment.org/sada/2014/02/18/new-generation-of-jordanian-jihadi-fighters/h17c.

2   David Schenker, "Countering the ISIS Threat to Jordan," *Wall Street Journal*, July 13, 2014.

3   Osama al-Sharif, "Jordan Rejects Land Offensive against ISIS for Now," *al-Monitor*, February 13, 2015.

4   Alami, "The New Generation of Jordanian Jihadi Fighters."

5   Sultan Barakat and Andrew Leber, "Fortress Jordan: Putting the Money to Work," Brookings Doha Center, Policy Briefings, February 2015, p. 10.

6   Lamis Andoni, "Not Our War: Jordan vs. the Islamic State Group," *al-Araby al-Jadeed*, December 30, 2014, and "Testing Jordan's Independence," *Middle East Monitor*, February 4, 2015, https://www.middleeastmonitor.com/articles/middle-east/16789-testing-jordans-independence.

7   Alice Su, "It Wasn't Their War," *The Atlantic*, February 5, 2015; Salah Nasrawi, "The Jordanian Option," *al-Ahram Weekly*, February 12-18, 2015.

8   Urayb al-Rantawi, "ISIS Will Be Consumed by the Flames of Its Own Radicalism"; *al-Dustur*, February 6, 2015; Fahd al-Fanik, "What Comes after the Shock?"; *al-Rai*, February 10, 2015; Jihad al-Muhaysin, "It's Their Ground War, Not Ours"; *al-Ghad*, February 11, 2015; King Abdallah interview with Fareed Zakaria, *CNN*, March 1, 2015, http://www.kingabdullah.jo/index.php/en_US/interviews/view/id/517/videoDisplay/0.html.

The Influence of the Islamic State on Israel's Arab Citizens and on Palestinians in Gaza and the West Bank

Aviad Mandelbaum and Yoram Schweitzer

The civil war that erupted in Syria in 2011 and the ongoing instability in Iraq have served as the backdrop for the growth of the ISIS organization and the ensuing establishment of the Islamic State, which contributed to the dissolution of the state structures in both Syria and Iraq. Abu Bakr al-Baghdadi's appointment of himself as caliph and the establishment of the Islamic State as the basis of his caliphate have inspired and driven tens of thousands of Muslim volunteers from all over the world to join the ranks of the Islamic State and perpetrate acts of terror in its name. This influence has not been lost on Israel's Arab citizens or the populations of the Gaza Strip and the West Bank.

In contrast to the large number of volunteers who flocked from all over the world to fight in Syria and join the ranks of the Islamic State, the response among Israel's Arab citizens has been relatively weak – although by late 2015 this phenomenon was clearly on the rise. According to reports in Israel, there have been 57 Arab citizens of Israel who have left Israel with the goal of joining the fighting in Syria, with at least 25 of those intending to join the ranks of Islamic State.[1] Most recently, one 23 year-old from Jaljuliya used a hang glider over the Golan Heights to cross the Israel-Syria border, allegedly to join the Islamic State.

In September 2014, Israel declared officially, as have various other Western countries, that any activity connected with the Islamic State is illegal, and accordingly, those who acted in its service were arrested and tried.[2] Over the last year alone over 40 Israeli Arabs who tried joining the Islamic State were arrested; some were caught when attempting to leave Israel, and some were caught upon their return from fighting in Syria and Iraq.[3] The age of the volunteers ranges from 19 to 30, and it is difficult to identify a common geographical thread regarding their places of origin, which include Hura in the Negev, Yasif and Yafia in the north, and central cities such as Umm al-Fahm and Tayibe.

The arrest in August 2015 of Iman Khanjo, an Israeli Arab woman who left Israel with the goal of joining Islamic State, exemplifies the diversity of the volunteers and their goals, as well as the role played by social networks in the recruitment process. Khanjo distributed propaganda materials on the internet, and through this activity was found by an Islamic State operative named Abu Ali Ashami, who contacted her online and assisted in her attempt to enter Syria.[4] Khanjo, a 44 year-old doctoral student in Islamic studies from Shfaram, is an example of the range in level of education, social standing, place of origin, and gender of the volunteers. Her ambition to educate young Muslims in accordance with *sharia* law goes hand-in-hand with the phenomenon of "immigration" to the Islamic State with the goal of taking part in the revival of the caliphate. This phenomenon appears among families relocating to Syria, and has occurred among families in Israel as well.[5] On a practical level, the arrest and return of Khanjo to Israel through the joint effort of Israeli and Turkish security and law enforcement authorities demonstrates how international cooperation can curtail this trend.[6]

Besides volunteering to fight in the ranks of the Islamic State, Arab citizens of Israel have engaged in various activities inspired by it, including supporting activities such as the financing of volunteers headed for Syria, contact with activists in the field, distribution of content identified with the Islamic State, and terror activities. On May 15, 2014, Adris Abu al-Qiyan was indicted on charges of conspiracy and assistance in the illegal exit of Israel. Al-Qiyan aided two volunteers, including his brother Othman Talib Ahmed Abu al-Qiyan, in leaving for Syria to enlist in the Islamic State.[7] Indictments submitted in July 2015 against six Israeli Arab citizens, including four teachers who lived in the villages of Rahat and Hura in the Negev, indicate that they were involved in the distribution of Islamic State propaganda in the schools in their villages.[8] There have also been cases of ideological support of the Islamic State on social networks.[9]

The fear of the transition from ideological support to actual terror activity within Israel's borders under the inspiration of the Islamic State was realized in January 2015: seven Israeli Arabs from Nazareth were indicted for association with the Islamic State and support of its actions. The head of this group was Adnan Sa'id Alla-a-Din, formerly an advocate with the public defender's office. Alla-a-Din recruited the group members, all in their twenties, lectured them on religion and taught them the main principles of Salafi jihadist ideology, preached to them about the need for preparation for military action and attacks against Jews, and trained and steeled them for such actions with the slaughter of sheep. One of those arrested admitted that he intended to carry out a shooting attack in Israel against security forces and members of the Druze community.[10]

In August 2015, security officials intercepted a cell of three men from Kafr Yafiya and Nazareth who had trained in shooting and had researched possible targets for terrorist attacks, including the police station in Migdal Haemek and an army base. They monitored businesses in Yafia and Nazareth that functioned "against the spirit of Islam" and sold alcoholic beverages. The cell was formed following Facebook encounters with contacts from Yafia who enlisted with the Islamic State in Syria and today are fighting in Iraq. These individuals were a source of inspiration and encouraged their contacts in Israel to launch terrorist attacks there. Indeed, this cell hoped to execute attacks in Israel, and then join the ranks of the Islamic State in Syria. One of the cell members was in contact with Ahmad Ali Khalil Ahmad, a Salafi jihadi resident of Nazareth, serving a life prison sentence in Israel for his involvement in the murder of an Israeli taxi driver in 2009.[11] Some individuals from that cell then went to Africa to train with the Somali al-Shaabab organization but were arrested in Kenya and extradited to Israel.[12]

In contrast to the influence on the Arab citizens of Israel, the Islamic State wields greater influence among the Palestinians in the Gaza Strip, where terror organizations identified with the Salafi jihadist stream have operated for a number of years. Such activity has led in the past to conflicts with Hamas, which has ruled Gaza since 2007, mainly involving challenges to the hegemony of the Hamas regime. The most prominent case occurred in August 2009, when Hamas activists raided the Ibn Taymia Mosque in Dir al-Balah, killing 24 Salafist operatives, including their leader Sheik Abed-al-Latif Musa, who was considered dangerous due to his declaration of the establishment of an Islamic emirate in the Gaza Strip. The strengthening of the Islamic State since the summer of 2014 has instilled renewed momentum among Salafi jihadist activists in Gaza, and has led to a cluster of organizations from this camp declaring their support for the radical stream. Since then, there has been a struggle underway between Hamas and Salafi jihadist elements, which involved Hamas security forces arresting dozens of their operatives and even destroying a Salafi mosque in Dir-al-Balah.

For their part, the Salafi jihadist operatives have planted bombs in public buildings and fired rockets toward Israel without Hamas approval, in order to cause friction between Hamas and Israel. Against the backdrop of the escalation of the internal struggle, an official Islamic State video clip was distributed on social networks in late June 2015 threatening Hamas and warning that the blood-drenched theater of war in the Levant will in the future be relocated to the Gaza Strip. The spokesman, Issa a-Lakta of the Sheik Raduan neighborhood in Gaza, who was formerly a Hamas operative, joined the ranks of the Islamic State in Syria in 2013. In his statement a-Lakta mentioned the slaughter carried out by Islamic State operatives last April in the Yarmouk Palestinian refugee camp near Damascus, when they beheaded several of the Hamas commanders in the camp; he further promised to bring down the infidel Palestinian governments in the West Bank and the Gaza Strip. The identity and blunt public threats of a former Hamas member against continued Hamas rule of Gaza demonstrate the criticism of Hamas by Salafi jihadists, and at the same time, the rising stature of the Islamic State among Gaza Strip residents. This is also reflected in the establishment of new Salafi jihadist groups in the Strip, such as the Sheik Omar Hadid Bait al-Maqdis Brigades[13] and Supporters of the Islamic State in Jerusalem.[14]

The unqualified support of these groups for the Islamic State was reflected in the establishment of ISIS in Gaza in 2014 and subsequently in their declaration of loyalty to al-Baghdadi, which to their disappointment was rejected and did not lead to their acceptance by the Islamic State as an independent Palestinian province. The refusal to recognize these groups as an exclusive province stems from their being marked by sectarianism and factionalism, their inability to establish an autonomy in Gaza ruled by *sharia* law, and lack of proof of their ability to fight Israel effectively. These circumstances violate the Islamic State admission requirements as specified in *Dabiq*, the Islamic State's English-language propaganda magazine.[15] Moreover, al-Baghdadi does not see Palestinian nationalism as an independent issue, and holds that its solution will be realized through the merging of the Palestinians into the broader Islamic State that he has established, or through cooperation with Wilayat Sinai – the Islamic State's proxy in Egypt. Nonetheless, the efforts by Salafi jihadist organizations in Egypt continues, and are reflected in attempts to unify the various Salafist organizations in the Gaza Strip, as evidenced by propaganda notices distributed in Gaza and in retaliatory strikes against Hamas symbols in Gaza, as well as in rocket fire toward Israel in an attempt to demonstrate stronger opposition to the enemy.

For its part, Hamas is fighting Islamic State supporters in Gaza, and is attempting to suppress any action undermining its hegemony over the Strip. Nevertheless, due to a variety of considerations and interests, Hamas sometimes allows operations from Gaza aiding Ansar Bait al-Maqdis in Sinai in their struggle against the Egyptian regime. This aid includes smuggling through the tunnels in Rafah, treatment of operatives wounded in battles against the Egyptian army, and sometimes even the transfer of combat intelligence.[16] The double standard in Hamas' attitude toward Islamic State supporters in the Gaza Strip and the operatives in Sinai suits the pragmatism of the Hamas movement, which is driven by a central strategic consideration of maintaining its rule over the Gaza Strip while continuing to maintain the "resistance," and preserve the possibility that in the future it may benefit from the cooperation of its counterparts in Sinai.

In contrast with Gaza, where there is a prominent Salafist presence, most of which identifies with the Islamic State, it is clear that among Palestinians in the West Bank the activity of Salafi jihadist elements is relatively marginal, and accordingly, so is the influence of the Islamic State. Only a few operatives from the West Bank have joined the fighting in Syria, and even fewer have joined the ranks of the Islamic State. Similarly, the West Bank has seen only isolated incidents that reflect the presence of Salafi jihadist elements operating secretly underground, awaiting a suitable time to act. Some of them have already attempted to act over the last few years. Thus, for example, in 2013 three operatives associated with Salafi jihadist elements in Hebron were killed in an IDF counterterrorism operation to prevent their attempt to carry out a large scale attack.[17] In January 2014, three operatives were arrested (one from East Jerusalem and two from Jenin) for planning attacks in Israel. The head of the terror cell was in contact with elements identified with al-Qaeda in Pakistan and Gaza, and intended to join operatives who took part in the fighting in Syria and were supposed to enter Israel to help him carry out attacks.[18]

Yet despite the only minor support for Islamic State that has surfaced so far, streams that identify with its ideology exist throughout the West Bank and may eventually attempt to act in its name, and perhaps even with its guidance. Such a scenario becomes more likely should there be a significant escalation in Israeli-Palestinian relations. In a round of arrests made by the Palestinian security services in February 2015, for example, some fifteen people were arrested, suspected of ties to the Islamic State – some out of ideological identification and some out of financial incentive. Dozens of individuals have been arrested since on similar charges; most have been released.[19]

Although Palestinian society in Gaza and the West Bank has for the most part rejected the Islamic State, there is evidence of growing support for it.[20] In recent years some 200 Palestinians have made their way to the Islamic State, and in 2015 an average of two Palestinians a month were killed on the various fronts – Syria, Iraq, and Libya, in suicide attacks, ground combat, or airstrikes. Most of those killed came from Gaza, with some from Hebron, Nablus, and Jenin. Most of these volunteers are in their twenties, claiming that they are headed abroad to continue their education; many are former Hamas operatives or members of Salafist factions in Gaza.

Thus the changes in the map of Salafi jihadist organizations that have occurred in various locations in the region, in the wake of the arrival and success of the Islamic State, have not eluded the Arabs residing in Israel, Gaza, and the West Bank. While in Israel and the West Bank this is a relatively marginal phenomenon, significant support for the Islamic State and its ideology can be found in the Gaza Strip. The background for this is the existing infrastructure in Gaza for Salafi jihadist ideas, which preceded the arrival of ISIS and subsequently the Islamic State. Hamas' failure to institute and forcibly enforce *sharia* law on all Gaza Strip residents, and its avoidance of continuous military confrontation with Israel due to survival considerations, has led to disappointed Hamas operatives leaving the movement and joining new Salafi jihadist organizations in Gaza, as well as to cooperate with jihadist elements in Sinai.

It appears, therefore, that the future support for Islamic State actions depends to a great extent on the organization's success in surviving and expanding its conquests, and broadcasting an image of success and power. The main support is expected to come from the direction of the organizations in Gaza, but there exists potential for activity by these elements also in Israel and the West Bank, depending on developments in Israeli-Palestinian relations. The Islamic State may well use the escalation in the Israeli-Palestinian arena in late 2015, with stabbing, vehicle, and shooting attacks, to broaden its influence, engage new recruits, or launch terror attacks in Israel. This is already reflected in video clips posted on the social media, which promise Israel's imminent obliteration, and in the establishment of a new communications platform – al-Musra – devoted specifically to the Palestinian issue.

Notes

1   Reported on Channel One news on July 7, 2015 by Amir Bar-Shalom, and confirmed in a private conversation with him. See also Yasir Okbi, "Three Israelis in Turkey Seek to Join ISIS," *Maariv*, July 23, 2015; Yehoshua Briner and Gali Ginat, "Two Israelis Accused of Trying to Join ISIS Ranks," *Walla*, August 13, 2015, http://news.walla.co.il/item/2881604; Yair Kraus, "Israeli Doctoral Student Accused of Joining ISIS," *NRG*, September 20, 2015, http://www.nrg.co.il/online/1/ART2/726/098.html?hp=1&cat=402&loc=2.

2   Gili Cohen, "Yaalon Declares Islamic State to be Unlawful Organization," *Haaretz*, September 3, 2014, http://www.haaretz.co.il/news/politics/1.2424208.

3   Briner and Ginat, "Two Israelis Accused of Trying to Join ISIS Ranks."

4   Kraus, "Israeli Doctoral Student Accused of Joining ISIS."

5   Yasir Okbi, "Israeli Arab Admits: I Eluded the GSS and Joined ISIS," *Maariv Online*, May 2, 2015, http://www.maariv.co.il/news/world/Article-473617.

6   Krauss, "Israeli Doctoral Student Accused of Joining ISIS."

7   "Hura Resident Arrested on Suspicion of Assisting in Recruitment for Organization Fighting Assad Regime," Israel Security Agency website, May 27, 2014, http://www.shabak.gov.il/publications/publications/Pages/NewItem270514.aspx.

8   "Six Residents of Hura in the Negev Arrested for their Support of ISIS," Israel Security Agency website, July 6, 2015, http://www.shabak.gov.il/publications/publications/Pages/NewItem060715.aspx.

9   Such was the case of Muhammed Jamal Suleiman Abu Ra'ad, 22, who was convicted on May 28, 2015 of supporting ISIS through Facebook. He was the first person in Israel convicted for supporting terror on social networks. See Yoav Zeitun and Hassan Shalan, "Umm al-Fah Resident Charged with 'Liking' ISIS," *Ynet*, May 28, 2015, http://www.ynet.co.il/articles/0,7340,L-4662477,00.html.

10 Furat Nassar and Nir Dvori, "Lawyer from North Recruited Israeli Youths for ISIS – and Trained in Slaughtering," Channel 2 News, January 15, 2015, http://www.mako.co.il/news-military/security-q1_2015/Article-9a71735488cfa41004.htm; "ISIS Activity in Israel Revealed."

11 "Terror Group from Yafia Involved with Establishment of ISIS Cell Arrested," Israel Security Agency website, October 1, 2015, https://www.shabak.gov.il/publications/publications/Pages/NewItem11015.aspx; Or Heller, Ali Levy, and Sami Abd al-Hamid, "Released for Publication: 7 Arab Israelis who Planned to Launch Terrorist Attacks and Join ISIS Arrested," *Nana 10*, October 1, 2015, http://

news.nana.co.il/Article/?ArticleID=1150642&sid=126; Adi Hashmonai and Amir Buhbut, "ISIS Cell that Operated in the Nazareth Area and Planned Attacks against Soldiers Arrested," *Walla*, October 1, 2015, http://news.walla.co.il/item/2893731.

12 "Seven Nazareth Residents Arrested on Nationalist-Related Offenses," Israel Security Agency website, June 28, 2010, www.shabak.gov.il/publications/publications/Pages/shotef280610.aspx; Ron Ben Yishai, "From the Mosque through the Internet, to Somalia: The Jihad Route," *Ynet*, June 28, 2010, http://www.ynet.co.il/articles/0,7340,L-3911797,00.html.

13 The Sheik Amr Hadid Bait al-Maqdis Brigades organization was named for the deputy of Abu Musab al-Zarqawi, leader of al-Qaeda in Iraq, known as a courageous fighter who was killed by the Americans in 2003.

14 The Supporters of the Islamic State in Jerusalem organization played a prominent role in escalation incidents in the Gaza Strip, with a leaflet distributed on April 9 presenting an ultimatum to Hamas to release Salafist operatives, including the well-known Salafist Sheik Adnan Elmit, who were arrested in wide-scale arrest campaigns in the strip. See "Terror News and the Israeli-Palestinian Conflict," Meir Amit Intelligence and Terrorism Information Center, January 14, 2015, http://www.terrorism-info.org.il/Data/articles/Art_20797/H_056_15_412793579.pdf. The Sheik Amr Hadid Bait al-Maqdis Brigades organization first appeared when in early June 2015 it published on its Twitter account a video claiming responsibility for the firing of a Grad missile at Israel. See Asaf Gibor, "Troubles at Homes: Salafi Organization Presented Hamas with an Ultimatum," *NRG*, June, 2, 2015, http://www.nrg.co.il/online/1/ART2/698/321.html.

15 *Dabiq* 5, https://azelin.files.wordpress.com/2015/02/the-islamic-state-e2809cdc481biq-magazine-522.pdf.

16 Avi Issacharoff, "Revealed: Hamas Continues to Transfer ISIS Wounded from Sinai to Gaza," *Walla*, July 8, 2015, http://news.walla.co.il/item/2871024; Avi Issacharoff, "Hamas UAV Revealed: Cooperation with ISIS Stronger than Ever," *Walla*, July 9, 2015, http://news.walla.co.il/item/2871353.

17 Yoav Zeitun, "3 Wanted for Planning Attack in Israel Killed," *Ynet*, November 26, 2013, http://www.ynet.co.il/articles/0,7340,L-4458357,00.html.

18 Amir Buhbut, "Al-Qaeda Leader Planned Attacks in Binyanei Haumah in Jerusalem," *Walla*, January 22, 2014, http://news.walla.co.il/item/2714361.

19 Avi Issacaharoff, "ISIS Threat: The Palestinian Authority Arrests some 15 Suspects in the West Bank," *Walla*, February 3, 2015, http://news.walla.co.il/item/2825879.

20 Sam Boutrous, "Does My Relative Support ISIS? 1 Million Palestinians in the West Bank and Gaza Support ISIS," Linga.org, July 4, 2015, https://www.linga.org/local-news/NzY4OQ.

Part IV

Regional Forces

Iran vs. the Islamic State:
The Enemy of My Enemy is also My Enemy

Ephraim Kam

According to the official annual publication of the US State Department, Iran has been defined since 1984 as the country most involved in terrorism around the world. Yet it too has faced terrorist attacks carried out by its various enemies and opponents.

Iran is a country of minorities. Indeed, half of the country's residents are not ethnic Persians, and some of these minorities exhibit a readiness to engage in terrorist activity against government targets. In the past, political groups opposed to the regime perpetrated terrorist acts as well. The scope and magnitude of such attacks in Iran since the stabilization of its Islamic regime has been limited, however. Most have been solely of tactical significance, and in any case, their numbers have waned over the years.

The threat posed by the Islamic State is of a different scale. It is multi-dimensional, affects Iran's most important regional interests, and jeopardizes its status and allies among particular groups in the three countries most important to it: the Shiites in Iraq, the Assad regime in Syria, and Hezbollah and the Shiite community in Lebanon.

As a Sunni entity, Iran regards the Islamic State as a Sunni threat to the Shiites, particularly as the Islamic State possesses immense sources of power: large territories that it has seized in Iraq and Syria; preliminary infiltration of other countries (Libya, Egypt, Lebanon, and even the Caucasus and Southeast Asia); military and terrorist capabilities; major financial assets; and an ability to attract young people to expand its manpower. The Islamic State vision of a large Islamic caliphate runs counter to the interests of Iran, which seeks to maintain the territorial integrity of Iraq and Syria, and certainly that of its own country.

The Islamic State, along with other organizations headed by Jabhat al-Nusra, poses a concrete threat to the Assad regime in Syria. For Iran, the meaning of this threat is clear. Syria, under the leadership of Assads Sr. and Jr., has been Iran's oldest ally. The alliance between them is based on important common interests, and has proven solid over the years. Syria also serves as a bridge between Iran and Lebanon and thus Hezbollah, and enables Iran to maintain an essential frontline against Israel. As such, the Assad regime is irreplaceable; its fall would not only be a severe blow to Iran, but also a victory for the United States, the Sunni Arab countries, Turkey, and the Islamic State. It would thus weaken Iran's regional status.

The Islamic State's current control of one quarter of Iraq, including some of its key cities, poses a threat to Iran. For the last decade, Iran has been the most important and influential external player in Iraq. Its standing has rested primarily on its close ties with Shiite organizations, leaders, and armed militias, and is reflected in its transfer of money and arms and its more limited ties with the Kurds. The Islamic State's rapid penetration of Iraq poses a critical threat to the Iraqi government, which has ties with Iran, and to the Shiite militias in the country. Like Iraqi security forces, these militias have already proven their inability to cope with the invasion.

In certain respects, Iran regards the Islamic State's threat to Iraq as even greater than its threat to Syria. Iraq borders Iran, and the Shiites constitute about 60 percent of the Iraqi population, albeit substantial numbers of them oppose Iran's growing influence. Two of the most holy Shiite cities, Najaf and Karbala, lie in Iraq. Iran's links with Iraq, including economic ties, are currently more extensive than its ties with Syria. The Assad regime is tottering, and its fate is unclear. The importance of Iraq to Iran is clearly reflected in the words of Iranian Foreign Minister Javad Zarif, who, after the Islamic State's penetration of Iraq, stated that "Iran regards the security of Iraq as its own."[1]

The Islamic State now constitutes – and likely never will – no direct threat to Iranian territory, thanks to Iran's military power, the stability of its regime, and the absence of a governmental vacuum in the country. In addition, Iran is a Shiite country with no real basis of popular support for the Islamic State. Indeed, in June 2014 Iranian Deputy Foreign Minister Hossein Amir Abdollahian declared that the Islamic State does not pose a threat to Iran's geographic borders.[2] However, Iran worries primarily about the lack of stability in Iraq, which might spill over to its own territory. Iranian sources warn that the splintering of Iraq would affect minorities in Iran, especially the Kurds, and encourage these groups to raise their demands to realize their national aspirations and break away. The Iranian press has also argued that the Islamic State is a creation of the United States, Saudi Arabia, and Israel, aimed at dividing Iraq and weakening Iran.[3] Against this backdrop, Iran is taking steps to prevent Islamic State forces in Iraq from nearing its territory, in part by stationing Iranian forces along the border with Iraq.

The deteriorating situation in Iraq and Syria has led Iran to grant substantial aid to both these countries in their struggle against the Islamic State – aid that actually began before the organization appeared on the scene. In November 2013, Iran and Iraq signed an arms agreement, which supplied artillery, mortar, and light arms to Iraq. Given the sanctions imposed on Iran, which banned it from selling arms, it is unclear whether all the ammunition included in the transaction was actually shipped. Yet after the fall of Mosul to the Islamic State in June 2014, Iran openly supplied the Iraqi government with Iranian-made rockets, UAVs, and other military equipment. In early July 2014, Iran also gave Iraq SU-25 warplanes, which had been smuggled to Iran by Saddam Hussein during the Gulf War in 1991. However, once it became clear that these munitions were not enough to stop the Islamic State, due to the weakness and lack of resolve on the part of the Iraqi army, Iran increased its military aid to Iraq.

The key figure in Iran's military aid to Iraq is General Qassem Suleimani, Commander of the Revolutionary Guard's al-Quds Force, Iran's chief agency for dealing with clandestine security activity abroad. Suleimani has traveled to Iraq frequently; since June 2014, his visits there have been public, accompanied by a public relations campaign that portrays him as the country's savior. Suleimani handled the training of the Shiite militias in Iraq, helped establish volunteer militias to fight alongside the weak local army, and presided over the establishment of joint operational centers, the transmission of intelligence, and the provision of military and organizational advice to the Iraqi government and security forces. He also granted military aid to the Kurdish militia while helping it defend Erbil and push Islamic State forces away from the city. In addition, he played a key role in breaking the Islamic State siege of the Shiite Turkoman city of Amirli in September 2014.[4]

Suleimani's appearance in Iraq is also associated with a shift in the nature of Iranian military involvement in the country. Like the US, Iran has tried to avoid sending ground troops into Iraq, and in case such a move proved necessary, to restrict it to a minimum. The goal was to assist the Iraqi government and the Shiite militias, but avoid open and direct military confrontations and thereby avoid entanglement and losses that might lead to internal criticism of its own regime. Thus initially, in June 2014, officials in Tehran denied the presence of any Iranian forces in Iraq. At the time, Iranian President Rouhani asserted that the country had never sent any forces to Iraq, and would most probably never do so in the future. When, however, it became evident that no party in the field was capable of stopping the Islamic State and forcing it to withdraw, and on the contrary, the Islamic State was moving toward the Iranian border, Iran grew more inclined to become involved in the actual fighting. Iran, for example, reportedly aided the Kurdish counterattack in northern Iraq by sending in military units, including tanks.[5]

The full extent of Iranian ground force involvement in Iraq is unclear. Presumably Suleimani brought Revolutionary Guard troops with him; some of its members may have taken part, albeit in a limited way, in military campaigns. In any case, in late November 2014, another form of Iranian involvement became evident when Iran officially confirmed that it began launching air strikes against Islamic State targets in eastern Iraq in order to help the Iraqi government.[6]

A similar picture of Iran's involvement emerges in Syria. Its military involvement there, likewise led by Suleimani, began in the second half of 2012 at a critical moment for the Assad regime and two years before the Islamic State entered the scene. Until that point, Iranian aid to Syria had been limited to military and communications-jamming equipment, and operational and organizational military advice. In the summer and fall of 2012, however, Iran sent Syria several hundred troops from the Revolutionary Guard and the al-Quds Force, allegedly for "non-military" purposes, or so it claimed after several of these soldiers were captured by the Syrian opposition. Hezbollah units, Shiite militiamen from Iraq, and Shiite fighters who had arrived from Afghanistan and Pakistan since 2013 at Iran's initiative, also took part in the fighting.

Little if any doubt exists that the Revolutionary Guard ground troops and al-Quds forces are involved in combat in Syria, though the extent of their involvement remains unclear. Funeral notices of Iranian, Afghan, and Pakistani Shiite soldiers killed in Syria between early 2013 and mid-2015 indicate the deaths of 113 troops from the al-Quds and Revolutionary

Guard ground forces, 121 Afghans, and 20 Pakistanis;[7] the actual numbers are likely higher. Whatever the case, it is difficult to believe that over 110 Iranian fighters not involved in the fighting, or at least not present in the combat zone, were killed. This pattern appears to have continued after the entrance of the Islamic State on the Syrian stage.

Iran's role in the military campaign against the Islamic State invites speculation about Iran's cooperation with other countries, particularly the United States. This possibility was raised in mid-2014, shortly after the Islamic State appeared on the scene, for two reasons: first, because the United States and Iran were the only two countries with the military capability to check the expansion of the Islamic State; and second, because most of the governments involved in the struggle realized that Iran was playing an important and influential role in the struggle against the Islamic State in both Iraq and Syria. Furthermore, the nuclear talks between the major powers and Iran were creating a channel for direct dialogue between the United States and Iran at a relatively high administrative level and thus granting Iran some degree of legitimacy as an international actor. At the same time, however, Iran's wish to limit the talks to the question of nuclear power in order to avoid other problematic issues made it difficult to hold a significant discussion on regional problems, such as that of the Islamic State.

Since the US administration was seeking allies to help it stop the Islamic State, it did not rule out the possibility of cooperation even with Iran, on condition that the country took a "constructive approach." Such cooperation in any case would not include direct military cooperation. Iran's public stance on cooperation with the United States in Iraq was vague, possibly due to internal disagreements over the matter. Nonetheless, Iran did not rule out military cooperation in Iraq.

American and Iranian officials did hold incidental discussions on the question of aid to Iraq during the nuclear talks. These were not concrete, however, and did not go beyond general statements. In September 2014, when the US administration refrained from including Iran in the coalition it had formed against the Islamic State, Iranian Supreme Leader Khamenei claimed that American officials had asked his country to discuss coordinated action against the Islamic State, but added that though several Iranian leaders had not opposed the proposal, he himself rejected it. In practice, limited coordination between the US and Iranian air forces, aimed at avoiding clashes during air raids in northern Iraq, has been conducted through the mediation of the Iraqi government since late 2014. Both sides, however, are intent on emphasizing that such precautionary measures do not constitute military cooperation.

The negative attitude of both the United States and Iran toward cooperation on Iraq despite their common interest in stopping the Islamic State is not merely a direct result of the usual suspicion that guides their relations; it also reflects their realization that their respective strategic goals in Iraq and Syria conflict. The United States is trying to shape the Iraqi regime into a moderate one, free of Iranian influence, with ties to the West. It believes that the stability of the Iraqi regime will require granting genuine representation to Sunnis and Kurds, and restricting the role of the armed militias. Iran, on the other hand, seeks to enhance its influence in Iraq, while relying on the power of the Shiite militias to make sure that the Shiites continue to dominate the country's leadership.

In Syria, the United States seeks the overthrow of the Assad regime, while Iran wishes to ensure its survival. Above all, the United States wishes to rein in Iran's growing influence in the Middle East, while Iran desires to reduce and eliminate the US military presence and influence in the region. As long as both sides cling to to these objectives, any real cooperation between them, beyond ad hoc occasions, is unlikely to develop despite their common interests.

In addition, although Iran is highly concerned about the rise of the Islamic State in Iraq and Syria, it may also profit from it in the future. The Iraqi government recognizes Iran's contribution to its own critical struggle against the Islamic State. Iran, in fact, was the first country to offer aid to both the Iraqi government and the Kurds while the United States was still hesitant to do so, even as Baghdad lay in jeopardy.[8] Iran also has a clear advantage over the United States in terms of their respective status and influence in the country. Despite all its efforts since 2003 to foster ties with Iraq, the United States is having trouble competing with Iran among Iraq's Shiites – even those who object to the Iranian regime. Iran also has the advantage of geographic proximity. For all these reasons, if the Islamic State is eventually defeated, the main beneficiary will presumably be Iran, which can then expand its influence in Iraq and help the Assad regime survive in Syria.

Thus although the United States and its allies in the West and the Middle East who are fighting the Islamic State are willing to weigh cooperation with the Iranian regime, they should consider the degree to which their actions will eventually play into Iran's hands. Defeating the Islamic State in Iraq means strengthening the Shiite militias linked to Iran, while defeating the Islamic State in Syria means strengthening the Assad regime, which the US and other nations deem illegitimate and which is also linked to Iran.

Notes

1   *IRNA*, August 24, 2014.
2   Dina Esfandiary and Ariane Tabatabai, "Iran's ISIS Policy," *International Affairs* 91, no. 1(2015): 1-15.
3   "Iranian Daily Hints at U.S. Plan to Divide Iran By Collapsing Iraq," *MEMRI*, special dispatch 5767, June 12, 2014, http://www.memri.org/report/en/0/0/0/0/0/0/8024.htm.
4   "Iran's General Qassem Suleimani Masterminds Iraq Ground War," *al-Arabiya News*, November 5, 2014, http://english.alarabiya.net/en/perspective/profiles/2014/11/05/Iran-s-General-Qassem-Suleimani-masterminds-Iraq-ground-war.html; Esfandiary and Tabatabai, "Iran's ISIS Policy."
5   Esfandiary and Tabatabai, "Iran's ISIS Policy."
6   "Iran Air Strikes against ISIS Requested by Iraqi Government, says Tehran," *The Guardian*, December 6, 2014, http://www.theguardian.com/world/2014/dec/05/iran-conducts-air-strikes-against-isis-exremists-iraq.
7   Ali Alfoneh, "Shiite Combat Casualties Show the Depth of Iran's Involvement in Syria," *PolicyWatch* 2458, Washington Institute for Near East Policy, August 3, 2015, http://www.washingtoninstitute.org/policy-analysis/view/shiite-combat-casualties-show-the-depth-of-irans-involvement-in-syria.
8   Tim Arango and Thomas Erdbrink, "U.S. and Iran Both Attack ISIS, But Try Not to Look Like Allies," *New York Times*, December 3, 2014, http://www.nytimes.com/2014/12/04/world/middleeast/iran-airstrikes-hit-islamic-state-in-iraq.html.

The Islamic State vs. the Saudi State

Yoel Guzansky

In June 2014, Abu Bakr al-Baghdadi announced the establishment of the Islamic caliphate, declaring it to be the true home of Islam and demanding that every Muslim move there. Both the Islamic State and al-Baghdadi portray themselves as the authentic heirs of Muslim leadership. This, an explicit challenge to Saudi Arabia and its kings, who claim to be the custodians of Islam's holy sites, prompted the Saudi grand mufti, the highest religious authority in the kingdom, to engage in the battle and declare the ideas of the Islamic State as a distortion of Islam and its largest threat.[1]

The threat posed by the Islamic State to Saudi Arabia and the Gulf states is essentially one of competitive ideology. Seeking to replace the existing political order with an "authentic" Islamic caliphate, the Islamic State views the Gulf monarchies as heretical, having veered off the true path of Islam, and as entities that therefore must be toppled. The Islamic State directs its challenge primarily at reactionary Sunni Islam, Wahhabism, represented by Saudi Arabia. The ideological enmity is manifest in the call by Islamic State leader Abu Bakr al-Baghdadi to topple the Saudi kingdom. This call to arms closely resembles the call made by Bin Laden in the previous decade.

The first public threat issued by the Islamic State to Saudi Arabia came in the form of a video released in November 2014, in which al-Baghdadi invoked his followers to attack Shiites, foreigners, and the royal household, while announcing the expansion of the Islamic State into the Najd Province of the Arabian Peninsula.[2] He did not refer to Saudi Arabia by name, lest by doing so he acknowledge the legitimacy of the rule of the House of Saud. Around the same time, the Islamic State proclaimed in its online magazine *Dabiq* that it would "raise the flag of the caliphate over Mecca and Medina...despite the wishes of the hypocrites and apostates." In the same issue, al-Baghdadi asked Saudis to remain in the kingdom and fight for the establishment of the caliphate from within, rather than leave for distant arenas of conflict.[3]

The Objective: Increasing Inter-Ethnic Tension

The Islamic State flourishes in areas where the Sunni-Shiite fault lines are deepest. Shiites comprise a significant portion of the population in the Gulf monarchies (15 percent of Saudi Arabia, 30 percent of Kuwait, 70 percent of Bahrain), and thereby constitute a regional soft underbelly. In November 2014, during the Shiite Ashura festival, the Islamic State conducted its first suicide attacks in the eastern province of Saudi Arabia, where the state's Shiites are concentrated. According to the Saudi Ministry of the Interior, the terrorist cell responsible for this attack, which killed nine Shiites at prayer, was dismantled.[4] Six months later, however, in May 2015, the Najd Province of the Islamic State claimed responsibility for the deadliest onslaught on Saudi soil in over a decade: two attacks in Shiite mosques in one week killed 25 civilians and injured dozens more.[5] A month later, in honor of the first anniversary of the caliphate, an Islamic State terrorist of Saudi origin blew himself up inside a crowded Shiite mosque in the capital of Kuwait, killing 26. In August 2015, the organization also took credit for an explosion that claimed 15 lives in a mosque serving Saudi security forces near the border of Yemen. The Islamic State has also tried to penetrate Saudi Arabian territory, as it did north of Arar in January 2015, and has fired rockets from Iraq onto the kingdom's territory.[6]

The Islamic State is doing its best to drive a wedge between the Shiite minority and the Sunni majority, hoping that any violent Shiite response will provoke a countermove by the regime and initiate a vicious cycle. Al-Baghdadi hopes that by attacking Shiites he can exploit Sunni hostility toward them and recruit fresh blood while weakening the legitimacy and stability of the royal household. The success and ideology of the Islamic State attracts many young Sunnis who might conceivably channel their fury at the Shiite population or at the royal household, should it be deemed conciliatory to the Shiites. Although the Shiites are viewed by many in Saudi Arabia as an Iranian fifth column, they have never challenged the regime; opponents of the regime have consistently been radical Sunnis. Moreover, the royal household bears some responsibility for the tension generated by its own anti-Shiite rhetoric, which it uses to enhance support for its objectives as its struggles against Iran and Iranian proxies in the region. A decision by Shiites to respond to attacks on them could play into the hands of the Islamic State, which would then be perceived as a defender of the Sunnis.

Close to two thirds of the Saudi population is below the age of thirty. Much of the country's youth is unemployed, ready to channel their frustrations to the virtual reality of social media, where many express support for the ideas of the Islamic State. As a result, the Saudi regime has stepped up its monitoring of the internet and the rhetoric from the mosques, and increased the sums it allocates to the housing, employment, and education for this sector.[7] In the past two years the Saudi security establishment has also killed or arrested hundreds of members (mostly Saudi) of the Islamic State who, according to authorities, were involved in recruitment, fundraising, and/or the planning of attacks and assassinations within the kingdom.[8]

Lessons from the War on al-Qaeda

In previous years, members of al-Qaeda returning from Afghanistan operated in the kingdom and carried out a series of showcase attacks. After a long struggle, the Saudis managed to curb al-Qaeda activity and arrest many of the organization's leaders, while others fled to Yemen. Yet despite that relative success, which occurred more than a decade ago, the challenge posed by the Islamic State today is likely to prove tougher. The return of "alumni" to Saudi Arabia from the battlefields of Syria and Iraq may test the relative efficacy of Saudi security forces in their war against terrorism. The wave of attacks that gripped the kingdom in the middle of the first decade of this century was halted in part through a means whose success rate is questionable, namely, terrorist rehabilitation. The Saudis now intend to open new rehabilitation centers in addition to the one already operating in Riyadh. The fact that the Saudis as well as other Gulf states are taking active measures indicates the seriousness of the threat both to these regimes and to Western interests.

More than 2,000 young Saudis have joined the Islamic State fighters in Syria and Iraq despite a royal decree imposing stiff penalties on anyone joining, funding, or supporting the Islamic State, or even identifying with its ideology.[9] The return of many of these young people (several hundred by September 2015), who constitute one of the largest groups of Islamic State fighters, could grow into a serious security problem for the Saudi kingdom. For this reason the royal household is concentrating its efforts on upsetting the local financing of the Islamic State, stopping the flow of young Saudis exiting and entering the kingdom, and disrupting the Islamic State's propaganda with the help of the religious establishment, the media, and the kingdom's law enforcement and judiciary system.

The Saudis worry that domestic Islamic opposition will increase with the return of more young Saudis to the kingdom and the territorial conquests of the Islamic State, which denies the integrity of the kingdom's political borders as well as its religious validity. The House of Saud believes that it has the tools to cope with the challenges posed by the Islamic State. However, it cannot as easily contend with the incitement by the Wahhabi establishment against the Shiites, as this would target its own support base. Furthermore, the kingdom's security today is worse than it was in 2002-2006 due to the number of Saudis who have left to fight for the Islamic State in Syria and Iraq as well as the fact that the arenas of operation are more geographically varied, spanning the entire kingdom.

Saudi Arabia's neighbors have also begun responding to the challenge. In Kuwait, some 200 preachers, who according to authorities were harboring radical ideas, were fired.[10] In addition, all 1.5 million residents and 3 million foreigners in the country were ordered by law to submit DNA samples, a measure that the kingdom claims will help track down terrorist suspects.[11] Like Saudi Arabia, the UAE has established a media staff to monitor social media and challenge the Islamic State narrative while providing a forum for moderate voices.[12] In Bahrain, however, the situation is somewhat different. Bahrain serves as a target of Islamic State activity due to inter-ethnic tensions in the country, which have been surfaced more since the spring of 2011. Yet because the royal household views Shiites as the most dangerous threat and aspires to preserve Sunni unity, it has turned a blind eye to Salafist Sunni activity.

Targeted assassinations of al-Qaeda's senior personnel and deserters from its ranks have helped the Islamic State draw recruits from the poorest and most populated country in the Arabian Peninsula, Yemen. The organization began its activities there in March 2015 with a dramatic double attack on Shiite mosques in Sana'a that killed 145 and wounded 357, exploiting the country's chaos and al-Qaeda's seemingly weakened status in the Arabian Peninsula after the US assassination of Nasser al-Wuhayshi,[13] al-Qaeda's former leader. Many of the Islamic State's attacks are directed at concentrations of Houthi forces and strategic locations, especially in the capital of Sana'a, controlled by the Houthis. As of the writing of this essay, the latest attack occurred in July 2015, when the Islamic State detonated a car bomb near the capital's hospital.[14] Al-Qaeda and the Islamic State seem to be competing over which group will strike hardest against the Houthis, who have made significant territorial gains. Yet it is not inconceivable that in the future al-Qaeda and the Islamic State will turn on each other and conduct attacks on Saudi Arabian targets.

The Islamic State's struggle in Saudi Arabia and its neighbors is primarily ideological. It presents a not insignificant challenge to the royal households, first and foremost, the House of Saud, even though initial surveys indicate that the number of Saudis embracing Islamic State ideology is relatively small.[15] One of the reasons for Riyadh's resolve to fight against the Islamic State both within Saudi borders and beyond may be the entity's ideological resemblance to the Wahhabi ideal and the challenge posed by the caliphate to the kingdom's pan-Islamic vision. Consequently, Saudi Arabia and its neighbors have invested many resources, particularly through its powerful religious establishment, in the effort to counter the Islamic State narrative.

Ricochets

The threat of the Islamic State will likely hang over Saudi Arabia and the Gulf states in the upcoming years. Although they joined the US aerial campaign against the Islamic State in September 2014,[16] the Gulf states did so mainly for political/diplomatic reasons and in order to polish their image; they gradually stopped almost all participation in the campaign since March-April 2015. In their perspective, the true danger lies at home. So far, the Islamic State has attacked Shiites in order to stir up inter-religious tensions and destabilize the Gulf states. It has already declared that its goal is to destroy the regimes, which in practice would mean targeting their production of oil as well as their refineries. In addition, Saudi youths who have thus far eluded security services may act as lone wolves, either on their own initiative or with guidance from abroad.

At this point, the Islamic State's presence in the Arabian Peninsula is limited in comparison to its presence in Iraq and Syria or even the Sinai Peninsula and Libya. Nevertheless, it can potentially entrench its hold for several reasons. First, the idea of the caliphate is attractive to the already conservative societies in the Gulf, especially among the younger population. Second, the idea is especially attractive to those of a Salafi jihadist orientation who have grown disillusioned with al-Qaeda. Third, the Saudi "reeducation program," which combines psychological treatment, financial aid, and religious instruction is problematic and does not always bear fruit. Fourth, security coordination among the Gulf states is lacking, and it is relatively easy for citizens to cross borders within the Gulf Cooperation Council borders. Fifth, the Islamic State is highly effective in disseminating its messages through social media (the number of social media users in Saudi Arabia is among the highest in the world).[17] Finally, the successes of the Islamic State are in and of themselves a selling point for many who view it as the standard bearer and frontline of Sunni Islam.

Some of the Gulf states have been involved in financing terrorism. Some have turned a blind eye or been less than zealous about checking the flow of money from private donors or Islamic charitable organizations to terrorists. The pressure exerted by the United States after 9/11 and a series of attacks in Saudi Arabia in the first half of the last decade have now prompted the kingdom to assume a more aggressive stance, if only to prevent more attacks on its soil. The campaign it spearheads today, which includes television programs and newspaper articles directed against the Islamic State and its ideology, is meant to harm domestic ties with such groups as well as to gainsay accusations that it has supported these groups in the past. Indeed, to demonstrate its sincerity, Saudi Arabia recently donated $100 million to the UN counterterrorism center.[18]

The kingdom can no longer isolate itself from the wars raging all around it, especially as it itself is deeply involved in regional conflicts that also exert influence on its domestic affairs. It must therefore work that much harder to provide a suitable response to the challenges posed by the Islamic State. If the kingdom does not undertake comprehensive reforms in curricula and launch an inter-ethnic dialogue, it will not be able to face this challenge in the future. Many young people are returning to their homes in the Gulf states burning with Salafist jihadist zeal. Having gained experience on the battlefield, they will soon test the stability of the monarchies still standing in the crumbling Middle East.

Notes

1   "Saudi Arabia Grand Mufti Says ISIS 'Enemy Number One of Islam,'" *al-Akhbar,* August 19, 2014.

2   "Islamic State Leader Urges Attacks in Saudi Arabia: Speech," *Reuters,* November 13, 2014.

3   *Dabiq* 5 (November 2014): 3.

4   "74 Held in Saudi for Involvement in Terror Activities," *al-Arabiya,* March 22, 2015.

5   "Suicide Blast Kills 21 at Mosque in Saudi Arabia," *al-Arabiya,* May 22, 2015; "Saudi Security Foils Terrorist Attack on Dammam Mosque," *a-Sharq al-Awsat,* May 29, 2015.

6   "Saudi Border Guards Killed in Attack," *al-Jazeera,* January 5, 2015; "Rocket Landings at Saud-Iraq Border Under Probe," *Arab News,* July 8, 2014.

7   "Online Imams under Scanner," *Arab News,* November 10, 2014.

8   "43 Killed, 431 Held as Saudi Crushes Daesh Network," *Khaleej Times,* July 20, 2015.

9   "Saudi King Issues Royal Decree Cracking Down on Terrorism," *a-Sharq al-Awsat,* February 4, 2014.

10 "Kuwait Sacks 198 Preachers, Including 7 Wanted by Authorities," *Khaleej Times,* July 8, 2015.

11 "Kuwait Detains 26 over ISIS Suicide Attack on Mosque: Newspaper," *Daily Star,* July 6, 2015.

12 "US, UAE Launch Anti-IS Online Messaging Center in Abu Dhabi," *Daily Star,* July 8, 2015.

13 "ISIS Video Claims 'We've Arrived' in Yemen," *al-Arabiya,* April 26, 2015.

14 "ISIS Claims Car Bombing Near Hospital in Yemeni Capital," *al-Arabiya,* July 29, 2015.

15 David Pollock, "New Poll Shows Majority of Saudis, Kuwaitis, Emiratis Reject ISIS, Back Two-State Solution with Israel, *PolicyWatch* 2329, Washington Institute for Near East Policy, October 23, 2014.

16 See more: "Operation Inherent Resolve: Targeted Operations Against ISIL Terrorist," US Department of Defense, http://www.defense.gov/News/Special-Reports/0814_ Inherent-Resolve.

17 "The Social Media Stars of Saudi Arabia," *Bloomberg,* July 31, 2015.

18 "Saudi Arabia Donates $100 Million to UN Counter-Terrorism Centre," Royal Embassy of Saudi Arabia, Washington, D.C., August 7, 2013.

Turkey in Face of the Threat from the Islamic State: Finally in Sync with its NATO Allies?

Gallia Lindenstrauss

Relations between Turkey and the Islamic State in the various incarnations of the entity reveal that notwithstanding the gains that both derive from the silent understanding between them, the Islamic State poses a significant threat to Turkey. What appeared for a long time to be Ankara's disregard of the scale of this threat perplexed Turkey's NATO allies. The country's initially hesitant policy toward the Islamic State, which could be summed up as "live and let live,"[1] is, however, attributable to several factors. First, the goal to overthrow the Bashar al-Assad regime in Syria made Turkey willing to cooperate with extremely radical groups that were willing to assist it in doing so. On this issue, the Turkish government has regarded – and still regards – United States policy as mistaken, and contends that the Islamic State is merely a symptom of the broader problem of Assad's retention of power. Furthermore, the Turks believe that the priority assigned to fighting the Islamic State while ignoring the horrors committed by the Syrian regime strengthens the Islamic State, especially its attractiveness among foreign volunteers eager to enlist in its ranks.[2]

Another consideration behind Turkey's cautious policy and reluctance to engage in conflict with the Islamic State is that the entity serves as a restraining element on the Kurds in Syria. An additional important matter is that shortly before the declaration of the establishment of the Islamic caliphate in June 2014, the organization abducted a number of Turkish citizens – a crisis that Ankara successfully resolved without harm to the hostages. The 46 civilians kidnapped from the Turkish consulate in Mosul following the city's conquest were freed in September 2014 after being held prisoner for over three months – in sharp contrast to citizens of other, often distant countries, such as Japan, who were beheaded. Thirty-two Turkish truck drivers kidnapped by the Islamic State were likewise released after a month of imprisonment.

Turkey's hesitant and cautious policy toward the Islamic State is reflected in part in its inadequate effort to obstruct the flow of volunteers crossing the border from Turkey into Syria, and its agreement to allow the Islamic State to use its territory as a center for its logistical needs. The city of Gaziantep in southeastern Turkey, for example, has been described as a "shopping center" for Islamic State fighters; according to some reports, the wounded are treated in Turkish hospitals.[3] Although most of the rumors about the transfer of supplies from Turkey to radical groups, including apparently the Islamic State, remain unconfirmed in open sources, there have been occasional reports implying that such aid is indeed granted. In January 2014, for example, the Turkish government imposed a news blackout on information regarding a convoy of trucks loaded with weapons that had been seized by the Turkish police in Adana. The convoy turned out to be an initiative by the Turkish secret service, which had organized it for the purpose of sending it to Syria.[4] On July 26, 2015, *The Guardian* reported that a raid in eastern Syria by US special forces on the stronghold of the person responsible for the Islamic State's oil smuggling had uncovered hundreds of documents and files linking Islamic State members to Turkish officials.[5]

In 2015, and especially after the July 7 visit to Ankara by General (ret.) John Allen, at the time the coordinator of the international coalition against the Islamic State, Turkey seemed to step up its campaign against the Islamic State, primarily by reinforcing its control of border crossings and increasing its arrests of Islamic State operatives in its territory. By mid-August 2015, 700 Islamic State personnel had been arrested and expelled from Turkey, compared to 520 in all of 2014.[6] Since October 2013, when Turkey first declared the Islamic State a terrorist organization, over 1,500 people linked to it were expelled from Turkey, while over 15,000 have been denied entry.[7] The most significant shift in Turkish policy, however, occurred after a terrorist attack in Suruc on July 20, 2015, which killed 32 people and was attributed by the Turkish government to the Islamic State. Following a telephone conversation between US President Barack Obama and Turkish President Recep Tayyip Erdogan on July 22, 2015, Turkey finally agreed – after months of refusal – to allow US and international coalition warplanes to operate against the Islamic State from the Incirlik airbase in Turkey.

To be sure, the Suruc attack was not the first terrorist attack in Turkey ascribed to the Islamic State. In May 2013, the Turkish government accused parties linked to Syrian President Assad of the car bombing in the town of Reyhanli that killed 53 people, but reports in the Turkish press stated that the Islamic State was behind the attack. In addition, on June 5, 2015, two days before the Turkish parliamentary elections, two bombs exploded at an election meeting of the pro-Kurdish party in the city of Diyarbakir in southeastern Turkey, and the leading suspect in planting the bomb was a member of the Islamic State.

Nonetheless, a number of factors may have prompted the change in Turkey's policy toward the Islamic State after the terrorist attack in Suruc. First, what had been perceived as an inadequate Turkish contribution to the struggle against the Islamic State had become a bone of contention between Turkey and its NATO allies, especially the United States. Second, the defeats suffered by the Islamic State at the hands of the Kurds, especially in Kobani and Tel Abyad, created positive momentum for the Kurds and aroused concern in Turkey, which hoped to disrupt this momentum through measured cooperation with the United States. Turkey is in fact making use of the Incirlik airbase conditional on specific approval for every operation departing from its runways. It also wanted warplanes from countries other than the United States to use the base, so that it appears to be a NATO operation.[8] Furthermore, though the Turks had apparently given up on United States cooperation toward a general solution to the Syrian problem, they expected at least the creation of a safe zone in northwestern Syria – with all that this implies – including protection against the forces of the Assad regime (the United States, on the other hand, only intended to create an area that is free of Islamic State presence; but these ideas have in any case become less relevant since the Russian military intervention in Syria after September 30, 2015). A fourth factor was the Turks' growing awareness of the magnitude of the threat posed by the Islamic State. In this case, the point of departure was the prior refusal by President Erdogan and Prime Minister Ahmet Davutoglu to publicly and clearly declare the Islamic State a terrorist organization.[9] Following the attack in Suruc, however, Turkish presidential spokesman Ibrahim Kalin stated, "The fact that Turkey is completely against any terrorist organization, including Daesh, is self explanatory…Along with that, there are also those trying to legitimize the PKK terrorist organization."[10]

Already in September 2014, the US shared information with Turkey about the existence of Islamic State sleeper cells in Istanbul, Ankara, Konya, and, apparently, other Turkish cities.[11] According to a Turkish government report prepared in 2015, approximately 1,300 Turkish citizens have joined the Islamic State (for the sake of comparison, 1,500 Turkish citizens joined the PYD – the PKK branch in Syria – during the same period).[12] Turkish authorities are also concerned about significant recruiting potential for the Islamic State among the two million refugees Turkey has absorbed from Syria. It was reported in August 2015 that Turkey had established a special unit for collecting information about these refugees.[13]

The Islamic State has also undertaken propaganda efforts at the Turkish public. In May 2015, it published a 46-page electronic magazine in Turkish for the first time; the main purpose of the publication was to recruit operatives and raise support. The magazine also contained veiled threats against the Turkish ruling Justice and Development Party.[14] The Islamic State likewise operates a Turkish-language website and Twitter accounts (which are closed from time to time, but then reopened with similar names). Following the airstrikes by Turkish warplanes against Islamic State targets, warnings were published on the social media operated by the Islamic State, including threats that the Turkish public would soon be punished. Note that in contrast to the PKK, whose attacks target primarily soldiers and police personnel, the Islamic State attacks primarily civilians. The Islamic State warned Turkey that it would be easy to undermine stability in the country with a few bombs laid in municipal and tourist areas, and even easier to launch attacks in Turkey than in Tunisia.[15] In addition, the social media operated by the Islamic State cast the Turkish leaders as "apostates," Turkish President Erdogan as "Satan," and Turkish Prime Minister Davutoglu as "Little Satan." The Islamic State alleges that the Turkish government is in effect supporting the PKK "atheistic gang," and that this "gang" is spreading the "lie" that Erdogan supports the Islamic State in order to recruit greater support for itself.[16]

A survey conducted by Metropoll in August 2014 found that a decisive majority of the Turkish population regarded the Islamic State as a terrorist organization. At the same time, 11.3 percent did not hold this opinion.[17] Another survey by the same company conducted in July 2015 found that most of the Turkish public would prefer to see northern Syria controlled by the PYD, rather than the Islamic State. Among supporters of the Justice and Development Party, however, 21 percent of those questioned answered that they preferred control by the Islamic State (compared with 35 percent who preferred control by the PYD).[18] It therefore appears that there is support among part of the Turkish public for the idea and activity of the Islamic State. Significant progress was achieved in Turkey's struggle against the Islamic State doctrine when Turkey's Directorate of Religious Affairs (Diyanet) – the official state religious body – published a report summarized by the Diyanet Head as follows: "It would be a major insult to Islam to claim all such terrorist activities stem from Islamic interpretation."[19]

It is still too early to assess the significance of the campaign by the international coalition (Turkey included) against the Islamic State. It does seem, however, that the Turkish attacks against PKK operatives in northern Iraq, which are conducted in parallel with attacks against Islamic State targets, are much more frequent and hence overshadow Turkish efforts vis-à-vis the Islamic state. Despite the tendency in the West to criticize Turkish policy as motivated solely by internal considerations (especially against the Kurdish minority), Turkish arguments about the international coalition's strategy and methods against the Islamic State can be regarded as legitimate criticism. On the other hand, it is no surprise that the contradictions in Turkish policy have made it a target of the Islamic State today,[20] which manifested itself most clearly in the Ankara bombings on October 10, 2015 that killed more than 100 people and were attributed to the Islamic State.

In view of the difficulty experienced by Turkey and the United States in cooperating on the issue of the Islamic State, it is doubtful whether the same issue can constitute potential for cooperation between Turkey and Israel, despite the threat to Turkey posed by the Islamic State. The level of suspicion between Turkey and Israel is even greater than between Turkey and the United States. Along with its offensive against the Islamic State, Turkey is continuing its cooperation with other radical groups in Syria – a matter that poses a problem for the United States and Israel alike. Furthermore, while both the United States and Israel see potential for cooperation with the minorities in Syria (the Kurds for example, and for Israel, also the Druze), Turkey regards this cooperation as problematic, and is likewise emphasizing the territorial integrity of Syria.

Turkey has a complicated array of considerations with respect to events in Syria, resulting not only from the fact that its neighboring country is involved, but also because the Kurdish issue transcends borders. From this perspective, Turkey's cooperation in the struggle against the Islamic State should not be taken for granted and needs ongoing maintenance, informed by an awareness of Turkish concerns about events in Syria in general, and especially those occurring in the proximity of the Turkish-Syrian border.

Notes

1   Mustafa Akyol, "Islamic State Ups Rhetoric against Ankara," *al-Monitor*, August 11, 2015.
2   Bill Park, "The Islamic State and Turkey's 'Precious Loneliness,'" *Defense-in-Depth*, April 1, 2015.
3   Sinan Ulgen and F. Doruk Ergun, "A Turkish Perspective on the Rise of the Islamic Caliphate," *EDAM Discussion Paper*, September 1, 2014, p. 3.
4   Burak Kadercan, "What's Eating Turkey? Ankara and the Islamic State," *War on the Rocks*, July 30, 2015.
5   Martin Chulov, "Turkey Sends in Jets as Syria's Agony Spills over Every Border," *The Guardian*, July 26, 2015.
6   "Turkey Has Arrested and Expelled More than 700 Foreign Terrorists This Year: Official," *Daily Sabah*, August 12, 2015.
7   "Turkey Puts Travel Ban on 15,000 Foreign Fighters," *Hurriyet Daily News*, July 15, 2015.
8   Metin Gurcan, "What the U.S. Is Really Doing at Turkey Incirlik Air Base," *al-Monitor*, August 7, 2015.
9   "Davutoglu Says ISIL is Driven by Anger, Avoids Calling it Terrorist," *Today's Zaman*, August 7, 2014.
10 "Turkey is Against All Kinds of Terror, Says Presidential Spokesman Ibrahim Kalin," *Daily Sabah*, July 22, 2015.
11 "Report: ISIL Has Sleeper Cells in Ankara, Istanbul, Konya," *Today's Zaman*, September 15, 2014.
12 "Government Report: 1,300 Turks Joined ISIL," *Today's Zaman*, July 31, 2015.
13 "Government to Launch Separate Intelligence Unit for Syrian Refugees," *Today's Zaman*, August 10, 2015.
14 Metin Gurcan, "Islamic State Releases First Turkish Publication," *al-Monitor*, June 8, 2015.
15 Omer Taspinar, "The Risk of ISIL Retaliation," *Today's Zaman*, August 9, 2015.
16 Aykol, "Islamic State Ups Rhetoric against Ankara."
17 Burak Bekdil, "Turkey's Double Game with ISIS," *Middle East Quarterly* (summer 2015): 3.
18 Arif Tekdal, "Majority of Turks Would Prefer Kurds over ISIL Controlling Northern Syria," *Today's Zaman*, July 29, 2015.
19 Joost Lagendijk, "Can We Trust Turkey on ISIL?" *Today's Zaman*, August 11, 2015.
20 Kadri Gursell, "Has Press Freedom Fallen Victim to AKP's Syria Policy?" *al-Monitor*, August 11, 2015.

Israel and the Islamic State

Shlomo Brom

The Islamic State arose on the regional stage as a significant actor threatening the continued existence of state frameworks and the regional order established following World War I. For Israel's government, which has focused on the threat from Tehran and Iran's allies and proxies, the Islamic State's prominence came at a critical period. It coincided with the heavy involvement of Iran and Hezbollah in the Syrian civil war, and the negotiations, followed by an agreement, between Tehran and the world powers over the Iranian nuclear program.

Israel's focus on Iran has made it difficult to isolate its complex attitude toward the Islamic State phenomenon. This is due both to the actual impact that the focus on the Iranian threat has had on how Israel perceives the Islamic State, and the fact that Israel sometimes seemed intent on avoiding statements on the issue. This apparently deliberate restraint regarding the Islamic State stems from Israel's tactical considerations, namely, not to distract the world's attention from the Iranian threat, and not to imply that there may be greater threats in the Middle East. Therefore, any attempt to understand the Israeli view of the Islamic State phenomenon cannot be based only on statements from Israeli sources on the issue, but must attempt to understand the operational steps that Israel has taken regarding the Islamic State question.

The Islamic State is perceived in Israel as one result of the weakened nation-state framework in the Arab Middle East, a natural consequence of the internal and regional upheavals in the Middle East since 2011. The weakening of the states has created a vacuum that non-state actors – for the most part, Islamist organizations – have penetrated. True, the Islamic State developed out of al-Qaeda in Iraq, which was a central player in the fight against American occupation of the country since 2003, with no connection to the Arab Spring phenomenon; but the organization's renewed awakening resulted from the transfer of its activities to Syria in the wake of the civil war there. Al-Qaeda in Iraq's involvement in the Syrian civil war was also a central device for recruitment of foreign volunteers from the region and beyond to the organization.

The uniqueness of the Islamic State phenomenon lies in the fact that it expanded beyond the borders of one Arab state, both in its ideology and its operations, and founded a cross-border state framework in Syria and Iraq. As in the case of al-Qaeda and its proxies, Islamic State proxies cropped up in other countries; in many cases, this was the result of local Islamist organizations deciding to affiliate themselves with the Islamic State. This process is what turned the Islamic State into more of a threatening power from Israel's perspective than other Islamist movements that were involved in the civil wars that developed in some Arab countries. Yet despite the fact that the discourse promoted by the Islamic State is unambiguously anti-Israel and anti-Jewish (as with other jihadist organizations), and despite the fact that the Islamic State casts Israel as a legitimate target for attack, the threat for now appears to be distant, given that the territories controlled by the Islamic State are in Iraq and eastern Syria, and its activities take place, at this point, far from Israel's border.

The concerns in Israel since the spread of the Islamic State have focused mainly on its potential impact in Jordan, which shares a long border with Israel. Jordan, in fact, has been a focus of Israeli concern since the onset of the Arab Spring – concern that stems from Jordan's demographic makeup, the massive number of Syrian refugees it has absorbed, and its precarious economic condition. Israel is troubled by the potential undermining of the Jordanian regime and destabilization of the kingdom, which would harm the strategic partnership between the countries and lead to Jordan becoming an operational base for jihadist elements against Israel. This fear on Israel's part is based, inter alia, on an assessment that conditions exist in Jordan that can turn significant portions of the population into Islamic State supporters.

Moreover, in Israel there are political elements that have an interest in emphasizing the danger in Jordan's destabilization, and even in overemphasizing it, for reasons connected to the Palestinian issue: according to these elements, the inherent lack of stability in Jordan does not allow Israel to agree to the establishment of a Palestinian state, or even more so, to concede an Israeli presence in the West Bank that can cope with the security dangers expected from the direction of Jordan. This argument, however, lacks substance, given the stability the Jordanian regime has demonstrated since the outbreak of the Arab Spring, and contravenes the well-developed system of security ties between Jordan and Israel.

A scenario where columns of armed Islamic State SUVs invade Jordan and take control of Jordanian territory, as occurred in Syria and Iraq, has not been taken seriously in Israel. According to those who have related to such a scenario, Jordan's professional military will remain loyal to the regime and prevent any such invasion. These assessments are more concerned with the formation of an underground movement supporting the Islamic State among the Jordanian populace, which would be composed of elements estranged from the regime – disappointed supporters of the Muslim Brotherhood, Palestinians with Salafist leanings, and Bedouin tribes who feel economically deprived. However, even should such a scenario play out, most analysts are confident that the Jordanian security services would be able to handle such phenomena effectively.

Since the fall of the Mubarak regime in Egypt, there has been concern in Israel regarding the terror groups in the Sinai Peninsula. These groups operate mainly against the Egyptian government, but have already also acted against Israel from Sinai. These are organizations that are a mix of local Bedouins and Salafi jihadist elements, who share resentment of the Egyptian regime and Egypt as a state for abandoning and discriminating against the Sinai population. Added to this resentment is the religious motivation of Salafi jihadist elements to undermine the current regime of President el-Sisi, due to the deposing of his Muslim Brotherhood predecessor Mohamed Morsi.

The implications for Israel of the alliance of Wilayat Sinai – formerly Ansar Bait al-Maqdis, the largest organization in the Sinai Peninsula fighting Egyptian forces effectively – with the Islamic State are still unclear. According to the limited information available, the Islamic State apparently transfers financial aid of an unknown extent to the organization. One question is whether the Islamic State transfers to Ansar Bait al-Maqdis aid and resources that it did not previously possess, thus making it a greater threat. Indeed, Ansar Bait al-Maqdis has demonstrated improved capabilities in its war against the Egyptian military, although it is possible that such capabilities would have developed even without Islamic State aid, simply from the cumulative experience of years of fighting against the Egyptian regime. The relatively small number of Ansar Bait al-Maqdis attacks in Israel since Morsi was deposed can be explained by the organization's current preference for the struggle against the el-Sisi regime, as well as its need to defend itself against Egyptian military actions, which are growing gradually more intense. Thus the concern in Israel relates to a future change of Wilayat Sinai's order of priorities, which would lead to a greater focus on Israel, especially in a situation where the Egyptian military experiences setbacks in its fight against this organization and others operating in Sinai. Such a change may be significant from Israel's perspective due to the many weak points on its long border with Egypt, although the topographical inferiority is balanced to a certain extent by the limited vulnerable Israeli civilian presence along this border.

The developments in the Sinai Peninsula have led to changes in IDF deployment along the border with Egypt. Initially a relatively simple fence was built with the goal of preventing the infiltration of illegal foreign workers, and the deployment of forces was based on this concept. Today the Egyptian border is viewed as a front that may become active with very little warning. This change has led to the reinforcement of the forces deployed along the Israel-Egypt border, and to improvements in the border fence.[1]

Further north, the involvement of Islamist organizations in fighting against the Syrian regime in the Golan Heights region has resulted in their taking control over most of the Syrian territory on the border with Israel (not including an enclave in the north of the Syrian Golan Heights, which includes, inter alia, the Quneitra region and the Druze village of Hader). This situation has sharpened the sense of threat to Israel from the Syrian front. While it is true that the most dominant organization currently operating in the area is the al-Nusra Front, and not the Islamic State, reports have already been received of a planned Islamic State attack against Jabal al-Druze in the south of Syria – a region, in which Israel has an interest because of the Druze lobby in Israel. Moreover, the Yarmouk Martyrs Brigade, which controls sections adjacent to the border with Israel in the southern Golan Heights, has declared its loyalty to the Islamic State. All of this has created a sense of fear of ensuing friction from the Islamic State advance toward Israeli territory. This joins the concern regarding Hezbollah aid to the forces of President al-Assad near the Golan Heights, which may be exploited as an opportunity to open an additional front with Israel.

The increased sense of threat on the Syrian border has led Israel toward better deployment in the Golan Heights. The threat that Israel had prepared for in the past on the Golan Heights was of a mechanized, armored attack by the Syrian military, and thus Israel's deployment was based mainly on armored forces. In the current reality, the asymmetrical threat from the direction of groups such as the al-Nusra Front and the Islamic State requires a different deployment. In this context, the border fence has been modernized, and forces suited to fighting the type of enemy that may be encountered there have been transferred to the region.[2]

These developments in Syria have led to the formation of two schools of thought in public and political discourse in Israel. The first holds that the main threat against Israel from the direction of Syria comes from the Iranian-led axis, and includes the Assad regime, Hezbollah, and Palestinian organizations – far different from the Islamic State threat, which can only create nuisances with limited damage potential, and with which Israel knows how to contend. The conclusion of the proponents of this school of thought is that Israel needs to be proactive against the al-Assad regime in Syria.[3] The second school of thought estimates that in the coming years Israel should expect to deal mainly with threats similar to the Islamic State and other non-state elements, while Iran and its proxies are effectively deterred by Israel and caught up in fighting for the survival of the al-Assad regime and the Shiite regime in Iraq. According to this approach, Israel must not underestimate the Islamic State threat, although the danger this threat poses to Israel itself should not be exaggerated.[4]

The Israeli government has thus far chosen not to embrace a specific school of thought: officials speak sparingly regarding all issues related to the Islamic State, while emphasizing the Iranian threat. The Israeli position regarding the Syrian civil war is that the State of Israel has no position: it supports no side and is not interested in being involved in what goes on in its northern neighbor. This lack of a position does not stop the two rival sides in Syria from accusing Israel of supporting the other side, in order to depict the "infidel" enemy as a collaborator with Israel. Israel's declarative policy is accompanied by steps to deal with the concrete threats facing it, in both the Egyptian and Golan Heights arenas. Statements regarding the need to construct a fence along Israel's eastern border – in the first phase along the southern section from Eilat and going northward – may reflect a growing Israeli sense of concern regarding the spread of the Islamic State and its proxies toward Jordan.[5]

Israel is acting aggressively regarding another aspect, albeit of limited scale, related to the group – attempts on the part of Arab volunteers who are citizens of Israel to enter Syria to join the ranks of the Islamic State.[6] Intelligence and police efforts are assigned to identify such people, who are arrested and put on trial, whether prior to leaving Israel or upon their return. While the number of such volunteers is still small, the concern is of the establishment of a terror infrastructure within Israel inspired by the Islamic State, which would be promoted by those volunteers returning from Syria and Iraq. Such a fear is not baseless, as the ideology disseminated by the Islamic State has the potential to appeal to elements among the Israeli Arab populace, as indicated by the number of cases already uncovered.[7]

Another aspect of the Islamic State phenomenon from Israel's perspective involves Israel's view of itself as responsible for the security of Jews throughout the world in the face of threats stemming from their Jewish identity and closeness to Israel. Israel is presumably investing resources, at least intelligence, in an effort to cope with the growing threat to Europe's Jews posed by Islamic State volunteers returning from Iraq and Syria. This threat has already been realized in attacks carried out by Islamic State activists and admirers against various Jewish communities throughout Europe.

The answer to the question of how Israel's view of the Islamic State threat will develop in the future depends on the success or failure of the international coalition established against the Islamic State. As of September 2015, it appears that the Islamic State in Iraq has been halted and even rolled back to a certain extent, thanks to the operations of this coalition. In Syria, on the other hand, the volume of operations against the Islamic State was smaller in the first place, and consequently, the international coalition's achievements have been more limited.

The more the Islamic State approaches Israel's borders, the more concrete Israel's attitude must become regarding the threat it poses. There is potential for Israel becoming entangled in fighting the Islamic State, especially if the latter threatens Druze communities in Syria and due to domestic considerations Israel decides to become involved to prevent the realization of such threats. The more troubling question in the long term regards the impact of Islamic State ideology on the internal stability of the two Arab states that have signed peace agreements with Israel – Egypt and Jordan.

The strengthening of elements that support the Islamic State in both of these countries may present a substantive threat to Israel.

Notes

1   Amir Buhbut, "The IDF Beefs Up Forces in the South, Given Concerns of Terrorism along the Egyptian Border," *Walla*, March 12, 2015, http://news.walla.co.il/item/2837407.

2   Yoav Zeitun, "Attack Exercise in Syria: The IDF's New Policy in the Golan," *Ynet*, August 16, 2015, http://www.ynet.co.il/articles/0,7340,L-4691341,00.html.

3   Maj. Gen. (ret.) Amos Yadlin, Executive Director of the Institute for National Security Studies, is a prominent representative of this school. Thus, for example, he claimed at an INSS conference on the Islamic State that "ISIS are experts at media and intimidation, but there is nothing to fear from them."

4   See for example "Eyes on Jerusalem: The Islamic State and the Global Jihad vs. Israel and the Jews," *Online Jihad Exposed,* August 8, 2014, http://www.onlinejihadexposed.com/2014/08/blog-post_8.html.

5   Barak Ravid and Gili Cohen, "The Cabinet Approves: Construction of a Fence will Begin on the Eastern Border, with Jordan," *Haaretz*, June 29, 2015, http://www.haaretz.co.il/news/politics/.premium-1.2671344.

6   This issue is analyzed extensively elsewhere in this volume.

7   Ahiya Rabad and Hasan Shalan, "Israeli Cell Uncovered: Lawyer Wants to be ISIS Chief of Staff in Palestine," *Ynet*, January 18, 2015, http://www.ynet.co.il/articles/0,7340,L-4616056,00.html.

Part V

The Sphere of Influence

Wilayat Sinai:
The Islamic State's Egyptian Affiliate

Zack Gold

For the Islamic State, bringing the Sinai-based Ansar Bait al-Maqdis ("Supporters of Jerusalem," ABM) into its fold was a major coup on two fronts. First, since its inception in 2011, ABM had leaned toward al-Qaeda – the Islamic State's rival for leadership of the global jihad movement. Second, ABM was already the most active and lethal jihadi group in Egypt, giving the Islamic State an immediate presence in the Arab world's most populous country.

Ansar Bait al-Maqdis emerged from a number of indigenous Salafi jihadist groups in the Sinai Peninsula. Some of these groups had ties to Salafi jihadis in Gaza or leaders that had previously fought abroad, including with al-Qaeda. ABM rose from the chaos in Sinai that began with the uprising against long-time president Husni Mubarak in January 2011.[1] In the summer of 2013, ABM shifted its main target from Israel to the Egyptian security forces (especially soldiers and military patrols and outposts in North Sinai), with additional attacks against state economic engines, such as internal gas pipelines and on one occasion, tourists. From September 2013 to late January 2014, ABM claimed responsibility for a rapid succession of mass-scale attacks throughout Cairo and the Nile Delta, including the attempted assassination of the Egyptian interior minister Mohamed Ibrahim.

From early 2014 onward, the Egyptian military managed, for the most part, to confine the group to the northeastern corner of the Sinai Peninsula. The massive pressure on ABM, however, did not destroy it; indeed, Sinai's militants continuously improved their capabilities. Yet while they continued to thrive in North Sinai, a combination of desperation over funds and leadership losses likely played a role in the group's eventual affiliation with the Islamic

State.[2] There was already a level of affinity among Sinai's Salafi jihadis for the Islamic State: both for what the latter stood and also because a number likely fought alongside Islamic State militants in Syria and Iraq. However, Egyptian, Israeli, and international officials all conclude that ABM's main reasoning for affiliating with the Islamic State was financial.

Personal contacts between ABM and Islamic State leaders paved the way toward the alliance.[3] According to the *New York Times*, in October 2014 two emissaries traveled from Sinai to Raqqa to negotiate how much money the Islamic State could provide to the Egyptian group.[4] Yet even if the affiliation was purely a financial decision, a major ensuing concern has been that the Islamic State's financial commitment and logistical support would noticeably affect the operations and targets of ABM, now known as Wilayat Sinai, the Sinai Province of the Islamic State.

There were early signs of ABM's organizational shift toward the Islamic State while the Syrian-based group courted Egypt's jihadis in the summer of 2014. For example, in his Eid al-Fitr sermon in July 2014, ABM spiritual guide Abu Usama al-Masri called for victory for the Islamic State.[5] The affiliation was not without controversy, however, and the struggle between pro- and anti-affiliation ABM cells poured out into the open with competing statements in early November 2014. Indeed, for Sinai's jihadis, affiliating publicly with a global organization, whether the Islamic State or al-Qaeda, created a number of risks, first among them the negative impact on local support. Despite its Salafi jihadi goal of forming an Islamic emirate in Sinai and its waging of jihad against Israel and the Egyptian army, ABM had always presented itself as a defender of the local Sinai population. In the first months as Wilayat Sinai, then, the group treaded carefully so as not to undermine its local support. Despite officially being directed by a foreign-based leadership, there was no operational difference from ABM: the group's targets remained the same.

The situation began to change slowly in January 2015, when over a dozen local civilians were killed by Wilayat Sinai.[6] With rare exception, ABM had avoided targeting civilians and even operated in a manner to limit civilian casualties. In contrast, in 2015 Wilayat Sinai became ruthless in killing those it accused of cooperating with the Egyptian military and Israel's Mossad. It is unclear if the increased targeting of civilians is related to the group's Islamic State affiliation or is a measure of its paranoia regarding infiltration. However, the brutal manner in which these killings took place shows a clear inspiration from the Islamic State, which is also responsible for the Sinai wing's messaging and propaganda.

Also unclear is whether Wilayat Sinai's major attacks in 2015 are results of Islamic State influence in arms and training or if they are arguably the natural progression of a militant group that has shown continuous advancement over the past two years. The Islamic State's provision of weapons, vehicles, and new uniforms to its Sinai-based affiliate may be beneficial, but such assistance may not actually make as strategic a difference as Islamic State-run propaganda suggests.

However, Wilayat Sinai has certainly attempted Islamic State-like operations in the Sinai Peninsula. Militarily, the group's July 1, 2015 siege of the town of Sheikh Zuweid in an apparent effort to control parts of the town, at least temporarily, resembled the manner in which Islamic State fighters have taken over cities in Iraq.[7] In its propaganda, the group presents itself as carrying out state-like functions: from handing out food and financial aid to countering drug trafficking and cigarette smuggling.

Both Egyptian and Israeli officials have drawn links between Wilayat Sinai's most proficient attacks and the group's connection to the Gaza Strip and to Hamas weapons. Egyptian security officials also believe that Sinai's militants have received training from former Egyptian special operations officers such as Hisham al-Ashmawi, who split off from ABM following its Islamic State affiliation.[8] In addition, Sinai fighters have seized weapons and explosives during operations in which they overran military checkpoints and police buildings.

While Wilayat Sinai increased its capabilities, the group for the most part limited its operations to the peninsula. One exception occurred on November 28, 2014 – a day of "Islamic rage" organized by a number of Egypt's Islamist political groups – when Wilayat Sinai claimed that a "detachment" of its fighters killed five soldiers, including two officers, in Cairo and Qalyubia governorates.

The Islamic State advanced on mainland Egypt in July 2015. That month, Wilayat Sinai took responsibility for a car bombing suicide attack at a military checkpoint on the Suez-Cairo road. Although Wilayat Sinai is the Egyptian-based arm of the Islamic State, the parent organization took responsibility for a July attack on the Italian consulate in Cairo. Given the historical and religious imagery of attacking the seat of Christendom, as Islamic State propaganda has made clear, perhaps Wilayat Sinai operatives were behind the attack on behalf of the greater Islamic State collective.[9]

More worrisome would be if fighters from the Islamic State affiliate in eastern Libya were dispatched to attack the relatively vulnerable consulate in the Egyptian capital. Certainly, an apparent Islamic State strategy has been to provoke Egypt into a two-front war. This was quite clear in February 2015, when Islamic State fighters in Libya slaughtered 20 Egyptian Copts. This action prompted Egypt to launch airstrikes on its western neighbor; and the Egyptian military has been alert on its western border, which distracts it from the internal battle against Islamic State forces in Sinai.[10] Another attack in Egypt's western desert, claimed by the Islamic State, raised the likelihood of a connection between Islamic State operations in Egypt and Libya. However, the fact that successive bombings in Cairo were also claimed by the Islamic State – and not Wilayat Sinai – suggests that at least one Islamic State cell is based in Egypt's capital.

The Islamic State crossed another line in Egypt in August 2015 with its "Message to the Egyptian Government." Coinciding with celebrations of the opening of new sections of the Suez Canal, Wilayat Sinai released a video of a Croatian worker kidnapped on the desert road from Cairo in July. As a masked, knife-wielding militant stood over him, the captive read a statement in English that Wilayat Sinai would kill him if Egypt did not release "Muslim women" from its prisons. Despite the video's title, the message was more clearly directed toward Western interests in Egypt, particularly to international companies that invest there.

Egyptian Response

Egyptian officials note that their country is not Iraq or Libya: the military will not run away or fall apart. As such, while it struggles to stop the Sinai insurgency, the Egyptian military has managed to contain it.

In addition to its military response, Cairo has enacted a number of laws aimed at stemming the flow of Egyptians trying to join the jihad in Syria and Iraq. All Egyptians age 18-40 must register with state security before boarding planes to Iraq, Jordan, or Syria. While focused on potential Islamic State recruits, Egypt's registration program also has political connotations, given the late 2014 additions of Turkey, known as a hub of Muslim Brotherhood members in exile; and Qatar, another pro-Brotherhood state.[11]

Consumed by its own counter-terrorism fight, Egypt's involvement in the anti-Islamic State coalition is non-military. At the same time, at every opportunity Egyptian diplomats call on the coalition to expand its mission to Islamic State affiliates in Libya and even to broaden further the scope of the alliance to counter the Brotherhood as well.[12]

In addition to intelligence sharing, the main contribution Egypt has put forward in the anti-Islamic State fight is the religious legitimacy of al-Azhar University, one of the oldest institutions of Islamic learning. However, there are two major flaws with this strategy. First, al-Azhar itself is a conservative institution that is slow to change. In July, six months after calling for a "revolution" in Islamic thinking, Sisi scolded al-Azhar for not following through.[13] A more fundamental problem with al-Azhar's religious legitimacy is that the institution is considered closely tied to the Egyptian state. As H. A. Hellyer told the Associated Press after Sisi's call for reform, "no one who is remotely inclined to a violent interpretation will be impressed by" a counter-radicalization message from al-Azhar.[14]

Policy Recommendations

The international community must support Egypt's efforts to counter its internal Islamic State threat, as Wilayat Sinai has the desire and proven capabilities to attack Egyptian, Israeli, and international interests. Such assistance includes intelligence sharing, border security cooperation, and efforts to stem weapons smuggling and financial transfers from the Islamic State to its operatives in Sinai.

At the same time, Israel and Egypt's other allies in the fight against Wilayat Sinai must encourage Egypt to follow through on plans to address the long term economic and developmental grievances in Sinai that fuel support for anti-state violence. It is also important to counter the Islamic State narrative of an Egyptian government that represses Muslims. For the international community, a major concern is the effect Egyptian political repression has on Islamic State recruitment, both to Wilayat Sinai and externally.

Notes

1   For an in-depth background on ABM, see Zack Gold, "Security in the Sinai: Present and Future," International Centre for Counter-Terrorism – The Hague, March 2014, http://www.icct.nl/download/file/ICCT-Gold-Security-In-The-Sinai-March-2014. pdf.

2   Daveed Gartenstein-Ross, "Ansar Bayt Al-Maqdis's Oath of Allegiance to the Islamic State," Wikistrat, February 2015, http://www.wikistrat.com/ansar-bayt-al-maqdiss-oath-of-allegiance-to-the-islamic-state-report-released/.

3   Ahmed Eleiba, "Not an Easy Scenario: How will Iraq Affect Sinai?" *Ahram Online*, July 13, 2014, http://english.ahram.org.eg/News/106137.aspx.

4   David Kirkpatrick, "Militant Group in Egypt Vows Loyalty to ISIS," *New York Times*, November 10, 2014, http://www.nytimes.com/2014/11/11/world/middleeast/egyptian-militant-group-pledges-loyalty-to-isis.html.

5   "New Video Message from Jamā'at Anṣār Bayt al-Maqdis' Abū Usāmah al-Maṣrī: 'Sermon of 'Īd from the Sinai,'" *Jihadology*, July 31, 2014, http://jihadology.net/2014/07/31/new-video-message-from-jamaat-an%E1%B9%A3ar-bayt-al-maqdis-abu-usamah-al-ma%E1%B9%A3ri-sermon-of-id-from-the-sinai/.

6   "Egypt Security Watch – Monthly Briefing 4: January 2015," Tahrir Institute for Middle East Policy, February 13, 2015, http://timep.org/esw/articles-analysis/egypt-security-watch-monthly-briefing-4-january-2015/.

7   "Assault in Sheikh Zuweid: A Turning Point in Egypt's Fight against Terrorism," Tahrir Institute for Middle East Policy, July 2, 2015, http://timep.org/commentary/assault-in-sheikh-zuwaid-a-turning-point-in-egypts-fight-against-terrorism.

8   "Wanted Egyptian Militant Urges Jihad against Sisi: SITE," *Reuters*, July 22, 2015, http://www.reuters.com/article/2015/07/22/us-egypt-militant-idUSKCN0PW0M220150722.

9   Damien McElroy, "Rome will be Conquered Next, Says Leader of 'Islamic State,'" *The Telegraph*, July 1, 2014, http://www.telegraph.co.uk/news/worldnews/middleeast/syria/10939235/Rome-will-be-conquered-next-says-leader-of-Islamic-State.html.

10 Mahmoud Mourad, "Egypt's Sisi Tours Border with Libya after Bombing IS Targets," *Reuters*, February 18, 2015, http://www.reuters.com/article/2015/02/18/us-egypt-libya-idUSKBN0LM1JK20150218.

11 "Country Reports on Terrorism 2014: Chapter 2. Country Reports: Middle East and North Africa Overview," U.S. Department of State, http://www.state.gov/j/ct/rls/crt/2014/239407.htm.

12 "Egyptian Rejection of Taking the Provisions of the International Coalition Strategy against ISIS," Egyptian Ministry of Foreign Affairs Facebook page, August 1, 2015, https://www.facebook.com/MFAEgypt/posts/902452593160021.

13 "El-Sisi says Al-Azhar has Failed to Renew Islamic Discourse," *Ahram Online*, July 14, 2015, http://english.ahram.org.eg/News/135369.aspx.

14 Sarah el Deeb and Lee Keath, "From Egypt's Leader, an Ambitious Call for Reform in Islam," *Associated Press*, January 8, 2015, http://bigstory.ap.org/article/d2f4ad0aefc742c0981575537818ffd5/egypts-leader-ambitious-call-reform-islam.

The Islamic State in Libya: Challenge and Response

Shaul Shay and Av Baras

The national uprisings in the Middle East and Africa that began in late 2010 did not bypass Libya; by early 2011 the Libyan regime had collapsed on the heels of a civilian revolt. Muammar Qaddafi, Libya's long-time leader, was caught and executed by the rebels in October 2011.[1] The governing vacuum created by the downfall of Qaddafi's regime led to violent struggles between armed militias and the Libyan army, particularly around Benghazi and Tripoli. In the democratic elections held in July 2012, representatives of the armed militias did poorly as compared to the secular leadership identified with the Libyan military. This led to even more fighting and chaotic governance, and cast the nation in a downward spiral.[2]

A new election was held in July 2014. The secular government won once again,[3] but the results were contested by the Islamists.[4] In August 2014, Islamic militias, united under the banner of Fajr Libya (Libyan Dawn), took Tripoli, forcing the parliament to move the seat of government to Tobruk on Libya's east coast. At the same time the Islamic militias also seized cities in eastern Libya. As a result, two different governments, parliaments, and militaries are currently in place. The state in Tobruk and Bayda is secular, has a parliament, and is recognized by the UN; the second entity, concentrated in Tripoli, is ruled by a government and parliament of an Islamic bent. The power struggle between the two rivals and the consequent chaos in the nation has enabled the Islamic State to seize control of certain areas, including Derna and Sirte on the Mediterranean coast.

Libya is important to the Islamic State for several reasons. First, like Syria and Iraq, it is a failed state with no effective central government or organized army capable of resisting the forces of the Islamic State and impeding their progress. Second, Libya sits at a critical geographical crossroads that allows terrorist movement throughout the Maghreb and the Sahel – areas perceived by the Islamic State as natural extensions of its caliphate. Third, Libya is a strategic location with quick and relatively easy access to Europe across the Mediterranean. The Islamic State can thus use the masses of refugees fleeing the country as a cover for exporting its activists and ideology to European shores. Fourth, Libya is rich in oil and gas, resources that can help finance Islamic State activities if it is able to seize control of them. And finally, the enormous munitions stores left behind by Qaddafi's regime are of inestimable value to the Islamic State, which can distribute these weapons not only to its operatives in Libya but also to those in other areas of the African continent and beyond.[5]

The Islamic State's presence in Libya was first exposed in October 2014 via a video clip that introduced several fighters who had joined the Young Muslims Shura Council, an organization that has sworn an oath of allegiance to Abu Bakr al-Baghdadi, the leader of the Islamic State. According to most reports, by the summer of 2015 the organization had several thousand fighters at its disposal in Libya. Many of these had served in other outfits before switching their loyalty to the Islamic State, while a relatively smaller number were Islamic State activists who had returned from the battlefields in Syria and Iraq.

The Battle over Derna

Until the spring of 2014, Derna, located in eastern Libya, was controlled by Ansar al-Shariah, an Islamic militia historically associated with al-Qaeda. However, during the protracted fighting in Libya, the group split both ideologically and geographically, with one faction occupying Benghazi, the other Derna. Significantly, this development reflects the consequences of the April 2013 rift between al-Qaeda in Syria, led by Abu Muhammad al-Julani, and al-Qaeda in Iraq, led by Abu Bakr al-Baghdadi.[6] Ansar al-Shariah in Benghazi continued to identify with al-Qaeda, while Ansar al-Shariah in Derna aligned itself with al-Baghdadi and the Islamic State.[7]

In the spring of 2014, a group of Islamic activists arrived in Derna, among them people who had fought in Syria and Iraq with the Islamic State. The group's announcement that it was founding an organization called the Young Muslims Shura Council led to battles for control of the city between those who supported the Islamic State and those who favored Salafist organizations such as the Derna Shura Council and the Abu Salim Brigades. The fighting continued until September 2014, when a large contingent of Islamic State activists arrived from Syria and won control of the city for the Islamic State.[8] Approximately one month later, the heads of the Ansar al-Shariah group in Derna swore allegiance to al-Baghdadi.[9] Derna was consequently declared a city controlled by the Islamic caliphate, in fact, the first outside of Syria or Iraq to be annexed to it.[10]

Beyond their pledge of allegiance, the Islamic State activists in Derna announced the establishment of an emirate, subdivided into three districts. This move was endorsed by the caliph, who called on all his supporters in Libya to join the Islamic State. In January 2015, al-Baghdadi announced three new provinces of the Islamic caliphate: Wilayat Tarabulus (Tripoli) in Libya's northwest, Wilayat Barqa (which included the major cities of Derna and Benghazi) in the country's northeast, and Wilayat Fazzan in the country's south.[11] While Wilayat Fazzan has been relatively peaceful and quiet, the other two provinces have witnessed several terrorist attacks and violent incidents, such as the execution of 21 Egyptian Copts in February 2015,[12] and a suicide attack involving three car bombs that led to 47 civilian deaths in al-Qubbah in March 2015.[13] In June 2015, the Islamic State in Derna made a move that cost it control over the city and the emirate it had established. Immediately after Islamic State supporters assassinated two opposition leaders, battles broke out between the sides. Fearing the spread of combat westwards, the army deployed its forces. During the first days of fighting, the organizations opposed to the Islamic State managed to oust its fighters from the center of Derna to an eastern suburb,[14] thereby bringing Islamic State control of the city to an end.

The Seizure of Sirte

In August 2015, the mufti of the Islamic State in Sirte, a city on the Mediterranean coast between Tripoli and Benghazi, announced the establishment of a new emirate[15] under the aegis of the caliphate as a replacement for the one lost in Derna. The announcement followed the total conquest of the city, most of which had already been taken in June 2015. Islamic State fighters invaded Sirte, repelled the militias still loyal to the government and parliament in Tripoli, and seized control of government buildings.[16] The fighters also occupied the Ghardabiya air base south of the city, a site that the Libyans still viewed as a strategic stronghold though it was all but razed to the ground by the NATO bombing of the Qaddafi regime in 2011. In the course of the takeover, hundreds of civilians in Sirte, mostly Salafist clerics who refused to swear an oath of allegiance to the Islamic State, were slaughtered.[17]

While the Libyan army chose not to intervene except through pinpoint airstrikes,[18] the militias headed by Fajr Libya and loyal to the Islamic parliament in Tripoli tried to move against the Islamic State, but to no avail.[19] Following its successes in Sirte, the Islamic State expanded its activities and tried to seize control of Misurata, Libya's third largest city.[20] The Islamic State conquest of Sirte, like its occupation of other strongholds in Libya, was accomplished with help from Salafist jihadists from other countries. The Nigerian Boko Haram, for example, sent hundreds of operatives to help the Islamic State in Libya.[21]

Regional Influences

The entrenchment of the Islamic State has not only affected Libya's internal affairs, but also caused reverberations in neighboring regions. For example, Egypt, which shares a border with Libya, is now forced to confront the Islamic State threat on two fronts – first, with respect to the damage that it has wrought on Egyptian citizens and interests in Libya (as in the case of Derna), and second, with respect to the terrorists infiltrating Egypt from Libya as well as the large scale smuggling of arms. These challenges join Egypt's bitter war against Ansar Bait al-Maqdis, an organization active mostly in the Sinai Peninsula, which took an oath of allegiance to the Islamic State already in November 2014 and announced the establishment of Wilayat Sinai, a new Islamic State province.[22] In light of these threats, Egypt has beefed up its forces along the Libyan border as well as its navy in the region. Its air force also bombed Islamic State targets in Libya after the murder of the Copts in Derna.

Tunisia too is affected by the Islamic State's presence in Libya. In this case, the danger is real and immediate, as hundreds of Tunisian volunteers are making their way home from Libya.[23] These activists undergo training in camps in western Libya, whence they continue to their various destinations, be they Syria, Iraq, Libya, or Tunisia.[24] Since 2013, an active group of Salafist jihadists has been calling itself the Uqba Ibn Nafi Brigade and operating against Tunisia's security forces along the country's border with Libya. In the past it was thought that the group identified with al-Qaeda of the Islamic

Maghreb, an extension of North Africa's "official" al-Qaeda, but in late 2014 it became known that the group's leadership had sworn allegiance to Caliph al-Baghdadi and the Islamic State. Two terrorist attacks took place in Tunisia in 2015, both targeting tourists. The first, in March 2015, at the Bardo National Museum in the capital city, killed 18;[25] the second, in the resort town of Sousse on the Mediterranean coast, took the lives of 38 vacationers, 30 of them British citizens.[26] Both acts were conducted by terrorists who had arrived from Libya, where they had been trained in camps before returning to Tunisia to launch the attacks.[27]

Another concern – to many Westerners in particular – regarding the Islamic State in Libya is the country's proximity to Europe.[28] The Islamic State not only recruits operatives in Europe to join its ranks in the Middle East and Africa, but also sends operatives into Europe. According to one Libyan source, the Islamic State allows immigrant smugglers to operate freely in the country in exchange for half their profits, and also exploits this route and has activists disguised as refugees infiltrate Europe.[29] The presence of the Islamic State in Libya thus undermines the stability of neighboring countries and represents a twofold danger to Europe. First, it encourages the flow of refugees in order to apply pressure on European countries, most of which are helping the US-led coalition against it. Second, its activists enter Europe purporting to be among the waves of refugees entering the continent. In this way it can establish terrorist infrastructures to use against European targets.

Conclusions

Four years after the ouster of Qaddafi, Libya remains a failed state without a functioning central government and subject to the throes of civil war. Two armed militias supporting two rival governments – a result of the last election – are fighting one another, instead of joining forces to defeat the Islamic State. Libya thus lacks a central government capable of stopping the entity's spread or even collaborating with the West's military initiatives against it. This reality poses a growing threat to Libya's neighbors – Egypt and Tunisia – as well as a substantive danger to Europe.

In Libya, the campaign against the Islamic State must take the form of a comprehensive war on all geographical fronts with the coordination of all nations involved. Militarily, the coalition's activities against the Islamic State in Iraq and Syria must be extended to Libya through airstrikes and naval blockades in order to stop the movement of Islamic State fighters and arms to and from the country. In addition, the Egyptian initiative to establish an Arab League military force to confront the Islamic State in Libya (modeled on the force against the Houthis in Yemen) must be implemented. Finally, illegal immigration into Europe must be more closely monitored with mechanisms designed to check and identify Islamic State activists trying to enter the continent under the guise of refugees and asylum seekers.

Given today's reality, it is clear that Libya and Tunisia are incapable of dealing effectively with the spread of the Islamic State on their soil. Egypt is engaged in a harsh struggle with the Islamic State's branch in Sinai and elsewhere within its country and is therefore unwilling to open another front on the Libyan border without external help. On November 14, 2015, a US airstrike in Derna is believed to have killed Iraqi national Abu Nabil, one of the top Islamic State commanders in Libya. The strike was the first US raid against an Islamic State leader in Libya, and it is not clear yet if it represents a change in US policy and greater American involvement in fighting the Islamic State in Libya.[30]

At present, the Islamic State in the region is still limited in power and influence, but if the West and/or the Arab League nations do not intervene militarily in the near future, the Islamic State will be able to be further entrenched and pose a serious threat that its opponents will find difficult to confront. They therefore need to act accordingly, and the sooner the better.

Notes

1 "Muammar Gaddafi Killed, Captured In Sirte," *World Post*, October 20, 2011.
2 Daniel Wigmore-Shepherd, "The Trend of Increasing Violence in Post-Gaddafi Libya," *ACLED*, August 6, 2014, http://goo.gl/IUcosb.
3 Cameron Glenn, "Libya's Islamists: Who They Are – And What They Want," Wilson Center, https://goo.gl/tBB9Ws.
4 Sasha Toperich, "Libya: New Parliament Set to Be Inaugurated in Tobruk," *World Post*, August 1, 2014, http://www.huffingtonpost.com/sasha-toperich/libya-new-parliament-set-_b_5640899.html.
5 Charlie Winter, "Libya: The Strategic Gateway for the Islamic State," February 2015, Quilliam Foundation, http://goo.gl/ZxBE6D.
6 "Qaeda in Iraq Confirms Syria's Nusra is Part of Network," *Global Post*, April 9, 2013, http:/goo.gl/3Kwumi.
7 "War in Libya and its Futures: State of Play – Islamist Forces (2)," The Red (Team) Analysis Society, February 26, 2015, http://goo.gl/0kGDbi.

8   Maggie Michael, "How a Libyan City Joined the Islamic State Group," *AP*, November 9, 2014, http://bigstory.ap.org/article/195a7ffb0090444785eb814a5bd a28c7/how-libyan-city-joined-islamic-state-group.

9   "Groups Pledge Allegiance to ISIS in Eastern Libya," *Vocativ*, October 5, 2014, http://www.vocativ.com/world/isis-2/isis-libya-parade/.

10 Michael, "How a Libyan City Joined the Islamic State Group."

11 Paul Cruickshank, Nic Robertson, Tim Lister, and Jomana Karadsheh, "ISIS Comes to Libya," *CNN*, http://edition.cnn.com/2014/11/18/world/isis-libya/.

12 "Egypt Eyes Revenge After ISIS Executes 21 Copts, Releases Video," *RT*, February 15, 2015, http://www.rt.com/news/232583-isis-video-execution-egyptians/.

13 "Triple Suicide Blasts Kill 47 in Libya's Qubbah," *Anadolu Agency*, February 20, 2015, http://www.aa.com.tr/en/headline/468248--20-killed-as-suicide-bombings-rock-libyas-qubbah.

14 "Libya: Shura Council Captures the Leader of the Islamic State in Derna and Allied with the Population," *France 24*, June 14, 2015, http://goo.gl/0gi9FL.

15 "The Organization of the Islamic State Declares Sirte Islamic Emirate as Belonging to the Ruler al-Baghdadi," *France 24*, August 29, 2015, http://goo.gl/ZbjV2J.

16 "ISIS Seizes Another Town in Libya," *al-Arabiya*, June 5, 2015, http://goo.gl/pxurv5.

17 "ISIS Victims in Sirte Exceed 169 Dead," *Sky News Arabia*, August 14, 2015, http://goo.gl/Xh5E4O.

18 "IS Kills Dozens in Libya's Sirte, Putting Down Uprising by Local Tribe," *Middle East Eye*, August 14, 2015, http://goo.gl/M212Nv.

19 "ISIS 'Beheads' 12 in Battle for Libya's Sirte: Media," *Daily Star*, August 15, 2015, http://goo.gl/MDcB3N.

20 Suliman Ali Zway and David D. Kirkpatrick, "Western Officials Alarmed as ISIS Expands Territory in Libya," May 31, 2015, *New York Times*, http://goo.gl/X65Nrz.

21 "Boko Haram Strengthens Ties with ISIS," *New York Post*, August 22, 2015, http://nypost.com/2015/08/22/boko-haram-strengthens-ties-with-isis.

22 Jon Lee Anderson, "Egypt, Libya, and ISIS," *New Yorker*, February 17, 2015, http://www.newyorker.com/news/news-desk/egypt-libya-isis.

23 "Libya a 'Magnet' for Jihadists from Tunisia and Beyond," *News 24*, July 4, 2015, http://goo.gl/BU9r0C.

24 Jack Moore, "5,000 Foreign Fighters Flock to Libya as ISIS Call for Jihadists," March 3, 2015, *Newsweek*, http://www.newsweek.com/5000-foreign-fighters-flock-libya-isis-call-jihadists-310948.

25 A. Khelifa and Katharina Wecker, "Accomplices Sought in Tunisia Terror Attack," *USA Today*, March 18, 2015, http://www.usatoday.com/story/news/world/2015/03/18/reports-shots-tunisia-parliament/24948295/.

26 Sam Webb, "Tunisia Attack: Latest Updates as Massacre British Death Toll May Rise Past 30," *Mirror*, June 29, 2015, http://goo.gl/0I0zO4.

27 "Tunisia Hotel Attack: Authorities Search for Libya-Trained Suspects," *Irish Times*, July 2, 2015, http://goo.gl/WtXKqy.

28 "The Second Front: ISIS Gaining Strength in North Africa," *NRG*, February 17, 2015.

29 "Worrisome: ISIS Fighters Entering Europe," *Israel Hayom*, May 17, 2015.

30 Jay Akbar, "ISIS Leader 'Killed' in American Airstrike in Libya while Paris Terror Attacks were Underway," *Mail Online*, November 14, 2015.

The Islamic State and its Intentions for Africa

Smadar Shaul and Yoram Schweitzer

As part of the Islamic State's aspiration to expand globally, the Nigerian Boko Haram, which was the first organization to express its desire to unite with the Islamic State, was selected as its regional representative for West Africa, and thus its pledge of allegiance was accepted. During the preparations for the official announcement of the merger between the two, Boko Haram's leader, Abu Bakar Shekau, gave the *bay'ah* to Abu Bakr al-Baghdadi. This was followed by a declaration several days later by the Islamic State spokesperson, Abu Muhammad al-Adnani, that the Nigerian organization was endorsed as an official province, designated as the Islamic State in West Africa. This unification process can serve as an example of the Islamic State's formation of its alliances with its other subordinates. It reflects the motives that underlie each side's eagerness for the alliance, and it also enables a better understanding of the Islamic State's intentions in Africa overall.

Boko Haram was founded in 2009 in northeastern Nigeria by a Muslim cleric named Muhammad Yousuf. Yousuf sought to create an Islamic state in this region based on the *sharia* (Islamic law); significantly, some of the group's members had begun operations for this purpose years earlier. The organization's official name was Jama'at Ahl as-Sunnah lid-Da'wah wa'l-Jihad (the Sunni Group for Islamic Preaching and Holy War); today it is widely known as Boko Haram, which means "Western education is forbidden." Following a violent clash between the organization's operatives and police forces in 2009, hundreds of members of the organization were arrested and their leader was executed. Abu Bakar Shekau, the organization's deputy leader, was appointed in his place. Shekau swore to avenge the death of his leader and to wage a total war against the Nigerian government and the state's institutions, and in 2010 the organization began to launch terrorist operations in Nigeria.[1]

After his nomination as the new leader, Shekau declared his support for al-Qaeda and Bin Laden, the renowned leader of the global jihad camp at the time.[2] As part of his efforts to tighten his links with the global jihad organization, Shekau wrote some letters addressed to Bin Laden that were found after the latter's death in May 2011 at his home in Abbottabad, Pakistan.[3] Boko Haram also maintained ties with al-Qaeda's other branches, al-Qaeda in the Islamic Maghreb and al-Shabaab in Somalia. These connections were reflected in the aid Boko Haram received from them in military training, manpower, and equipment.[4] For its part, the Nigerian organization sent its fighters to assist the branch of al-Qaeda in the Islamic Maghreb in the clashes in Mali in 2011.[5]

The influence of al-Qaeda on Boko Haram's operations was already apparent in 2011, when the Nigerian organization adopted the al-Qaeda inspired tactic of suicide bombings. Since its first use by Boko Haram in June 2011, it has become a common tactic in the organization's repertoire. Boko Haram has launched nearly 200 suicide bombings in the last four and a half years, mostly in Nigeria, with some in Cameroon, Chad, and Niger.[6] The first suicide attacks on the police station and the UN building in the Nigerian capital of Abuja carried out by Boko Haram were assisted with guidance by al-Qaeda in the Islamic Maghreb, which may have supplied Boko Haram with the explosives for the attacks.[7] The Nigerian organization seems also to have received training from al-Qaeda's branches in its propaganda and communications activities. This influence can be seen in the rhetoric used by Shekau and his threats toward Western countries, with an emphasis on the United States, and against Israel.[8]

Despite Boko Haram's ties with al-Qaeda branches, the organization was not officially accepted as part of the al-Qaeda network of alliances. Presumably Boko Haram's conduct did not fit the strategy of Bin Laden, or that of his successor, Ayman al-Zawahiri, particularly because of the Nigerian organization's *takfiri* policy (declaring Muslims to be heretics, which sanctions killing them). Al-Qaeda leaders also objected to Boko Haram's indiscriminate attacks against innocent Muslims, fearing a loss of support from Muslims around the world. In addition, the undisguised ambition of Boko Haram's leader to declare the establishment of an Islamic emirate in northeastern Nigeria opposed Bin Laden's position, which argued that the timing was not appropriate for such a move.[9] However, due to the relations between Boko Haram and al-Qaeda's branches and to the absence of any alternatives, the Nigerian organization continued to support al-Qaeda. This situation changed with the appearance of ISIS, which later became the Islamic State, and especially after the announcement on June 29, 2014 of the newly established caliphate, with Abu Bakr al-Baghdadi as caliph.

The first sign of Boko Haram's weakening support for al-Qaeda and its intention to unite with the Islamic State and be part of its caliphate came shortly after this announcement. In July 2014, Boko Haram's leader expressed his support for the Islamic caliphate and al-Baghdadi, whom he called the "leader of all Muslims everywhere." At this stage, Shekau did not officially abandon the al-Qaeda camp, and still expressed his support of al-Zawahiri and the leader of the Taliban, Mullah Omar.[10] Addressing al-Baghdadi as the "leader of all Muslims," however, reflected Boko Haram's support for the establishment of the caliphate by the Islamic State, and its inclination to accept al-Baghdadi as the new leader of the global jihad. Another expression of Boko Haram's support for the idea of the caliphate was indicated by Shekau's announcement in August 2014 of the establishment of an Islamic emirate in northeastern Nigeria over an area of 50,000 square kilometers.[11] This declaration reflected Shekau's own intention to be recognized as an emir of the Islamic state in Nigeria, and highlighted Boko Haram's strength, as it would be portrayed as the preferred representative of the Islamic State in West Africa. The Nigerian organization appeared to be at the peak of its power in late 2014, and a declaration that an Islamic emirate was established in a large territory constituted a significant projection of power and enabled Shekau to display his qualifications as emir – not only in theory, but also in practice. The Islamic State's response was swift: in September 2014, *Dabiq*, the Islamic State's English-language propaganda magazine, published its conditions for accepting loyalty from various organizations, and mentioned Boko Haram as a potential candidate to fulfill that position.[12]

The effect of Boko Haram's warming ties with the Islamic State became apparent in October 2014, and was expressed in changes in the Nigerian organization's media activity, manifested in video clips distributed by Boko Haram over the internet. The video clips were inspired by Islamic State videos: from the display of the black flag, which serves as the symbol identified with the Islamic State, to the high quality videos that were screened. These indicators supported the assessment that the Islamic State was assisting the

Nigerian organization in improving its communication capabilities.[13] The Islamic State also assisted the Nigerian organization in establishing its own professional media division. As part of this effort, an Islamic State social media specialist was assigned to assist Boko Haram. In January 2015 this operative created a Twitter account for the Nigerian organization and began distributing Boko Haram's messages, some of which were also distributed through the personal accounts of Islamic State operatives and on the official Islamic State media channels. This enabled the Islamic State to monitor the messages sent in the name of Boko Haram and ensure they were acceptable to the Islamic State policy. A month later, Boko Haram was entrusted with managing the Twitter account, which became the official voice for the Islamic State in West Africa.[14]

When the conditions were ripe for a union between the two, the Islamic State sent a team to Nigeria in February 2015 to negotiate the terms of Boko Haram's declaration of loyalty.[15] When the negotiations were concluded on March 7, 2015, the Nigerian organization swore allegiance to the caliphate and its leader, Caliph Abu Bakr al-Baghdadi.[16] On March 12 the Islamic State made an announcement accepting this declaration of loyalty.[17] As part of the completion of the union between Boko Haram and the Islamic State, the latter published a video clip in late April 2015 announcing that the name of the Nigerian organization had been changed to Islamic State's West Africa Province (ISWAP), and that it had been integrated into the emerging Islamic caliphate.[18]

The union between Boko Haram and the Islamic State took place at a time when the Nigerian organization was under attack by a multinational military offensive headed by Nigeria and a coalition of countries in the region. This resulted in Boko Haram losing most of the territory it had controlled, and putting it at risk of defeat.[19] Following the union with the Islamic State, Boko Haram's capabilities improved. These improvements were reflected in a broader scope of activity and in the effectiveness and geographic deployment of its attacks. These changes positioned the Nigerian organization as a regional threat that had to be destroyed and demanded a comprehensive effort on the part of all the countries in the region. These countries formed a multinational force led by new Nigerian President Muhammadu Buhari, a Muslim who was elected in late March 2015, when he defeated incumbent President Goodluck Jonathan, a Christian who had ruled Nigeria since 2010.

For the Islamic State, accepting Boko Haram into its system of alliances gave the Islamic State its first substantial foothold in West Africa that enabled its ultimate goal to expand the caliphate globally. In addition, the union with the Nigerian organization provides the Islamic State with territorial contiguity with its northern districts in Africa, including Libya and Algeria, while extending its influence to additional African countries. The implementation of this can already be seen in Boko Haram's suicide bombings outside Nigeria, which began only in 2015.[20]

As part of its expansion in Africa, the Islamic State it is also trying to extend the caliphate to East Africa, hoping to do this by recruiting the Somali organization al-Shabaab,[21] even though the Somali organization has become allied to al-Qaeda since February 2012.[22] Al-Shabaab, known for its internal disputes that led to assassinations within the organization in the past – that may also have contributed to the assassination of its leader Ahmed Abdi Godane, in September 2014[23] – is now embroiled in an internal dispute over whether to maintain its loyalty to al-Qaeda or to switch its allegiance to the Islamic State. Al-Shabaab's current leadership is making efforts to silence the voices calling on it to shift its alliance from al-Qaeda to the Islamic State in order to avoid a split. However, a union with the Islamic State, which has gained a worldwide reputation as victorious, identifies with the caliphate vision, and enjoys a wide range of resources and materials, is very tempting for the Somali organization, or at least for some of its members. For the Islamic State, this union, if successful – beyond the territorial advantage – could constitute a significant triumph in its struggle with al-Qaeda for leadership of the global jihad, a struggle that is also underway in Africa. The dissolution of the alliance between the Somali al-Shabaab and al-Qaeda is also likely to undermine al-Qaeda's alliances with its other branches, including al-Qaeda in the Islamic Maghreb and al-Qaeda in the Arabian Peninsula, both of which are closely linked to the Somali organization.

In conclusion, at the present time Boko Haram is the central player in the Islamic State's strategy in West Africa. Nonetheless, the Islamic State is striving to expand its influence in East Africa and attract additional organizations, such as al-Shabaab in Somalia, in order to convince them to shift their loyalty to the Islamic State camp. Salafi organizations in North Africa are also included among the ranks of the Islamic State, especially in Libya and Tunisia. The Islamic State's decision to adopt this strategy is, to a large extent, a direct consequence of the rivalry within the global jihadi camp, and is designed to unravel al-Qaeda's system of alliances, in order to establish and consolidate the Islamic State's leading role.

Despite what appears to be the Islamic State's momentum of success in parts of Africa, Boko Haram, its main representative in West Africa, also suffers from internal rivalries and unstable leadership, and faces a united and well integrated regional offensive. Therefore, there is no certainty of its success and achieving absolute loyalty to the Islamic State. In addition, al-Qaeda, the Islamic State's sworn enemy, has not given up on the struggle with the Islamic State over the leadership of the jihadi camp in Africa. This competition leaves an opening for countermeasures by the regional coalition, in cooperation with the international Western coalition, aimed at driving a wedge between the two organizations, increasing the friction between them, and weakening them in order to defeat them. At the same time, the African continent will almost certainly continue to be a key region for terrorism by both the Islamic State and al-Qaeda in the coming years, and the campaign against them is not expected to be easy or quick.

Notes

We wish to thank Einav Yogev, a research associate in the Terror and Low Intensity Conflict Research Program at INSS, for her help in preparing this article.

1   David Doukhan, "Who Are You, Boko Haram?" International Institute for Counter-Terrorism (ICT) website, December 12, 2012, http://www.ict.org.il/Article/991/Who-Are-You-Boko-Haram.

2   "Profile: Boko Haram," *al-Jazeera English*, December 31, 2010, http://www.aljazeera.com/news/africa/2010/12/2010123115425609851.html.

3   Eli Lake, "Boko Haram's Bin Laden Connection," *Daily Beast*, May 11, 2014, http://www.thedailybeast.com/articles/2014/05/11/boko-haram-s-bin-laden-connection.html.

4   Ely Karmon, "Boko Haram's International Reach," *Perspectives on Terrorism* 8, no. 1 (2014), http://www.terrorismanalysts.com/pt/index.php/pot/article/view/326/html.

5   Sudarsan Raghavan, "Nigerian Islamist Militants Return from Mali with Weapons, Skills," *Washington Post*, May 31, 2013, https://www.washingtonpost.com/world/africa/nigerian-islamist-militants-return-from-mali-with-weapons-skills/2013/05/31/d377579e-c628-11e2-9cd9-3b9a22a4000a_story.html.

6   Virginia Comolli, "The Regional Problem of Boko Haram," *Survival: Global Politics and Strategy* 4, no. 57 (2015): 109-17.

7   "Boko Haram: Growing Threat to the U.S.," *Homeland*, U.S. House of Representatives – Committee on Homeland Security, September 13, 2013.

8   Ibid.

9   Don Rassler, Gabriel Koehler-Derrick, Liam Collins, Muhammas al-Obaidi, and Nelly Lahoud, "Letters from Abbottabad: Bin Ladin Sidelined?" Combating Terrorism Center, May 3, 2015, https://www.ctc.usma.edu/posts/letters-from-abbottabad-bin-ladin-sidelined.

10 "Boko Haram Voices Support for ISIS' Baghdadi," *al-Arabiya News*, July 13, 2014, http://english.alarabiya.net/en/News/africa/2014/07/13/Boko-Haram-voices-support-for-ISIS-Baghdadi.html.

11 "Nigerian Town Seized by Boko Haram 'Part of Islamic Caliphate,' Leader Says," *The Telegraph*, August 24, 2014, www.telegraph.co.uk/news/worldnews/africaandindianocean/nigeria/11054219/Nigerian-town-seized-by-Boko-Haram-part-of-Islamic-caliphate-leader-says.html.

12 *Dabiq Magazine*, al-Hayat Media Center, October 5, 2014.

13 Gbenga Akingbule and Drew Hinshaw, "Boko Haram Denies Nigeria Cease-Fire Claim," *Wall Street Journal*, November 1, 2014, http://www.wsj.com/articles/boko-haram-denies-nigeria-cease-fire-claim-1414846770.

14 Jacob Zenn, "A Biography of Boko Haram and the Bay'a to Al Baghdadi," *Combating Terrorism Center*, March 19, 2015, https://www.ctc.usma.edu/posts/a-biography-of-boko-haram-and-the-baya-to-al-baghdadi.

15 Ibid.

16 "Nigeria's Boko Haram Pledges Allegiance to Islamic State: Audio Clip," *Reuters*, March 7, 2015, http://www.reuters.com/article/2015/03/07/us-nigeria-boko-haram-caliphate-idUSKBN0M30TH20150307.

17 "Islamic State Accepts' Boko Haram's Allegiance Pledge," *BBC NEWS*, March 13, 2015, http://www.bbc.com/news/world-africa-31862992.

18 Tomi Oladipo, "Analysis: Islamic State Strengthens Ties with Boko Haram," *BBC*, April 24, 2015, http://www.bbc.com/news/world-africa-32435614.

19 Colin Freeman, "Inside Boko Haram's 'Caliphate' in Nigeria," *The Telegraph*, May 11, 2015, http://www.telegraph.co.uk/news/worldnews/africaandindianocean/nigeria/11596614/Inside-Boko-Harams-caliphate-in-Nigeria.html.

20 Comolli, "The Regional Problem of Boko Haram."

21 Robyn Kriel and Lillian Leposo, "In Video, Somali ISIS Members Court al–Shabaab," *CNN*, May 22, 2015, http://edition.cnn.com/2015/05/22/world/somalia-isis-al-shabaab-video.

22 Rassler et al., "Letters from Abbottabad: Bin Ladin Sidelined?"

23 Isma'il Kushkush and Jeffrey Gettleman, "As Power of Terror Group Declines, Once-Feared Fighters Defect," *New York Times*, November 4, 2014, http://www.nytimes.com/2014/11/05/world/africa/shabab-somalia-fighters-leave-terror-group-behind.html?_r=0.

The Spread of the Islamic State in Southern Asia: Between Vision and Reality

Meirav Mishali-Ram

Background

In recent decades, South Asia has been a key battlefield for regional and global jihadist organizations. The war in Afghanistan in the 1980s between the mujahidin and the Soviet Union marked a turning point in the spread of global terrorist groups, built around the cross-border commitment to the jihadist cause by Muslims of various nations. After the war, two prominent organizations representing two central ideologies of radical Islam established themselves in Afghanistan: al-Qaeda, which bore the standard of global jihad against a US-led West, and the Taliban, which aimed to institute an Islamic emirate in Afghanistan. Before long, their influence spread throughout the region, especially in neighboring Pakistan, which was drawn into escalating warfare against Islamic terrorism. Embroiled in a longstanding conflict with Pakistan, India too has had to confront the ramifications of Islamic terrorism in the region.

The Islamic State's entry into the South Asia arena in 2014 coincided with political violence in Afghanistan, which intensified as US and NATO forces scaled back their involvement in the country, and as Afghanistan and Pakistan – both engaged in internal political struggles – grew increasingly incapable of stemming the rising tide of Islamic terrorism. Taking advantage of the situation, the Islamic State, which had originally drawn its inspiration from al-Qaeda's global jihadism and for a time had even served as that organization's extension in Iraq, severed the alliance to become its rival.

This essay surveys the Islamic State's penetration of Afghanistan, Pakistan, and India, and examines the ensuing threat to the area's dominant movements that until recently had been partners in jihad. It also outlines the Islamic

State's vision for expansion throughout South Asia as well as the practical limitations of that vision, while analyzing the ramifications of the struggles among the various actors in the terrorism arena.

The Afghan Arena: The Taliban versus the Islamic State

The first signs of the Islamic State's intention to spread to Afghanistan emerged in the second half of 2014, a few months after the Iraqi city of Mosul fell to the Islamic State. The Islamic State's independence, brutality, and expansionist ambitions were seen as a threat by dominant Sunni movements in Afghanistan. The leaders of the Afghan Taliban thus rushed to swear an oath of allegiance to Mullah Muhammad Omar (whose death was not yet common knowledge),[1] insisting that the war against the United States and its allies had to be conducted under a single authority, i.e., the Taliban.[2] This was the earliest evidence of the power struggle between the Taliban and the Islamic State – the result of the latter's challenge to the older organization on three key issues: control of the Afghan arena, ideology, and control of the Islamic struggle as a whole.

On the practical level, the rivalry between the Afghan Taliban and the Islamic State revolved around their struggle over the control and recruitment of fighters. In early 2015, a few months after the Islamic State made its first appearance in Afghanistan, a local Taliban leader deserted and opened an Islamic State training camp in Farah Province. Afterwards, jihadists began flying the black Islamic State flag in other Afghan provinces, though whether this was the result of official Islamic State policy is unclear. Mutual negative propaganda has played a role in the battle for loyalty and active support. In June 2015, for example, a spokesman for the Islamic State accused the Afghan Taliban of serving as an agent in the Pakistani intelligence service.

In his attempt to avoid clashes between the two organizations, the deputy chief of the Taliban asked Abu Bakr al-Baghdadi, the leader of the Islamic State, to operate in Afghanistan under the Taliban's leadership. The Islamic State, however, refused subservience to any other entity. Armed confrontations soon broke out between the Taliban and the Islamic State in Nangarhar, Helmand, and Farah;[3] in April 2015 each declared jihad against its opponent.

The Taliban and the Islamic State share an ideological platform. Like the Islamic State, the Taliban wants to make *sharia* the law of the land, and it ruthlessly enforced strict Islamic rulings when it ruled Afghanistan in the 1990s. Moreover, like its current rival, the Taliban has attacked the Shiite minority, destroyed historic temples and sites, and treated anyone it viewed as an enemy of Islam with brutality. Nonetheless, ideological differences exist between the two. The Taliban has established an Islamic emirate in Afghanistan that is based on a combination of Hanafi Sunni Islamic Law and the Pashtunwali, an unwritten Pashtun code of ethics and traditional life.[4] The puritan and uncompromising Islamic State, on the other hand, rejects any integration of Islamic law and cultural codes, and promotes a global Islamic caliphate, which al-Baghdadi announced in mid-2014. The Islamic State also aims at far greater territorial expansion than the Taliban ever envisioned. In addition, the brutality that has become a trademark of the Islamic State far exceeds Taliban tactics, and the Islamic State's rejection of any cooperation with all those deemed enemies of Islam leads it to condemn the Taliban's willingness to cooperate with the Pakistani intelligence service and engage in talks with both the United States and the Afghan government.

Such ideological differences between the Taliban and the Islamic State, however, are mostly window-dressing that conceals personal power struggles and competition over leadership. Prominent jihadist organizations, including al-Qaeda – under both Osama Bin Laden and Ayman al-Zawahiri – have long regarded Mullah Omar as their supreme leader. However, once al-Baghdadi declared himself caliph of the Islamic State, he openly challenged the status of Omar, the "emir of the believers." Since then, rivalry has led to hostile declarations that have at times assumed a personal tone. In April 2015, for example, a Taliban spokesman referred to al-Baghdadi as a "false caliph," and claimed that loyalty to him was forbidden by Islamic law. In turn, al-Baghdadi responded by calling Mullah Omar an "illiterate warlord."[5]

The Islamic State's entry into the Afghan arena has significant implications, both on a regional and global level. The Taliban is securely entrenched in the local population, especially among the Pashtuns in the south. Assessments of the Islamic State in Afghanistan reveal that it is still a minor power, attracting mostly foreigners and Taliban deserters. Nonetheless, the extreme brutality of the organization has damaged the delicate fabric of Taliban relations with the local population.[6] The emergence of the Islamic State in Afghanistan thus complicates the situation and escalates the struggle over the country's future. To remain relevant, the Taliban must now commit itself to violent and persistent combat instead of engagement in dialogue with the Afghan government, a course that has thus far yielded no significant results.[7] The announcement of Mullah Omar's death and the tug-of-war within the Taliban over his replacement is also bound to undermine any attempts at peace talks with the regime.

From a broader international perspective, the Islamic State's spread to Afghanistan, which coincides with the departure of US and NATO troops from the country, has created some new and surprising bedfellows. Changing circumstances are driving the Taliban, a radical Sunni organization, into accepting assistance from Shiite Iran, something unthinkable only a few years ago. What began as financial aid has now extended to the recruitment, training, and armament of Taliban fighters. No one knows what will become of Afghanistan following the US withdrawal, but it seems that Iran has already bet on the Taliban.[8] Cooperation between Iran and the Taliban, undoubtedly a matter of mutual convenience, aims to cut the United States out of the picture and disrupt the influence of the Islamic State – a challenge both to the Taliban and Iran – over the Afghan arena.

Khorasan Province: Pakistani Taliban Factions in Support of the Islamic State

While Afghanistan is the crown jewel of the South Asian jihad, it cannot remain isolated from the jihad in neighboring Pakistan. In fact, the border region, which is largely inhabited by Pashtun tribes, is one of the busiest centers of regional and international terrorist activity. Pakistan nurtured Afghanistan's Taliban in the madrassas that took in Afghani refugees during the war against the Soviet Union. In addition, dozens of Pakistani jihad organizations were established in the tribal area of Pakistan from the early 2000s, when the United States invaded Afghanistan, until 2007, when the Pakistan Taliban became the umbrella organization for the country's broad range of Islamist movements. The Taliban has operated and spread throughout Pakistan, enjoying cooperation with both its Afghan counterpart and al-Qaeda forces in the area. In late 2014, these groups were joined by the Islamic State, which cast its entrance into Pakistan as a natural continuation of its expansion throughout Afghanistan.

Although the Pakistani Taliban has its share of internal struggles and offshoots, it is solidly integrated into Pakistan's tribal areas, where its various branches do not pose a concrete threat to one another. However, the Islamic State's appearance in Pakistan disrupted this balance, destabilized power relations, and threatened the country's Taliban. Among the reactions to the Islamic State's entry into Pakistan was the attempt by the Taliban leaders to join forces. In October 2014, Abu Omar Maqbool, the spokesman for the Pakistani Taliban, declared his loyalty to al-Baghdadi; the leaders of five other organizations joined him. In response, Mullah Fazlullah, the emir of the Pakistani Taliban, immediately announced that Maqbool was no longer the organization's spokesman and confirmed the Pakistani Taliban's oath of loyalty to Mullah Omar. A month later, Jundallah, an organization affiliated with the Pakistani Taliban, swore allegiance to the caliphate, while its leaders declared their loyalty to al-Baghdadi.

It is not inconceivable that the defection of senior Taliban personnel to the Islamic State has been partly motivated by bribery as well as by the disappearance of Mullah Omar, who was not seen in public since 2001. Those who left the Pakistani Taliban have founded the Khorashan Province in order to control the Islamic State in Pakistan. Khorashan is a geographical region that has historically included Afghanistan, Pakistan, and parts of neighboring nations. Although the Islamic State has attained only limited power and control in Afghanistan and Pakistan, the declaration of the province offers further evidence of its expansionist ambitions and serious intent.

Al-Qaeda toward the Islamic State: From Patron to Bitter Enemy

Osama Bin Laden linked the fate of his organization to the Taliban under the rule of Mullah Omar, who hosted him and granted his men refuge in his country. Nonetheless, al-Qaeda is ideologically closer to the Islamic State than any other Salafist jihadist organization. Indeed, the two actually collaborated in the past. Abu Musab al-Zarqawi, the founder of the Islamic State, for example, made a pact with al-Qaeda and turned his organization into al-Qaeda's proxy in Iraq from 2004 until 2013. However, like the Taliban, al-Qaeda has opposed the Islamic State's expansion under al-Baghdadi. In Iraq, the Islamic State's growing power, accompanied by horrendous displays of violence against all – fighters and civilians, locals and foreigners – has prompted al-Qaeda to express its reservations very clearly. The split between the patron and its emissary in Iraq was officially announced in February 2014, when the Islamic State threatened al-Qaeda's status within the global jihad movement.

It is therefore not surprising that al-Qaeda has joined the Taliban's aggressive fight against the Islamic State in Afghanistan and Pakistan. Entering the struggle over control of South Asia, al-Qaeda leader al-Zawahiri actually announced the establishment of an al-Qaeda umbrella organization on the Indian subcontinent – AQIS. Cooperation in Afghanistan and Pakistan between the two veteran organizations, the Taliban and al-Qaeda, is likely to make it very difficult for the Islamic State to realize its hopes of expansion and growth in these areas.

India: An Inseparable Part of the Caliphate

While the Islamist discourse gains hold in the Muslim nations in South Asia, India, with a substantial Muslim minority of 177 million people, remains an enigma. Muslims in India are historically and often ethnically linked to those in Pakistan. Nonetheless, radical Muslim organizations operating in India outside the conflict zone of Kashmir are of relatively limited scope. Estimates on the numbers joining the ranks of global jihad indicate that very few volunteers come from India. At the same time, India has a long history of radical Islam. The Deobandi sect, for example, which provides the ideological basis of some of the most radical organizations in South Asia, has its roots in India.[9] The country's encounter with Islamic terrorism, which has largely been linked to its conflict with Pakistan, began with the war that the latter has been waging on India through the proxies of its various terrorist organizations.

The doctrine of global jihad and the notion of the caliphate are forcing the Islamic State to test the limits of its vision and operative goals. India, a strategic target in Osama Bin Laden's holy war, has become a target of the Islamic State as well, at least on a rhetorical level. In a speech announcing the caliphate, Abu Bakr al-Baghdadi made reference to India three times. Like Bin Laden, he sees India as an enemy state that oppresses Muslims, but emphasizes its natural place within the Islamic caliphate.[10]

A document in Urdu, captured in the tribal region of Pakistan, sheds further light on the Islamic State's vision as it describes a working program for uniting dozens of factions of the region's jihadist organizations into a single entity that will attack India in order to touch off an apocalyptic confrontation with the United States.[11] Yet though the document offers evidence of grandiose ambitions, it says nothing at all about real capabilities. In fact, the presence of the Islamic State in India is currently limited to sporadic associations between individuals and local groups that vary in their behavior. Expressions of sympathy appear primarily in social media. However, even if the Islamic State's hold on India is insubstantial and far from what the Islamic State would like, the inherent threat of its influence on this vast and complex nation cannot be ignored.

Conclusion

The activity of the Islamic State and the rhetoric of its leadership leave no doubt as to its expansionist vision, as well as its desire to make South Asia a significant part of the caliphate. While the governments of Afghanistan and Pakistan stagger under the burden of combating the older jihadist organizations that have settled in their countries, it seems that the main effort to stop the Islamic State is being shouldered by dominant organizations in the region, i.e., the Taliban and al-Qaeda. These two are openly expressing their concern over the Islamic State's inroads into South Asia and are engaging in both propaganda and military warfare in order to preserve their dominance in the regional and global jihadist movement.

The Islamic State's hold on South Asia is far weaker than its vision. Nonetheless, its entry in the region has enhanced Salafist jihadist ideology and made the arena more complex and violent than before. As the international community has learned in the last couple of decades, such developments may well lead to further radicalization, even in countries where the Islamic State lacks significant power. The international effort to stop the Islamic State in its principal loci of power, Iraq and Syria, must therefore be swifter and more decisive than it has been so that it may stop it before it takes permanent root in the seething jihadist arenas of South Asia.

Notes

1   In July 2015, the Afghani government issued a statement on the death of Mullah Omar, which seems to have already occurred in 2013. Sources in the Afghani Taliban confirmed the statement, and Akhtar Mansour, Omar's deputy, was named the organization's new leader.

2   Sharifi Najib, "ISIS Makes Inroads in Afghanistan, Pakistan," *Foreign Policy*, October 1, 2014, http://foreignpolicy.com/2014/10/01/isis-makes-inroads-in-afghanistan-pakistan/.

3   Bill Roggio, "Pakistani Taliban Confirms Death of Khorasan Province Spokesman," *Long War Journal*, July 14, 2015, http://www.longwarjournal.org/archives/2015/07/pakistani-taliban-confirms-death-of-khorasan-province-spokesman-calls-for-afghan-taliban-and-islamic-state-to-end-their-dispute.php.

4   Meirav Mishali-Ram, "When Ethnicity and Religion Meet: Kinship Ties and Cross-Border Dynamics in the Afghan-Pakistani Conflict Zone," *Nationalism and Ethnic Politics* 17 (2011): 1-19.

5   "Taliban Leader: Allegiance to ISIS 'Haram,'" *Rudaw Middle East*, April 13, 2015, http://rudaw.net/english/middleeast/130420151.

6   Talha Ibrahim, "Islamic State, Afghanistan and Pakistan!!" Centre for Strategic Research and Analysis – CESRAN, February 25, 2015, http://cesran.org/islamic-state-afghanistan-and-pakistan.html.

7   Vanda Felbab-Brown, "Blood and Hope in Afghanistan: A June 2015 Update," Brookings, May 26, 2015, http://www.brookings.edu/research/papers/2015/05/26-isis-taliban-afghanistan-felbabbrown.

8   Margherita Stancati, "Iran Backs Taliban with Cash and Arms," *Wall Street Journal*, June 11, 2015, http://www.wsj.com/articles/iran-backs-taliban-with-cash-and-arms-1434065528.

9   "Jihadi Recruitment and Return: Asian Threat and Response," Middle East Institute, January 16, 2015, http://www.mei.edu/content/map/jihadi-recruitment-and-return-asian-threat-and-response.

10   Christine C. Fair, "Is Pakistan in ISIS' Crosshairs?" *Boston Review*, October 16, 2014, http://bostonreview.net/world/c-christine-fair-isis-pakistan-militant-foreign-policy.

11   Sara A. Carter, "Islamic State Recruitment Document Seeks to Provoke 'End of the World,'" American Media Institute, July 28, 2015, http://www.usatoday.com/story/news/world/2015/07/28/ami-isil-document-pakistan-threatens-india/30674099.

Part VI

The World Powers

The United States vs. the Islamic State

Oded Eran and Afik Barak

Paradoxically, the United States finds itself in the conflict against the Islamic State partly because of the 2003 American invasion of Iraq, which destroyed the country's military and state infrastructure and enabled the subsequent territorial consolidation of the Islamic State in the resulting vacuum. The war in Iraq and its consequences, combined with the US failure in Afghanistan, highlight the dilemma posed by the new conflict with the Islamic State, namely, should the US continue to maintain a presence in the Middle East, and if so, for what purpose and at what level. On the one hand, the United States has experienced a series of failures in its attempt to design regimes in the region, shape policy, and defeat opponents with military force. On the other hand, it has experienced the limitations that arise from avoiding military force – including ground combat – and from relying on international and regional organizations to achieve policy goals. The dilemma has become all the clearer ever since Russia assumed the freedom in Syria that the US hitherto claimed for itself, and began using force primarily in order to support its ally, Assad, the formal ruler of Syria, rather than fight the Islamic State. This situation, in which Russia, the US, the military forces of neighboring countries such as Jordan and Turkey, and Hezbollah forces from Lebanon have been conducting ground operations in Syria for quite some time, is analogous to that of Spain in the 1930s, when it served as a midpoint on the road to a larger conflagration. From the US perspective, these factors complicate any efforts to devise a policy on Syria that will yield positive results.

President Obama gave the definitive framework for the US political and military operation against the Islamic State in an address to the nation on December 6, 2015. Key messages included: "Our military will continue to hunt down terrorist plotters in any country where it is necessary"; "in Iraq and Syria, airstrikes are taking out ISIL leaders, heavy weapons, oil tankers, infrastructure"; "we will continue to provide training in equipment to tens of thousands of Iraqi and Syrian forces fighting ISIL on the ground so that we take away their safe havens"; "in both countries, we're deploying Special Operations Forces who can accelerate that offensive"; and "we're working with friends and allies to stop ISIL's operations – to disrupt plots, cut off their financing, and prevent them from recruiting more fighters....We're working with Turkey to seal its border with Syria."[1]

At this stage, dealing with the internal problems created by the Islamic State is relatively simple for the United States; coping with the consequences of the Islamic State's success in the Middle East, however, is more problematic. The wars in Afghanistan and Iraq have made the US decidedly reluctant to intervene in situations leading to ambiguous political achievements, and even if the Islamic State were totally defeated, it is not clear whether any political entity – Syrian or Iraqi – acceptable to the US administration would be able to take control of the evacuated territory. The profound objection to sending ground forces into combat is a result of past failures, or as the President said, "We should not be drawn once more into a long and costly ground war in Iraq and Syria…and it won't require us sending a new generation of Americans overseas to fight and die for another decade on foreign soil."[2] Aerial operations, however effective, are of limited value without troops on the ground. The Islamic State's activity in built up areas reduces US willingness to engage in aerial attacks, as these are liable to increase the number of civilian casualties. Furthermore, aerial warfare does not impede the Islamic State from expanding its influence gradually in other countries of the Middle East, such as Jordan.

Fighting against the Islamic State

In order to fight the Islamic State without any significant ground operations, the United States has created two campaign frameworks. The first is local, comprising armed residents of Iraq and Syria. The second is international, which includes over sixty countries and various organizations that have joined a military coalition designed to defeat the forces of the Islamic State.

In the local framework, the United States has included various allies whom it can support with training, exercises, and a supply of military equipment. Initially, it chose the Free Syrian Army – a large opposition group founded by Syrian army deserters during the Arab Spring uprising – to represent Syria. This group was included in the United States' Syria Train and Equip Program, which was widely criticized because though designed to train 3,500 local Syrian combatants, by late 2015, a few months after the program was established, only 54 of them had completed the course. Kurdish organizations in Syria have likewise received training through the program.[3]

Participants in the Syria Train and Equip Program were assigned three objectives: to protect the Syrian people against attacks by the Islamic State and guard the territory controlled by the Syrian opposition; to defend the training forces of the United States army, its allies, and the Syrian people against terrorist threats in Syria; and to promote conditions for a negotiated settlement that would end the conflict in Syria.[4] By October 2015, once it became clear that the program had failed to achieve its goals, it was terminated. The Obama administration decided that all the bases used to train opposition organizations in Syria would be closed and replaced by one small base in Turkey, which would train only commanders of opposition organizations. At the time this article was written, the details of the new American policy had not yet been made clear.[5]

Events in Iraq have developed differently, but the situation framework is similar to that in Syria. The groups supported by the United States include the security forces of the Iraqi government, which unlike the Syrian regime, is Washington's ally. At the same time, US support also reaches groups similar to those that are cooperating with it in Syria: the Kurdish Peshmerga militia and clusters of volunteers from among Sunni tribes who support the Iraqi security forces in their war against the Islamic State. The program for the Iraqi forces includes a supply of American weapons and training on how to use them, and is conducted by a team of 3,100 American soldiers who are scheduled to prepare 23 Iraqi battalions for duty.[6]

Along with establishing the local combat framework, President Obama initiated the Coalition to Degrade and Defeat ISIL, which he announced on September 10, 2014 while announcing American military involvement in the war against the Islamic State. To date, over 60 countries and various organizations have joined this coalition, including Canada, Australia, the Arab League, Germany, and other European Union states. Some countries – including the United States, Canada, Australia, Germany, Saudi Arabia, Turkey, France, Jordan – are actively taking part in air attacks against the Islamic State; others are contributing to the war effort by training local forces, supplying equipment and ammunition, and providing economic aid. The five goals of the coalition are to provide military support for local coalition partners; to strike at the flow of foreign combatants arriving in Iraq and Syria; to halt the Islamic State's sources of financing; to deal with the humanitarian crises in the region; and to expose the true nature of the Islamic State and damage its propaganda capabilities.[7] Differences among the coalition members exist based on their respective approaches to the political and operational levels of the two arenas – Syria and Iraq. Turkey, for example, takes a different approach toward the Kurds in northern Iraq, and accepts their de facto autonomy there, while using nearly all available means to prevent the emergence of a similar identity among the Kurds of northern Syria. By contrast, France is operating in Iraq but avoiding military intervention in Syria.

A list of prior conditions posed by the US for groups seeking to join the Train and Equip Program in Syria, now defunct, has recently been revealed. One of these conditions was that the rebels were to use military force solely against Islamic State targets, and refrain from attacking the forces of Assad or his allies.[8] The list reflects the dilemmas faced by President Obama in deciding which enemies to target among the many forces fighting in Iraq and Syria, since it is clear that any attack on one leads to the immediate strengthening of another. A similar problem arose with the addition of the latest member of the coalition, Turkey.[9] The United States has paid a price for Turkey's membership and aid to the coalition forces, which have included the use of Turkish air force bases as departure points for the coalition's aerial attacks against the Islamic State. The Turks have taken advantage of this agreement to attack Kurdish forces that have been fighting its regime for years, but who at the same time have been loyal allies of the US in its war against the Islamic State.[10]

In 2015, ongoing fighting against the Islamic State in Syria generated another problem: friction between the United States and Russia. In an effort to retain its two related footholds in Syria – the Assad regime and a military base on the Mediterranean coast – Russia stationed additional units on Syrian soil and, as of the writing of this article, used airborne and ballistic missiles. The United States will have to deal with this political signal and its operative consequences. Having grown accustomed to the Russian military presence in Syria over the years, the US will presumably attempt to detect the potential for antagonism and reinforce the informal pattern that has hitherto prevailed so that its activity in Syria will not jeopardize Russian interests. Possible friction generated by Israeli and Russian aerial activity in Syria is ostensibly not of direct concern to the US, but the administration cannot afford to ignore the consequences of such. At this stage, Israeli-Russian coordination has helped reduce the risk.

Another question on the agenda with no clear cut solution is the effect of the nuclear agreement between Iran and the major powers, and relations between Tehran and Washington. In the foreseeable future, the United States will most likely seek to limit the visibility of any possible cooperation between the two countries on both fronts – Syria and Iraq. The 2016 US presidential campaign requires that there be extra caution regarding attempts to achieve understandings and arrangements.

The Islamic State Threat in the Internal American Theater

The Islamic State has long extended beyond the borders of Syria and Iraq. Its effective use of mass media, especially social networks, has helped it spread its message and pose a genuine threat to its enemies, even those distant from Syria and Iraq. This has led to two phenomena that may well threaten the internal security of the United States.

The first pertains to the foreign volunteers who are joining the ranks of the Islamic State. These constitute a threat as they may return to their countries of origin after acquiring experience in battle and undergoing Salafi jihad indoctrination. At this stage, however, the threat is perceived as extremely marginal, as the number of American foreign fighters who have thus far tried to join the Islamic State stands at approximately 200 – an extremely low figure compared to the number of volunteers from other Western countries. Furthermore, only a small number of them have actually succeeded in enlisting in Islamic State ranks. The return of the few who did manage to join the conflict is also expected to be difficult – even impossible – given the intense scrutiny of US intelligence services.[11]

The second threat consists of attacks carried out by individual terrorists, in most cases unaffiliated with any established organizational structure – "lone wolf terrorism." Such individuals have not managed to join the Islamic State itself, and are thus choosing an alternative course of action, namely, local attacks in their country of origin. FBI head of counterterrorism Michael Steinbach discussed the possibility of a terrorist attack inside the United States by a "lone wolf" influenced by Islamic State doctrine. He noted that the threat is significant and concrete, as tens of thousands of American citizens have been exposed to Islamic State propaganda and are thus liable to engage in such actions. Indeed, Islamic State spokesmen have declared that 71 separate terrorist cells exist in 15 US states – a figure that is a source of concern to US security services.[12]

A number of facts support the suspicion that the internal terrorist threat is greater than that of returning foreign combatants. Until now, at least three terrorist attacks have been conducted within the borders of the United States by perpetrators who identified with or were directly guided by the Islamic State. One took place in Tennessee in July 2015, where a naturalized American Muslim citizen shot and killed five US marines.[13] Another occurred in Texas in May 2015, when two Muslims fired shots at a building where a contest on caricatures of the Prophet Muhammad was underway. The two gunmen were killed, and one person was moderately wounded.[14] The third occurred in San Bernardino on Decmber 2, 2015, when a married couple killed 14 people in a mass shooting attack at a holiday party at the Inland Regional Center. Further evidence of the Islamic State's attempts to penetrate the United States emerged the following month, when the FBI arrested some ten people suspected of belonging to the Islamic State and planning to carry out a terrorist attack against various targets in the United States on July 4, 2015.[15] Both the US administration and FBI sources have repeatedly declared that the supreme objective in dealing with the spread of the Islamic State inside the United States is countering its influence among its potential target population.

Although the Islamic State does not constitute a threat to US sovereignty within its own borders, the US does play an essential role in affecting the Islamic State's success and survival in the war in Iraq and Syria. According to statements made by the State Department in August 2015, the total number of Islamic State targets hit during aerial attacks by the US-led coalition was 10,684.[16] For the sake of comparison, the number of attacks carried out by NATO forces against various targets in Libya in 2011 was estimated at 1,500.[17] Nonetheless, senior American officials have reportedly admitted that the Islamic State has managed to replenish its ranks, so that its current number of combatants is now equal to what it was at the beginning of the campaign despite the fact that over 10,000 of its fighters have been killed in these bombings.[18]

Conclusion

United States success against the Islamic State has thus far been limited. Although a significant number – approximately 10,000 – of Islamic State fighters have been killed, and some of the territory it has conquered has been seized by the various forces fighting against it, the Islamic State continues to recruit volunteers and control resources and a great deal of money. Turkey's participation in the attacks against the Islamic State, and its provision of an airport on its territory for use by American planes has improved the international coalition's military capability and eased the situation of the land forces fighting the Islamic State, but to date no substantial change has taken place in the balance of power between the sides. In the end, an increase in military aid to local forces and an acceleration of the process of training ground troops cannot compensate for the inherent weaknesses of the ethnic-religious-demographic divisions in either Iraq or Syria. Even if America sends in ground troops, it cannot insure a military victory over the Islamic State that will be followed by an acceptable political compromise among the various local forces, their willingness to cooperate within a single state framework, and the end of involvement by other countries in the region, such as Turkey, Saudi Arabia, and Iran, all of which are meddling in Iraq and Syria.

In the absence of a concrete threat on its soil, and due to the military constraints it has imposed on itself, the United States will have to choose from among three alternatives: (1) dispatching a significant force of American ground troops into combat; (2) stationing US soldiers along the front in order to bolster the effectiveness of its air strikes and the performance of local fighting forces; and (3) increasing its aid to local forces, even if these are not cooperating with each other and the chances of having them cooperate politically in the long term are limited. One possible blueprint lies in strengthening the fighting forces of Sunnis, Shiites, and Kurds, though this is tantamount to ignoring other considerations, i.e., sacrificing them at the altar in hope of defeating the Islamic State.

An assessment of American action thus far indicates that no dramatic change in its policy is expected from the Obama administration. The 2016 budget for equipment and training submitted to Congress is modest – less than $1.5 billion; as far as is known, no change in the nature of military involvement against the Islamic State is under consideration. On the other hand, a number of Republican candidates in the presidential campaign have announced that if elected, they would inject enough force into the campaign to achieve military victory. The current Russian military buildup in Syria, and the possibility that Russia will succeed not only in maintaining the Assad regime, but also in repelling the Islamic State, if only partially, and thus enhance its own status in the Middle East, may highlight the cogency of the Republican argument that President Obama's hesitant policy in the entire Syrian theater has damaged the image of the United States as a deterrent power.

The balance of local and regional forces operating against the Islamic State has created a situation in which there is no way out of the labyrinth and – from the administration's perspective – no ideal solution. Each of the parties involved accepts the existing situation and is unwilling to fathom any drastic change and its possible consequences. Will a change of administration and ideology in Washington break through this magic circle? Time – and the American voter – will tell.

Notes

1   "President Obama Addresses the Nation on Keeping the American People Safe," The White House, December 6, 2015, https://www.whitehouse.gov/blog/2015/12/05/president-obama-addresses-nation-keeping-american-people-safe.

2   Ibid.

3   Nick Paton Walsh, "Syrian Rebels: This Is What Almost $1M of U.S. Training Looks Like," *CNN News,* August 18, 2015, http://edition.cnn.com/2015/08/18/middleeast/new-syria-force-fighter-abu-iskander/index.html.

4   Christopher M. Blanchard and Amy Belasco, "Train and Equip Program for Syria: Authorities, Funding, and Issues for Congress," Congressional Research Service, June 9, 2015, https://www.fas.org/sgp/crs/natsec/R43727.pdf.

5   Helene Cooper and Eric Schmitt, "Obama Administration Ends Pentagon Program to Train Syrian Rebels," *New York Times,* October 9, 2015, http://www.nytimes.com/2015/10/10/world/middleeast/pentagon-program-islamic-state-syria.html?emc=edit_na_20151009&nlid=57604295&ref=cta.

6   Office of the Secretary of Defense, "FY 2016 Overseas Contingency Operations (OCO) Iraq Train and Equip Fund (ITEF)," March 2015, http://comptroller.defense.gov/Portals/45/Documents/defbudget/fy2016/FY16_ITEF_J_Book.pdf.

7   U.S. Department of State, "The Global Coalition to Counter ISIL," http://www.state.gov/s/seci/.

8   "The Hidden Side of the US Train and Equip Program for Syria's Opposition," *Middle East Briefing,* June 11, 2015, http://mebriefing.com/?p=1746.

9   Gordon Lubold and Dion Nissenbaum, "Turkey to Join Coalition's Airstrikes Against ISIS," *Wall Street Journal*, August 25, 2015, http://www.wsj.com/articles/turkey-to-join-coalitions-airstrikes-against-isis-1440535062.

10 Dion Nissenbaum and Ayla Albayrak, "U.S. Concerns Grow about Turkish Bombardment of Kurdish Separatists," *Wall Street Journal*, August 12, 2015, http://www.wsj.com/articles/u-s-concerns-grow-over-turkish-bombardment-of-kurdish-separatists-1439422676.

11 James B. Comey, "Statement Before the Senate Select Committee on Intelligence Washington, D.C.," FBI website, July 8, 2015, https://www.fbi.gov/news/testimony/counterterrorism-counterintelligence-and-the-challenges-of-going-dark.

12 Catherine Herridge, "Purported ISIS Warning Claims Terror Cells in Place in 15 States," *Fox News*, May 6, 2015, http://www.foxnews.com/us/2015/05/06/purported-isis-warning-claims-terror-cells-in-place-in-15-states/.

13 "Terror in Tennessee," Soufan Group, July 17, 2015, http://soufangroup.com/tsg-intelbrief-terror-in-tennessee/.

14 Holly Yan, "ISIS Claims Responsibility for Texas Shooting, But Offers no Proof," *CNN News*, May 6, 2015, http://edition.cnn.com/2015/05/05/us/garland-texas-prophet-mohammed-contest-shooting/index.html.

15 Kevin Johnson, "Comey: Federal Authorities Disrupted Islamic State-Linked July 4 Plots," *USA Today*, July 9, 2015, http://www.usatoday.com/story/news/nation/2015/07/09/james-comey-july-fourth-terror-islamic-state/29916253/?csp=breakingnews.

16 U.S. Department of Defense, "Operation Inherent Resolve – Air Strikes in Iraq and Syria," June 22, 2015, http://www.defense.gov/home/features/2014/0814_iraq/.

17 "NATO Operations in Libya: Data Journalism Breaks Down which Country Does What," *The Guardian*, May 22, 2015, http://www.theguardian.com/news/datablog/2011/may/22/nato-libya-data-journalism-operations-country; for a complete table of NATO fighting in Libya, see https://docs.google.com/spreadsheets/d/11-MRQdTRy8iUeBsbptkRDF92fL6Zd7oFbSGxUQUSuJ0/edit?hl=en_US#gid=0.

18 Rob Crilly, "US Officials Admit ISIL Just as Strong as when Air Campaign Began," *The Telegraph*, July 31, 2015, http://www.telegraph.co.uk/news/worldnews/islamic-state/11776346/US-officials-admit-Isil-just-as-strong-as-when-air-campaign-began.html.

Russia and the Islamic State Challenge

Zvi Magen, Sarah Fainberg, and Ilan Shklarsky

For nearly two decades, Russia has confronted Salafi Islam on a number of fronts: within its sovereign territory, in the Middle East, and in the international arena. The threat, which continues to develop in its territory and in its sphere of interests in the countries of the former Soviet Union, includes ongoing terrorism, guerilla warfare, and conventional war. As part of its activity in the Middle East, Russia has had to cope with this threat and prevent its penetration into Russian territory, while at the same time exploiting it as a lever for promoting its goals in the region.

Russia has shaped its position toward the Islamic State according to these considerations. Moscow initially regarded the Islamic State as merely one of many jihad organizations. Since the declaration of the caliphate in June 2014, however, which transformed ISIS into a different type of challenge, Russia's position has shifted and Russia's leadership has improvised moves that affect general Russian policy in the Middle East.

Currently Russia is home to some 16 million Muslim citizens, in addition to several million Muslim foreign workers from Central Asia and the Caucasus.[1] The Muslims are concentrated in two main areas: the northern Caucasus and the Volga and Ural districts (Bashkortostan and Tatarstan). Since the breakup of the Soviet Union more than twenty years ago, Moscow has conducted ongoing warfare against Muslim groups, mainly in the northern Caucasus, including two wars in Chechnya (in 1994-1996 and 1999-2003). Since roughly 2010, the Russian Muslim population in the Caucasus and the Volga-Ural has been under the influence of foreign Salafi Islam.[2] In addition to the young Muslims in these regions, Salafi influence is also strong among young Russians converts to Islam, as well as among Central Asian migrant workers in Russia.

Over the past two decades, Russia failed to generate a unified Muslim clergy capable of ruling Russia's Islam. Since Ramzan Kadyrov rose to become the head of the Chechen Republic in 2007, however, some improvement has been noticeable in relations between the Muslim population and the Russian establishment. This is particularly prominent in the general siding of the Chechens and other Muslims from the northern Caucasian districts with the central Russian administration – a development led by Kadyrov himself. It appears that many branches of Russia's Muslim clergy also support this trend. Nevertheless, opposition to Russian rule continues and is even growing in other parts of the Muslim population, including among Chechens, who are attracted to Salafi ideas and are thronging to the rival camps. A number of Muslim brigades are fighting against the Russian separatists in Ukraine, while others are active in various combat frameworks, most noticeably in the Caucasus Emirate. This regional Muslim association has supported al-Qaeda since it was founded in 2007, and is the principal source of belligerency, with an emphasis on terrorism directed against the Russian regime in both the Caucasus and in areas of Russia. Approximately 900 terror attacks throughout Russia have been attributed to it since it began operating.[3]

In June 2015, the Islamic State announced that the Caucasus Emirate had sworn allegiance to it and was accepted as a subordinate partner. This determined the status of the Caucasus Emirate, but the struggle in the Caucasus between the various terrorist groups continues, as it does between various global jihad groups all over the world, a struggle that has bolstered the position of the Islamic State throughout Russia. The organization directs propaganda efforts (including publications in Russian) aimed at expanding its influence among young people in the country. Concomitantly, the Islamic State pursues its efforts to form alliances with other Salafi jihad terrorist groups. Indeed, authorities in Russia and Central Asian countries that were part of the Soviet Union are increasingly alarmed at the spread of this phenomenon to the Central Asian countries – a process that began in 2014 – and from there to all over Russia. Individuals in Russia itself have enlisted as combatants in the Islamic State: Russian security services report that over 3,000 Russian citizens are engaged in the combat zones of the Middle East (this number is constantly growing) in addition to the numerous fighters coming from the post-Soviet space.[4] As time passes, anxiety increases about their expected return to Russia and the role they will play in establishing terrorist and guerilla infrastructures in their local areas.

At this juncture, Russia faces a potential crisis. Russian authorities are aware that a major declaration of war against Salafi Islam is liable to increase instability and lead to another conflict in the northern Caucasus, this time against a better trained and tougher foe than in the past, in view of the heightened experience of the combatants returning from the battlefields of the Middle East. Furthermore, another crisis in the northern Caucasus could bring about a conflict between the Russian security forces and Kadyrov and his associates, in which case the situation is liable to spiral entirely out of control.

Despite these obstacles and in view of the severe and immediate threat posed by the Islamic State to Russia in its own territory, Russia's attitude toward this problem underwent a fundamental change in the summer of 2015. Russia had regarded the Islamic State as a negligible and passing phenomenon – merely one of the many opposition organizations in Syria fighting against Assad, Russia's protégé. For this reason, despite the announcement of the caliphate and the subsequent threat to Assad posed by the Islamic State, the Russians did not regard a declaration of war against it as justified, and certainly not the formation of a broad based Western-led international coalition. For Russia, the main challenge in the Middle East was the West itself, and various streams in Russia still adhere to this approach. However, concern about the Islamic State has risen due to the Islamic State's proximity to Russia and the declarations by its leaders of their intention to conquer Russia in the future. It was further catalyzed by gradual Islamic State penetration into the northern Caucasus. All these factors have created a tangible threat to Russia's security, both external and internal, and the Russian leadership regards them as requesting a policy change.

While Russia was busy with the Ukrainian crisis, the developing crisis involving the Islamic State presented it with new challenges but possibly new opportunities as well. As part of the change in Russian policy on the Islamic State, Russia stridently declared that the Islamic State was its main enemy and the main threat to the Middle East in general. In this framework, Moscow decided to intervene militarily in Syria for the purpose of combating Salafi jihadi Islam, and to aid the Assad regime. Russian intervention in Syria is in effect a continuation of its political activism in the Middle East, which has been fairly successful in rehabilitating Russia's status vis-à-vis the countries in the region. The current intervention involves Russia's best forces, including MIG-31 and Sukhoi Su-34 warplanes (which were added to the Russian air force only in the past two years), advanced electronic warfare devices, and Kalibr cruise missiles (the Russian answer to the Tomahawk missiles that the US planned to launch) launched from its flagship, the Dagestan frigate, the newest missile boat in the Russian fleet. The use of these and other means is designed to pose a substantial challenge to the West and the Islamic State, and "to impress the audience at home," who like to feel that they are once again citizens of a major power.

In practice, the Russian offensive has consisted primarily (as of this writing) of air attacks against targets belonging to the various types of rebels, including a relatively small proportion against Islamic State targets. Although it is expected that these attacks will be expanded, at the current stage it appears that Russia has an interest in helping Assad through attacks against the more "moderate" rebels threatening the Latakia district. This policy is designed primarily to help the Syrian regime gain control of areas held by the rebels in order to facilitate the consolidation of future areas of control for the regime in the Syrian coastal area. At a more advanced stage, this measure is also designed to help promote an internal Syrian dialogue between the regime and the rebels and allow negotiations toward an agreement acceptable to Russia.

Russia's traditional policy in the Middle East is to be an active regional player, and it is taking action both to reclaim its status of an influential power and enhance its international standing. Following the upheavals of the Arab Spring, Assad remains Russia's main ally in the region, and Syria possesses the only logistics infrastructure in the Middle East available to Russia. Throughout the civil war in Syria, Russia has supported Assad, whose survival is critical from its perspective, and has reaped benefits for itself from the resulting situation.

Yet along with Moscow's regional interests, it appears that Russia's policy constitutes a response to other difficult challenges that it faces in the international arena. It appears that Russia is taking advantage of the situation in the region to deflect international attention away from the Ukrainian theater to the Middle East, and to create an additional area of friction with the West in order to divert attention from the Ukrainian question. Furthermore, Russia is directing its efforts to facilitate a possible dialogue with the West by promoting the idea of give and take on the Syrian question (Russian willingness to sacrifice Assad, for example) versus the Ukrainian question (easing of the economic sanctions imposed on Russia by the Western countries, which are gradually posing a threat to the stability of the Russian regime). In this give-and-take approach, Russia has both persisted in its support for Assad and refrained from joining the coalition fighting against the Islamic State. It is possible that from the beginning, this was intended as an additional bargaining chip, probably in order to increase pressure on the West for the sake of promoting the equation that includes concessions to Russia on the Ukrainian question.

It has been argued that Russia intends to change its policy of support for Assad, but in practice, it appears that Russia is opting for a more sophisticated compromise formula. The preferred procedure for Russia is likely to be based on the struggle against the Islamic State as its main axis in order to combine a number of interests by linking the Syrian crisis with the Ukrainian crisis, and achieving beneficial solutions for Russia in both, together with action against the Islamic State in order to remove the threat aimed at Russia.[5]

It therefore seems that all the actors in the region, including the other powers involved in the Middle East, are interested in making the Islamic State a lever for achieving their regional objectives. These include Iran, which is involved in Syria, together with Russia, which is supporting Assad and is probably also interested in using this card in the regional arrangements. The same is true of the West, which regards it as an opportunity, as part of the settlement with Iran, to saddle Iran with this task. The possibility that this matter has been coordinated among the "international six," i.e., between Russia and the West, also cannot be ruled out. Russian-Western cooperation on the Islamic State, and probably also on Syria in general, is an increasingly viable option in the emerging circumstances. Furthermore, it is possible that under the new circumstances, the situation gives Russia an opportunity for rapprochement and the beginning of general cooperation with the West. In addition to Russia's stepped-up rhetoric on the Islamic State, concrete contacts between senior Russian and American officials can be discerned concerning all regional affairs as a combined and coordinated package, including the Iranian question, the Syrian question, and the Islamic State. Presumably Russia is continuing its efforts to include the Ukrainian question, especially the easing of Western economic sanctions against Russia. In the wake of these processes, Russian willingness to withdraw its support for the Assad regime therefore cannot be ruled out.

In conclusion, Russia indeed faces a combined challenge at home and abroad from the Islamic State, which can be expected to escalate. The Russian decision to embark on a military campaign against the Islamic state serves its desire to contain the threat on its territory, while simultaneously finding a suitable solution compatible with its interests in Syria.

It is premature to attempt an analysis of the results and consequences of the Russian involvement in Syria with respect to its fighting against the Islamic State. Russian attempts at creating a link between the above aspects are evident, including Russian willingness to cooperate with the other players in the region and in the West to halt the buildup and spread of the Islamic State – both in the Middle East and in the direction of Russian territory. It is difficult, however, to assess Russia's ability, with the help of its allies in the region, to eliminate the Islamic State. It is clear that this will not be a short and easy struggle, and will very likely spread to Russia itself, bringing with it a host of related challenges.

Notes

1   The figure is an estimate. According to official Russian sources, approximately 20 million Muslims live in Russia, 80 percent of whom are Russian citizens and the rest immigrants from Central Asia and Azerbaijan. Nevertheless, the exact number of Muslims in Russia is probably higher than the official figure, because the Russian immigration authority does not regularly monitor Muslim foreign workers from Central Asia and the northern Caucasus. The true number of Russian Muslims is almost certainly higher: about 20 million Muslim citizens and several million foreign workers of Muslim extraction in Russia.

2   Alexey Malashenko, "Islamic Challenges to Russia, From the Caucasus to the Volga and the Urals," American Enterprise Institute, May 13, 2015, http://carnegie. ru/2015/05/13/islamic-challenges-to-russia-from-caucasus-to-volga-and-urals/i9l4.

3   "Caucasus Emirate," Global Security.org, http://www.globalsecurity.org/military/ world/para/ik.htm.

4   "Demand Action Based on National Interests, Not Personal Desires," *Kommersant*, June 30, 2015, http://www.kommersant.ru/doc/2778226.

5   Even though some believe that Russia is really playing a double game toward the Islamic State, and argue that the Russian secret service has turned a blind eye to the movement of jihad followers from the northern Caucasus to Syria; see Michael Weiss, "Russia is Sending Jihadis to Join ISIS," *The Daily Beast*, August 23, 2015, http://www.thedailybeast.com/articles/2015/08/23/russia-s-playing-a-double-game-with-islamic-terror0.html.

The European Union and the Rise of the Islamic State

Shimon Stein

Since the outbreak of the Arab Spring, the European Union has found it difficult to find a solution for the political chaos and the accompanying violence that has overtaken much of the region south of its border – the Middle East and North Africa. The policy with which the EU has attempted to stabilize the region socio-politically and economically for nearly two decades has failed. In the course of 2016, the EU is supposed to formulate yet another policy to resolve problems within the region, which is currently in the throes of "violent transformation."

The emergence of the Islamic State[1] as an actor with aspirations vis-à-vis the world as a whole and the Middle East in particular has created a new geopolitical reality that requires the European Union to take more urgent action. This article frames the threat posed by the Islamic State to the EU and its member states, and surveys the European efforts to formulate a solution. It discusses the issues as they relate to both the Middle East and Europe, and also examines the humanitarian problem that has resulted from the crisis.

The collapse of Syria, Iraq, Libya, and Yemen has accelerated the disintegration of the Middle East established by the Sykes-Picot agreement, which was in effect for close to a century. The rise of the Islamic State, a consequence of events in Syria and Iraq, threatens to nullify the principle of territorial integrity and national borders in the region, a principle that has served as the bedrock of international order. Were the Islamic State comparable to other terrorist organizations operating in the Middle East, it could be tackled with the standard means used to deal with such struggles: a direct military campaign against it. However, by declaring itself a caliphate and challenging the old order, the Islamic State has aggravated the situation and impeded efforts to combat it. The Islamic State phenomenon also complicates all attempts – and the European Union is a party to these efforts – to resolve internal conflicts in Syria and Iraq and restore the previous situation while preventing the collapse of the old state order. The establishment of branches of the Islamic State in an ever-growing number of Arab countries that are highly important to European interests, such as Egypt, Lebanon, and Jordan, threatens to heighten the instability in Iraq and Syria, as well as the region as a whole.

Although the threat posed by the Islamic State is central to the Middle East, it is not limited to its borders. A string of attacks carried out by supporters of the Islamic State in several European capitals (Brussels, Paris, and Copenhagen) in 2014 and 2015 have made the destructive potential of this group entirely clear to EU member states and illustrated the danger of ignoring or attempting to downplay its severity.

The extreme violence surrounding the sectarian struggle in Iraq and the civil war in Syria, both caused in part by the Islamic State's seizure of substantial parts of territory in the two countries, has led to the most serious global humanitarian crisis since World War II. Millions of Syrians have abandoned their homes and migrated elsewhere in Syria or beyond to neighboring states (Turkey, Lebanon, Jordan, Iraq, and Egypt). Many others have attempted to make their way, via difficult routes, to the safer shores of Europe. Thus far, the European Union has extended approximately €3.7 billion in humanitarian aid to the refugees, and intends to allocate an additional €1 billion in 2015-2016. The scope of this assistance has placed the EU at the top of the list of states providing aid to the refugees. In addition to the aid flowing from the EU as a whole, member states are providing bilateral aid to huge numbers of refugees.

The number of refugees who have moved and will continue to move to the countries neighboring Syria and Iraq is much higher than the number of those who have reached and are still expected to reach Europe. Nonetheless, for a variety of reasons the 28 members of the European Union have found it difficult to contend with the influx. In 2015, nearly one million asylum seekers arrived in Germany.[2] Other European countries serving as magnets for refugees include Sweden, Italy, France, and Hungary. This unprecedented flow of refugees caught Europe by surprise – and unprepared. The more than 850 refugees who drowned off the coast of Libya in April 2015[3] forced the

Europeans and their decision makers to deal (not for the first time) with the urgent need for a multi-systemic solution to the growing problem.

In addition to its humanitarian dimension, the problem poses an internal threat caused by the appeal of the Islamic State narrative to young European Muslims who are joining the ranks of the Islamic State in ever-growing numbers. Alienation, unemployment, difficulties with integration, access to social networks that revile the decadent West, and the heroism assured to those who join the Islamic State – against the hopelessness and unclear future that face those who remain in their home countries – create fertile ground for Islamic State recruitment. According to a report by the International Red Cross, approximately 3,850 of the 20,000 foreign fighters in Syria and Iraq in the second half of 2014 hailed from European Union states. The threat becomes even graver given the expectation that these fighters, steeped in anti-Western ideology, will eventually return to Europe, equipped with combat experience and prepared to carry out attacks at any time.[4] Another threat is posed by "lone wolves" – those who have not been on the battlefield but have been exposed to the narrative of the Islamic State through social media and, inspired, are prepared to carry out attacks.

The working assumption of EU states dealing with the threat is that the crisis caused by the Islamic State and the religious and ethnic rivalries in Iraq and Syria is rooted in internal crises within these countries. Consequently, they feel that all efforts must be directed toward stabilizing the situation in the Middle East. The key word in this context is "inclusiveness," that is, the inclusion of all relevant forces in the formulation of a political solution that is based on the desire to preserve the multinational, multi-religious, and multi-ethnic character of Iraqi and Syrian society.

As the Islamic State poses a threat not only to Syria and Iraq but also to the region as a whole and European stability, the quest for a political solution is conducted in tandem with military campaigns against the Islamic State. The European Union has developed a strategy for fighting terrorism and apprehending foreign fighters (the terrorists recruited into the service of the Islamic State) and has formulated two documents that in effect constitute a detailed working plan to resolve the crisis and prevent its spread.[5] According to one document, the EU's ability to achieve its aim hinges on developments on the ground, which include resistance to the Islamic State and the willingness of international and regional actors to take action to oppose it. The document also stresses that a resolution to the crises in Syria or Iraq will not in itself promote political stability or economic prosperity in the region. In an attempt to avoid the errors of the past (e.g., the wars in Iraq and Afghanistan), the EU has again clarified the need for the states in the region to play a greater role in dealing with the crisis and leading the effort to resolve it. As part of the international community, the EU can provide assistance to military, political, and humanitarian efforts. However, the lion's share of the burden and responsibility should fall on the shoulders of the states in question.

While the EU recognizes, however, that military force should be an important (though not exclusive) tool in the eradication of the Islamic State, it has so far been unable to reach a consensus on the issue. Therefore it has permitted each of its member states to proceed as it sees fit. The EU has welcomed the decisions of its various member states to contribute their share to the struggle, but as an organization, it has stressed its non-involvement in either the actual fighting or the coordination of actions by member states that have chosen to engage in the situation. In fact, most EU members have extended their assistance to the campaign against the Islamic State, albeit not on a large scale; some are also helping to train soldiers in the Iraqi army and the Kurdish Peshmerga. A small number of member states (Britain, France, Belgium, Holland, and Denmark) are also playing an active role in the airstrikes staged under US leadership against the Islamic State in Iraq.

The lack of a mandate from the UN Security Council is preventing the EU states from participating in the attack against the Islamic State in Syria. (This has not prevented the British air force from undertaking reconnaissance missions over Syria, however.[6]) Moreover, the scope of the airstrikes in Iraq (as compared to NATO strikes in Yugoslavia or air strikes in Afghanistan) attests to the fact that the effort is currently not a high priority among the countries involved. Furthermore, as of late 2015, no EU state has declared its intention to send its own ground forces ("put boots on the ground") to Iraq or Syria. This stance effectively expresses the policy noted above, namely, that the states in the region should deal with these challenges and not expect the international community to do the work for them. This fundamental position must also be understood within the domestic context of EU member states, in which many are fundamentally opposed to sending troops to the Middle East. Such an approach is likely to change (if at all) only in the event of a mass casualty terrorist attack directly attributable to the Islamic State, or with a significant increase in the threat posed to the political and economic interests of European countries.

Aside from their support of military efforts to defeat the Islamic State, EU member states clearly understand that any effort to contend with the phenomenon must be multidimensional; hence a strategy that brings together the many realms that must be addressed simultaneously: ideology, communications, economics, financial resources, and terrorism. The aim of this integrated strategy is to close all the possible cracks and loopholes that can be exploited by the Islamic State.

On the internal European level, the induction of thousands of EU citizens into the ranks of the Islamic State and the showcase executions broadcast over the media, as well as the terrorist attacks in Europe and elsewhere in which EU citizens have taken part (with the most recent and deadly attack in Tunisia in June 2015) have increased awareness of the threat posed by the Islamic State among European political leaders and their publics and intensified the need for an appropriate response to this threat. The formulation of an all-encompassing strategy that would address the threat on the ground is one way to deal with the phenomenon. Another equally important issue is to introduce measures to deal with the threat of "veterans," some of whom have returned to their countries of origin or are expected to do so, and "lone wolves," who never left Europe but may nonetheless attempt to carry out terrorist attacks on behalf of Islamic State guiding principles. The appeal of the Islamic State narrative, combined with the difficulty of dealing – in the short term – with the roots of the problem in its economic, social, and educational context, will presumably increase the number of new European recruits to the ranks of the Islamic State. The higher the numbers, the greater the threat posed by returning veterans and lone wolves.

Like other internal threats posed by extremists of the political left and right, that of the Islamic State inside Europe raises the dilemma that faces democratic societies in the struggle against terrorism. At its heart lies the desire to achieve a balance between individual freedom and the necessity of imposing limitations on individual liberties so as to minimize the threat of terrorism.

The terrorist acts perpetrated in France and Tunisia in 2015 may have raised awareness of the threat posed by the Islamic State, but most countries in Europe that are home to large Muslim populations – the main source for recruits in the ranks of the Islamic State – have yet to take adequate measures to address the problem. This is particularly true of Germany, Belgium, Austria, Denmark, and Sweden. In contrast, France and Britain, which have already experienced attacks, are now better prepared to deal with the threat. This does not suffice, however. British Prime Minister David Cameron has recently emphasized the need to contend with the Islamic State's radical narrative, which he views as poisoning young minds.[7] In a speech delivered before the British Parliament following the terrorist attack in Tunisia, he compared the challenge presented by Salafi jihadist Islam to the challenge posed by communism during the Cold War.

The "poisoning" of these young people – most of whom were born in North Africa and the Middle East, or are children to immigrants from North Africa and the Middle East – is the consequence of the failure of integration efforts by the respective European states. This failure has led to radicalization, which provides fertile ground for the Islamic State and similar groups. European countries with large concentrations of citizens from Muslim countries urgently need to adopt active economic, social, and educational measures to integrate these young people into local society. Prime Minister Cameron was correct in pointing out that this is a struggle that will last for generations.

Regarding the ever-mounting flow of refugees and asylum seekers, the continent is not prepared to absorb these masses and deal with the phenomenon in the short, let alone the long term. At present, the European Union and its member states are still unable to formulate policy on the issue.[8] The drowning of many refugees in the Mediterranean Sea has forced the EU to adopt a number of measures aimed at preventing, to the extent possible, the recurrence of such incidents. Within this context, unrealistic suggestions have been made, such as the need to address the roots of the problem, that is, the political and economic situations, in the countries of origin.

European helplessness vis-à-vis the refugee problem is reflected in the decision by EU member states, following long discussions, to spread 40,000 asylum seekers among various nations, with the brunt of the burden falling on Germany, Sweden, France, Italy, Greece, and Hungary.[9] Without a doubt, it was the media coverage on the extent of the crisis that compelled the European political leaders to recognize the need for a short term solution. A long term solution that would significantly reduce the number of asylum seekers seems nowhere on the horizon. Side by side with the sympathy for the refugees demonstrated by some sectors of the European public and their willingness to help, lies a policy, advocated by those following the lead of populist parties, that will drastically limit immigration into Europe.

The handling of this issue will certainly not be liberal Europe's finest hour, which, true to form, continues to hope that solutions to the ethical and political dilemmas posed by the refugee problem will gradually emerge.

Conclusion

Since the launching of the Barcelona Process in 1995,[10] the European Union has attempted to deal with the ongoing crises of its southern neighbors, thus far without much success. The collapse of the state system in the Middle East, and especially the crises in Syria and Iraq, which gave birth to threats such as the Islamic State, are forcing the EU to make another attempt, on grounds of self-interest, at a solution. The comprehensive strategy it has formulated is meant to help Syria and Iraq implement a multi-systemic solution for the crises facing the two countries and, at the same time, to enable the countries of Europe to tackle the threat posed by their own citizens who support the Islamic State.

The European Union's ability to help resolve the crisis in Syria and Iraq and consequently reduce the scale of the threat posed by the Islamic State will depend on its determination and perseverance as well as its understanding that a long struggle lies ahead that requires the allocation of extensive resources. All of these efforts have one general goal: to ensure that the reality that Europe is gradually beginning to sense – and that can be summed up in the aphorism "if Europe does not visit the Middle East, the Middle East will visit Europe" – does not turn into a situation that spirals out of control.

Notes

The author would like to express his gratitude to Noa Saltzman for her help in assembling the material for this article.

1   The use of the term "Islamic State" reflects the interest in using unified terminology in this volume. The European Union uses the term ISIS. British Prime Minister David Cameron stated that the term "Islamic State" is an offense to many Muslims, and therefore prefers the ISIS acronym.

2   In addition to Syrians and Iraqis, the numbers of asylum seekers also include those from the Western Balkans, who constitute the largest group of refugees, as well as those from Somalia, Eritrea, Sudan, and Afghanistan.

3   According to UN reports, by late July 2015, the number of refugees who drowned reached approximately 2000.

4   Daniel Byman has claimed that the threat posed by foreign fighters returning to their countries of origin is less serious then generally believed. Among his reasons is the fact that many fighters are killed in battle; that others refrain from returning

to their home countries and continue on to the next conflict; and that yet others sober up and cease to pose a threat. See Daniel L. Byman and Jeremy Shapiro, "Be Afraid. Be a Little Afraid: The Therapy of Terrorism from Western Foreign Fighters in Syria and Iraq," The Brookings Institute, January 2015.

5   See European Council, Council of the European Union, "Council Conclusions on the E.U. Regional Strategy for Syria and Iraq as Well as the ISIL/Da'esh Threat," March 16, 2015; "Response to Foreign Terrorist Fighters and Recent Terrorist Attacks in Europe."

6   For details regarding the involvement of EU members, see Justine Drennan, "Who Has Contributed What in the Coalition against the Islamic State," *Foreign Policy,* November 12, 2014.

7   See David Cameron's "Extremism Speech" in Birmingham in *The Independent,* July 20, 2015. In this programmatic speech, Cameron presented his ambitious five-year plan to address the roots of the problem of radicalism.

8   Although the number of refugees from Syria is constantly increasing, they are only part of a larger number of refugees, most of whom are arriving from the Western Balkans. The tendency in Europe is to send these refugees back to their countries of origin, which are considered to be politically secure.

9   For additional information, see "Which EU Countries had the Most Asylum Seekers," *The Guardian,* May 11, 2015; "Mediterranean Crisis: The Facts So Far," *Migrant Report,* 2015.

10 The Barcelona Process (the "Euro-Mediterranean Partnership") is the European Union's policy on the Mediterranean region. In 1995, this policy led to the signing of the Barcelona Declaration by fifteen EU countries and twelve Mediterranean countries: Morocco, Algeria, Tunisia, Egypt, Israel, Jordan, Lebanon, Syria, Cyprus, Malta, Turkey, and the Palestinian Authority. The aim of the document was to establish a European-Mediterranean partnership based primarily on the creation of a joint area of peace, stability, and prosperity (including the establishment of a free trade zone by 2010), as well as the improvement of mutual understanding between its peoples.

The Islamic State:
The Danger that China Would Rather Not Name

Eyal Propper

The growth and expansion of the Islamic State over the past two years, as well as its power to transcend borders, has been watched by the entire world with much alarm. For its part, China too has extended its activity during this period, and consequently, its economic and political interests in many regions, including the Middle East. Chinese companies and citizens are thus potential targets for extremist terrorist groups – a point made poignantly by the leader of the Islamic State, who referred to "our suffering brethren" in his Ramadan speech of July 2014 and began the list of guilty countries with the Chinese,[1] "who are hurting our (Uyghur) brethren" in the province of Xinjiang.[2]

In November 2015, China strongly condemned the Islamic State, which executed a Chinese hostage in Syria, and the jihadist al-Murabitoun group in Bamako, Mali, which killed 27 people, including three Chinese nationals. At the same time, the global media's comparison of the brutality and evil of the Islamic State with the cruelty of Genghis Khan, who at his peak controlled Central Asia and China, has almost certainly not escaped Chinese attention.[3] It is therefore worth considering whether Chinese attitudes toward the Islamic State have changed over the course of the past two years, and if so, in what way; how growing alarm about the influence of the Islamic State on the stability of China is expressed; and how the regime is preparing to meet this new threat, especially in terms of international cooperation in the struggle against terrorism.

Activity by the Islamic State and its Proxies in China

At a press conference toward the end of the annual meeting of the Chinese Parliament in March 2015, Zhang Chunxian, Communist Party Secretary of the Xinjiang Uyghur Autonomous Region and a member of the Chinese Communist Party Politburo, confirmed – in a statement published in the official Chinese media – that "some Xinjiang residents have crossed the border illegally to join the Islamic State. The group currently has a growing international influence, and Xinjiang is affected by it, too."[4] Zhang did not disclose information on the number of Muslims who had joined the Salafi jihad forces, but Chinese publications indicated that approximately 300 Chinese had joined the circle of foreign combatants in Syria and Iraq.[5]

Turkey serves as a center for recruiting students and young Muslims from China, who are then sent to training camps and operations in Syria and Iraq. In an article that appeared in December 2014 in the *Global Times*, a publication sometimes used to deliver blunt party messages, a Chinese expert on terrorism claimed that Turkey's ambiguous policies made it possible for young Chinese of Uyghur origin to obtain passports, which enabled them to go to Syria and join the Islamic State.[6] A clip published by the organization in Syria in early 2015 showed an 80-year-old Uyghur, a former imam in Xinjiang, who had left the province with his family in order to join the fighters after, in his words, "60 years of Chinese oppression." The clip also depicted 10 year-old children training to "drive the Chinese heretics out of Turkistan."[7]

Responding to a question about reports of Chinese joining the Islamic State, a spokesperson from the Chinese Foreign Ministry replied: "We have noted the recent report about Chinese citizens joining the ISIS. We are verifying and will follow up on this." She proceeded immediately to add that China was in direct danger of terrorism by the East Turkistan Islamic Movement (ETIM).[8] Cheng Guoping, Chinese Vice Minister of Foreign Affairs, recently clarified his country's position at a press conference published only outside China by confirming that there was a concrete connection between the East Turkistan Islamic Movement and the Islamic State.[9]

Terrorist Attacks in China

Over the past two years, both Chinese citizens and foreign visitors have been injured in a number of terrorist attacks inside China, which the government has been quick to ascribe to the East Turkistan Islamic Movement. In contrast to earlier attacks, which had been aimed at government buildings and security forces in Xinjiang, these occurred in various locations in China, including Beijing, and were aimed at civilians.[10]

On October 28, 2013, a car driven by a Muslim from Xinjiang hit pedestrians in Tiananmen Square and caught fire. All three people inside the car and two passersby were killed in the attack, and about 40 were injured. The terrorist attack, which occurred near the government buildings in central Beijing, was a warning sign for Chinese Communist Party leaders. The government accused the East Turkistan Islamic Movement and arrested some of its operatives.[11] On March 1, 2014, a group armed with knives attacked passengers in the railway station of Kunming, the capital of Yunnan Province in southwestern China, killing 29 civilians, and wounding 140. On April 30, 2014, a bomb exploded in the railway station of Urumqi, the capital of Xinjiang Province; one person was killed and 79 injured. A month later, on May 20, 2014, a number of explosive devices were thrown into a market square in Urumqi, killing 39 civilians and wounding 94.[12] This series of attacks induced the party leadership, led by Party General Secretary and President Xi Jinping, to hold a special two-day meeting of the "main working group on the subject of Xinjiang" immediately after the May 2014 attack. Following the meeting, Xi was quoted in the media as saying that China would step up its international cooperation in the struggle against terrorism and build "walls made of copper and steel" and "nets spread from the earth to the sky" in order to capture terrorists.[13]

In accordance with decisions made at the meeting, security forces were reinforced in those parts of Xinjiang where Muslims were a majority, and a tough stance was taken against them. Communications networks used by Muslims were heavily monitored, and the ban on women wearing burkas and veils in public places as well as men growing beards was strictly enforced.[14] Students and Muslim government employees were reportedly forbidden to fast during the month of Ramadan.[15] In addition, China is preparing for the possibility of a terrorist offensive in its major cities, and its security forces conduct terrorist attack emergency drills in key public spaces.[16]

International Cooperation in the Struggle against Terrorism

Has China decided to bolster its cooperation with Western countries against Islamic State elements due to its growing anxiety over the potential spread of terrorist attacks on its territory? The answer to this question lies in China's consistent refusal to join coalitions and alliances, partly due to its traditional policy of non-intervention in the internal affairs of other countries. In this case too, China is portraying its policy as independent and distinct from that of the United States and other Western countries. The Chinese argue that not all Muslim believers should be classified as enemies, and that those committing terrorist attacks should be isolated as criminals, but they do not represent true Islam. According to this argument, the spread of a phenomenon such as the Islamic State in Syria and Iraq results in part from the instability caused by the United States, which has resorted to military force instead of proceeding with sensitivity and relying on cooperation with the Muslim world.[17] As a display of its independent policy, China has not yet joined any international coalition in Iraq and Syria, and has not involved itself in military actions against Salafi groups outside of China.[18]

The detailed statement by the United States and China at the conclusion of their annual high level strategic dialogue in late June 2015 exposes the gaps between the two countries. Despite direct US involvement in the struggle against the Islamic State and President Obama's clear statements on the global effort to combat the phenomenon, the joint sections in the document that discuss the situation in Syria, Iraq, and the war on terrorism do not include any direct mention of the danger of the Islamic State – almost certainly due to Chinese opposition. The section addressing the situation in Syria and Iraq notes that the two countries "reaffirmed their joint commitment to resolve the Syrian issue through political means…and called on the international community to step up humanitarian assistance." The statement on the struggle against terrorism simply asserts; "The United States and China condemn all forms of terrorism and concur on the global threat posed by terrorist organizations."[19]

As a permanent member of the United Nations Security Council, China supported the resolutions taken by consensus against Salafi jihad organizations. These as well as UN Security Council Resolution 2170, passed on August 10, 2014, and Resolution 2199, passed on February 10, 2015, were directed against the Islamic State and its operations. The first of these was in fact passed when China held the presidency of the Security Council. Chinese Ambassador to the UN Liu Jieyi was quoted in the Chinese media as saying: "China actively participated and played a constructive role in the consultations on the draft resolution," which were designed to extend sanctions against "relevant terrorist groups." His remarks as reported do not refer explicitly to the Islamic State.[20] The same is true of the UN Security Council Summit on Terrorism, held during the UN General Assembly in September 2014. Here Chinese Foreign Minister Wang Yi spoke about the dangers of international terrorism and mentioned the East Turkistan Islamic Movement's use of violence within China. Although he spoke about China's intention to allocate 60 million yuan for emergency humanitarian assistance in Iraq, he did not specify the reason behind this need.[21] Perhaps the earliest sign of a shift in this cautious attitude lies in the summary declaration of the seventh BRICS summit of five countries in Ufa, Russia, in July 2015, which condemned terrorism, violence, and severe human rights violation by the Islamic State.[22] A test of this shift will be China's policy following the execution of a Chinese citizen by the Islamic State in November 2015, an act that was condemned sharply by President Xi.

Conclusion

Since the turn of the millennium, the political and economic status of China has improved gradually and consistently, transforming the country into the world's second leading economic power. China's companies have expanded their business, and its citizens are now working and traveling all over the globe, including the Middle East. The American call to China a decade ago to behave as a "responsible shareholder" with respect to global problems has become ever more relevant over the years.[23]

China's traditional policy of refraining from open intervention in the internal issues of other countries is thus put to the test at a time when borders between countries in the Middle East are being erased, and the destructive forces responsible continue to blur even more borders and may perhaps affect China itself. Yet an examination of China's statements and mode of operation in both the multilateral and bilateral sphere indicates that despite growing challenges, China has not altered its policy of "restraint," which includes maintaining a low media profile and avoiding involvement in alliances and coalitions that could mark it as a key player in the combat against Salafi Islam, along with a focus on its own terrorist challenges and resistance to calls for independence in Xinjiang.

China's use of force against the Uyghurs in Xinjiang makes the country a potential target of the Islamic State and makes terrorism a concrete threat to its citizens. Official information on Chinese Uyghurs joining the foreign fighters in Syria and Iraq, and the danger to which they allegedly expose China upon their return home, indicates that Beijing is worried about the effects of the Islamic State on the stability of Xinjiang Province as well as attacks against Chinese on foreign soil. Nonetheless, China prefers to act independently, as it has done in other situations and with discreet cooperation that allows it to upgrade its capabilities without disclosing information on its methods for dealing with Muslims and other groups regarded by the Communist Party as liable to jeopardize stability and the Party's rule.

As part of its plan to strengthen its control over hostile factions, the regime expedited discussions on the formulation of a new bill on the struggle against terrorism. A draft of the "Terrorism Law," presented in March 2015 at the annual plenum of the Chinese Parliament, revealed that the regime intends to tighten further its supervision of social media and the flow of information. The draft evoked severe criticism outside of China, mainly relating to the option of unlimited monitoring of internet traffic and foreign companies inside China. This will force the Beijing regime to reconsider the new bill before giving it final approval.[24]

In the international arena, China has more than once expressed its disappointment with the West, as led by the United States, which, instead of supporting the struggle against Uyghur terrorism, has questioned the accuracy of the information coming from Beijing, while criticizing the country's human rights record and the tough measures taken against the Muslim population in Xinjiang. China therefore prefers to pursue cooperation with countries (such as the BRICS states) that do not intervene in its internal affairs and can also teach it methods to fight terrorism. Among other moves, China is conducting joint maneuvers with Russia and a number of other countries in Central Asia within the framework of the Shanghai Cooperation Organization (SCO), and is seeking cooperation with Middle East regimes that it regards as stable, such as Iran and Israel.[25]

The ideal solution for China is to find a path that will dissociate it from the chaos that reigns in large expanses of the Middle East, distance itself from Salafi jihad terrorists, and prevent them from penetrating Chinese territory. This will make it possible for China to maintain internal stability and Party rule, by building operational capabilities in counterterrorism and firewalls for controlling the flow of information, as well as additional, complementary capabilities.

The return to China of Uyghur veterans with a revolutionary attitude molded by the Islamic State, with training and experience in terrorist funding and attacks as well as organizational and interpersonal connections, could jeopardize stability in Xinjiang and inspire terrorist activity within China and against Chinese citizens abroad. As a result, China is likely to step up its security and intelligence coordination with other countries threatened by Salafi terrorism, such as Israel. The possibility of recruiting China as an active member in the international coalition depends on the coalition's ability to persuade decision makers in Beijing that cooperation of this kind would strengthen China in its war against separatism, bolster the legitimacy of its regime in the struggle against terrorism, and help it preserve internal stability. The more the threat increases, the clearer these points will become to Chinese Communist Party leaders.

Notes

1   Abdallah Suleiman Ali, "Baghdadi Vows Revenge in Announcing 'Islamic State,'" *al-Monitor*, July 3, 2014, http://www.al-monitor.com/pulse/security/2014/07/iraq-syria-baghdadi-call-muslims-caliphate.html#.

2   The Uyghurs are Muslims of Turkish origin. Approximately 10 million of the 22 million residents of Xinjiang Province are Uyghurs.

3   Dan Murphy, "ISIS Leader Baghdadi Cementing Reputation as the New Hulagu Khan," *Christian Science Monitor*, February 5, 2015, http://www.csmonitor.com/World/Security-Watch/Backchannels/2015/0205/ISIS-leader-Baghdadi-cementing-reputation-as-the-new-Hulagu-Khan.

4   Cui Jia, "IS Recruits Xinjiang Residents," *China Daily*, March 10, 2015, http://www.chinadaily.com.cn/china/2015twosession/2015-03/10/content_19770997.htm.

5   The figure of 300 is based on Chinese publications. One report states that in a single year, 800 Uyghurs were arrested in Vietnam trying to cross the border in order to continue from there to the Middle East and that the Chinese had established a special police unit called 4.29 to combat illegal border crossings. See Kyle Mizokami, "China has an ISIS Problem," *The Week*, March 2, 2105, http://theweek.com/articles/541531/china-isis-problem. Thailand recently returned 100 Uyghurs to China who had crossed the border illegally. See Oliver Homes and agencies, "Thailand Forcibly Sends Nearly 100 Uighur Muslims Back to China," *The Guardian*, July 9, 2015, http://www.theguardian.com/world/2015/jul/09/thailand-forcibly-sends-nearly-100-uighur-muslims-back-to-china.

6   See Qiu Yongzheng, "Turkey's Ambiguous Policies Help Terrorists Join IS Jihadist Group: Analyst," *Global Times*, December 15, 2014, http://www.globaltimes.cn/content/896765.shtml. Another report speaks of seven Chinese arrested on the Turkish border while trying to join Islamic State forces. See Mizokami, "China has an ISIS Problem."

7   "O Chinese kaffar (non-believers), know that we are preparing in the land of the khilafah (caliphate) and we will come to you and raise this flag in Turkestan with the permission of Allah." See Tom Wyke and Jenny Stanton, "Is this the Oldest Jihadi in ISIS? Elderly Man Flees China with his Family to Fight Alongside

Terror Group in Syria," *Mail Online*, June 3, 2015, http://www.dailymail.co.uk/news/article-3110022/Is-ISIS-oldest-jihadi-Elderly-man-flees-China-family-fight-alongside-terror-group-Syria.html.

8   "FM Press Conference on September 10," http://news.xinhuanet.com/english/bilingual/2014-09/11/c_133635859.htm. East Turkistan is another name for Xinjiang Province in northwestern China. East Turkistan existed as an independent country for short periods when Chinese rule was weak (e.g., in 1933-34 and 1944-49). The Muslim residents are currently fighting for independence.

9   "Rivals Pakistan, India to Start Process of Joining China Security Bloc," *Reuters*, July 6, 2015, http://www.reuters.com/article/2015/07/06/us-china-russia-pakistan-india-idUSKCN0PG09120150706. The Chinese news agency did not quote the statement about the Islamic State. See "Acceptance of India, Pakistan into SCO on Ufa Summit Agenda," *English.news.cn*, July 6, 2015, http://news.xinhuanet.com/english/2015-07/06/c_134387348.htm.

10   "Update: China's Xi Demands Action after 3 Killed in Attack," *Asahi Shimbun*, May 1, 2014, http://ajw.asahi.com/article/asia/china/AJ201405010022.

11   "Five Detained over Tian'anmen Terrorist Attack," *English.news.cn*, October 30, 2013, http://news.xinhuanet.com/english/china/2013-10/30/c_132845415.htm.

12   "Xi Urges Anti-Terrorism 'Nets' for Xinjiang," *English.news.cn,* May 29, 2014, http://www.chinadaily.com.cn/china/2014-05/29/content_17552457.htm.

13   Ibid.

14   An article by the Director of the Research Center of Ethnic and Religious Studies at the Party School of the Central Committee of the Communist Party of China claims that extreme terrorist groups persuade people to use these coverings to boost support, and confirms that the Party is acting against this phenomenon. See "Burqas, Hijabs and Beards in the Governance of Xinjiang," China policy Institute Blog, April 29, 2015, http://blogs.nottingham.ac.uk/chinapolicyinstitute/2015/04/29/regulating-burqas-hijabs-and-beards-to-push-or-pul.

15   "China Bans Ramadan Fasting in Muslim Province," *al-Jazeera*, July 3, 2014, http://www.aljazeera.com/news/asia-pacific/2014/07/china-bans-ramadan-fasting-muslim-province-20147371648541558.html.

16   "Counter-Terrorism Exercise in Shanghai," CCTV News, July 3, 2015, https://www.youtube.com/watch?v=Ua-nsce4Zv4.

17   "Commentary: Muslims, their Religion should not Take Blame for Terrorists' Crimes," *English.news.cn*, June 28, 2015, http://news.xinhuanet.com/english/2015-06/28/c_134362926.htm. Its statement of support for Islam did not help China, which was condemned by the Turkish government following reports that the regime was forcing Muslims to eat during the month of Ramadan. These condemnations incited violence against Chinese throughout Turkey, including the burning of Chinese flags and vandalism directed against Chinese-owned restaurants. See "Turkey Expresses Concern over China's Ramadan Bans on Uighurs," *Today's Zaman*, June 30, 2015,

http://www.todayszaman.com/diplomacy_turkey-expresses-concern-over-chinas-ramadan-bans-on-uighurs_392385.html. See also Ivan Watson and Steven Jiang, "Beijing Issues Travel Warning after Turkey Protests Target Chinese," CNN, July 8, 2015, http://edition.cnn.com/2015/07/06/asia/china-turkey-warning/.

18   Joint Statement Issued by Partners at the Counter-ISIL Coalition Ministerial Meeting," US Department of State, December 3, 2014, http://www.state.gov/r/pa/prs/ps/2014/12/234627.htm. In a press interview the Iraqi Foreign Minister claimed that at the UN General Assembly in New York in September 2014, Chinese Foreign Minister Wang Yi told him that China's political principles did not allow it to join a coalition, and that it would aid Iraq outside the coalition. Asked about this claim, the Chinese Foreign Ministry spokesperson responded ambiguously: "China has been fighting terrorism and has been providing support and assistance to Iraq, including the Kurdish region," RT, December 14, 2015, http://rt.com/news/214243-china-iraq-military-isis.

19   U.S.-China Strategic & Economic Dialogue Outcomes of the Strategic Track, US Department of State, June 24, 2015, http://www.state.gov/r/pa/prs/ps/2015/06/244205.htm.

20   Amy He, "China More Proactive at UN," China Daily, November 30, 2015, http://usa.chinadaily.com.cn/epaper/2015-03/02/content_19692303.htm.

21   Working Together to Address the New Threat of Terrorism-Statement by Wang Yi At the UN Security Council Summit on Terrorism, September 24, 2014, http://www.china-un.ch/eng/zywjyjh/t1196288.htm.

22   VII BRICS Summit Ufa Declaration, July 9, 2015, http://www.china-embassy.org/eng/zgyw/t1282066.htm. The BRICS countries are Brazil, Russia, India, China, and South Africa.

23   Robert B. Zoellick, "Whither China: From Membership to Responsibility?" Remarks to National Committee on U.S.-China Relations, Washington, September 21, 2005, http://2001-2009.state.gov/s/d/former/zoellick/rem/53682.htm.

24   See Counter-Terrorism Law (Initial Draft) at http://chinalawtranslate.com/en/ctldraft/; and Scott D. Livingston, "Will China's New Anti-Terrorism Law Mean the End of Privacy?" China File, April 22, 2015, http://www.chinafile.com/reporting-opinion/viewpoint/will-chinas-new-anti-terrorism-law-mean-end-privacy.

25   See the report on the dispatch of a special messenger on behalf of President Xi to promote cooperation with Iran in the struggle against terrorism, Ciao Siqi, "Beijing, Tehran to Fight Terrorism," Global Times, November 19, 2014, http://www.globaltimes.cn/content/892520.shtml. On Israel, see the report on the training of Chinese armed policemen in anti-terrorism military exercises at an Israel Border Police base, "What Were Armed Chinese Officers Doing with the Border Police," JDN, December 29, 2011, http://www.jdn.co.il/news/24139.

Part VII

Threat Assessment and Strategic Confrontation

The Strategic Challenge:
Contending with the Islamic State

Udi Dekel

The Current Situation

The United States, the West, and Israel were all caught off guard by the emergence of the Islamic State (ISIS, ISIL) – primarily by its scope, its power, and the expansion of its influence throughout the Middle East and beyond. The Islamic State is a new kind of hybrid actor combining a number of different forms: a terrorist organization, a religious ideological movement, and an Islamic state operating in accordance with *sharia* law. It performs governing functions, controls large swaths of land, and aspires to impose an Islamic caliphate on and beyond the entire Arab world. The wide variety of logics, dimensions, forms, and challenges with which the Islamic State presents the region and the world necessitates the formulation of a multidimensional response for contending with the phenomenon.

The United States found itself with no strategy for grappling with the rise of the Islamic State, despite defining it as the "primary strategic problem" of the Middle East[1] with negative implications for the international system. The aim presented by President Obama – defeating the Islamic State – proved to be overly ambitious, certainly in the short term. More than a year later, President Obama, updating the strategy, said: "The United States and our Armed Forces continue to lead the global coalition in our mission to destroy the terrorist group ISIL….Our strategy is moving forward with a great sense of urgency on four fronts – hunting down and taking out these terrorists; training and equipping Iraqi and Syrian forces to fight ISIL on the ground; stopping ISIL's operations by disrupting their recruiting, financing and propaganda; and, finally, persistent diplomacy to end the Syrian civil war so that everyone can focus on destroying ISIL."[2]

However, the US commitment to quash the Islamic State stemmed from a degree of responsibility for the very phenomenon and its effects: the Islamic State emerged out of the Sunni uprising waged in response to the American invasion of Iraq and the establishment, within its territory, of a Shiite dominated regime that subsequently joined the Iranian-led Shiite axis. The entity's growth was also bolstered by the quick US withdrawal from Iraq, the poor performance of the states in the region, and the power vacuum that resulted within states lacking effective governance (Syria) and suffering from a failed regime (Iraq). The Islamic State's spread to additional areas such as Yemen, Libya, and the Sinai Peninsula exploits this vacuum in these governance-lacking regions and is also based on their access to weapons and money.

After the initial surprise, the United States formulated a sequential strategic approach, whereby it would first be necessary to address the problems in Iraq – the Islamic State's home base – and then deal with Syria, where the struggle is more complex due to the large number of foreign actors and rebel forces involved. It quickly became clear that the Islamic State has made effective use of its ability to move between the two spheres – Iraq and Syria – in order to seize control of additional territories and populations and build itself an image of success.

As long as there is no solution to the crisis in Syria, which constitutes a main battlefield between Sunnis and Shiites and is subject to intensive Iranian and Russian intervention, the motivation of Sunni forces to join the Salafi jihadist organizations in general, and the Islamic State and the al-Nusra Front in particular, continues to rise.[3] Concomitantly, Sunni states continue to support the opposition groups in Syria with the aim of reducing Iranian influence and toppling the regime led by President Bashar al-Assad. The Islamic State is taking advantage of the struggles between the various forces in Syria, and when it observes that the different sides are wearing each other down, it sends in advance forces with the aim of establishing control over additional regions, or at least demonstrating an ability to reach almost all parts of Syria.

Building a Coalition and an Operational Concept

Although the United States has succeeded in building a broad coalition of more than 60 states that committed themselves to join the fight against the Islamic State, the goal of defeating it has proven to be difficult to achieve and is likely to take more than a decade if the campaign continues to be conducted in its current form (as of the summer of 2015).[4] The interim goal of halting the expansion of the Islamic State is also likely to take a significant amount of time – between three and five years.

Moreover, despite the establishment of the broad international and regional coalition against the Islamic State, a critical mass of forces and capabilities has not yet been achieved. Particularly conspicuous is the absence of ground forces ("boots on the ground"[5]) possessing capabilities typical of special forces and the determination and motivation required to fight the forces of the Islamic State. Most coalition airstrikes against Islamic State targets have been carried out by American squadrons and, as of August 2015, had injured approximately 12,500 Islamic State operatives and struck 7,600 Islamic State targets.[6] However, the Islamic State numbers more than 30,000 fighters, and according to varying estimates continues to recruit approximately 1,000 new volunteers each month from a large number of countries around the world. At the same time, it continues to control large regions of Iraq and Syria and to expand its influence in additional regions by means of Salafi jihadist groups that express an oath of allegiance to the Islamic State and proclaim the areas in question to be under its control, as in Libya and the Sinai Peninsula.

Potential American capabilities are far greater than those used in the current US military offensive against the Islamic State. American airpower is capable of destroying 7,600 targets in less than one week of consolidated effort. For example, in the 2003 air campaign against the Iraqi army, the US Air Force dropped an average of 1,039 munitions per day with an average of 600 daily sorties. In contrast, by the summer 2015, in its operation against the Islamic State, the average rate of American attacks stands at 43 munitions and 11 attack sorties per day. This lack of operational effectiveness also stems from a lack of intelligence regarding targets, holes in intelligence coverage, distance from the regions of fighting, the failure to establish no-fly and no-movement zones, difficulty forging satisfactory cooperation with local actors, and the absence of ground forces.

In practice, the operational concept of the war against the Islamic State that was drawn up in Washington has not reached full implementation, not to mention maximum use of all its components. This concept, based in part on ground operations by Iraqi government forces against the Islamic State, quickly proved to be flawed. These forces are weak and lack the motivation to fight, and have been superseded by Shiite militias operated primarily by Iran and Kurdish militias operating primarily in their own areas. The US effort to build up the Sunni militias of tribes has also failed as a result of the Sunni population's lack of faith in the United States and the Iraqi government. At the same time, the United States is reluctant to transfer weapons to Sunni militias opposing the Islamic State following cases in which such weapons were plundered and ultimately fell into the hands of enemies of the United States.

The building of opposition forces to the Assad regime in Syria based on non-Salafi jihadist elements has also proven to be a virtually impossible task. It has been underway for an extensive period and is contingent to a great extent on the goodwill of Jordan and especially Turkey, both of which share borders with Syria. The first forces that were sent to the battlefield in Syria were immediately destroyed or disarmed by the al-Nusra Front. More significant, however, is that the Islamic State has also proven to be capable of quick learning and rapid adaptation to new conditions. These attributes have hampered the effectiveness of the fighting conducted against it and the ability of the coalition forces to curb and contain it.

The more critical the need for special forces and special ground operations against the Islamic State, the greater the difficulties involved with recruiting forces from among the members of the international coalition, due particularly to their reluctance to send forces to engage in combat. Increased airstrikes have also turned out to be less effective than originally anticipated. In addition to the intelligence shortage, this has stemmed from the desire to avoid harming the non-combatant population; the lack of centers of gravity; and the need for aircraft to take off from distant airports without an ability to sustain a continuous presence over the areas of fighting. Also ineffective has been the increase in the number of American forces allocated to the training and operational instruction of Iraqi forces, including the allocation of American observation and operational mentoring personnel and coordinators for front line Iraqi operational units.

The bottom line is that to date, the US coalition effort against the Islamic State has not generated the desired outcome. The defeat of the Islamic State, the termination of its influence in Iraq and Syria, and the failure to prevent its influence from spreading to other areas have been hindered primarily by the failure to actualize components of the operational concept and its limited implementation.

A major problem of the international effort against the Islamic State has been the partial mobilization of some of the coalition members. Turkey, which as a result of its geostrategic location, and in addition to its membership in NATO, plays an important role in the struggle against the Islamic State, has conducted itself in a highly equivocal manner, and most of the time has actually helped the Islamic State. Turkey regards the Islamic State as a means of achieving Erdogan's ultimate goal of toppling the Assad regime in Syria and, under the cover of the war against the Islamic State, is pursuing its own private war against the Kurdish underground (PKK) and the Kurdish militias in northern Iraq and northern Syria.[7]

Other members of the international coalition, including Saudi Arabia and the Gulf states, are likewise playing a two-faced game. On the one hand, they regard the Islamic State as a major threat, but on the other hand, they also recognize that it constitutes a threat to the Shiites in the region, particularly for Iran – their main enemy.[8]

Finally, the United States itself – the leader of the international coalition – lacks sufficient determination in the fight against the Islamic State. The United States is capable of defeating the Islamic State on the battlefield in Iraq and most likely also in Syria, but the chances of the Obama administration's undertaking the necessary effort to do so appear extremely slim. After years of military intervention in the Middle East (Afghanistan and Iraq) that have yielded no positive return, opposition to unnecessary risks is on the rise within the American public and Congress.[9] Under such conditions, there is no reason to believe that the United States will succeed this time in places where it has failed in the past.

What Is Required to Curb, Weaken, and Dismantle the Islamic State

Achieving the strategic goal of curbing and ultimately defeating the Islamic State will require the promotion of a new multidimensional strategic concept based on the stipulation of clearly defined accomplishments required in a variety of areas: from the presentation of an idea that can compete with that of the Islamic State to the employment of smart power in combination with political, military, economic, social, ideological, infrastructural, and consciousness-oriented means. What follows are ten required efforts:

a. *The implementation of consciousness-oriented warfare.* The first and immediate aim is to prevent all possible successes of the Islamic State, which seeks to foster an image of ongoing success while minimizing the impact of its failures. The Islamic State's successes have been the product of the element of surprise, the parallel operation on three geographical levels (local, regional, and global), the high mobility of its forces, the assistance of forces on the ground, and use of the element of fear, which causes rival forces to flee prior to battle (as in the city of Ramadi in Iraq[10]). In addition, the Islamic State takes advantage of regions with power vacuums or weak regimes and seizes control of them with relative ease. In Syria, for example, the Islamic State stands on the sidelines watching the struggles among the different groups of rebels and against the forces of President Assad, and when the fighting forces reach a significant level of mutual destruction, it launches a surprise attack not necessarily aimed at holding territory over the course of time but, first and foremost, at demonstrating success. The continuity of successes in turn encourages organizations, groups, and individuals to join the ranks of the Islamic State. It is therefore critical to formulate an opposing consciousness of Islamic State failures and to taint its leadership with the image of a group of failed criminals. It will also be necessary to demonstrate its limited strength on the battlefield, to deepen its isolation, and to prove that its efforts are not improving the living conditions or addressing the needs of the Sunni population in the territories under its control.

b. *The need for high quality ground forces.* Achieving operational effectiveness against Islamic State forces will require the use of ground forces with enhanced capabilities, with an emphasis on special forces relying on intelligence-guided warfare. The West fears sending ground forces based on the desire to avoid becoming bogged down by the anticipated subsequent mobilization of local forces against the foreign forces, and in light of its failures in Afghanistan and Iraq. Therefore, as a first step, and in light of the precedent in Yemen, it will be necessary to make use of the ground forces of Sunni countries (not Iran, whose involvement encourages mobilization into the ranks of the Islamic State), closely guided by joint commands that include American forces and that will provide them with air support. Such countries include Turkey, Jordan, Saudi Arabia, Egypt, the Gulf states, and minority militias, such as those of the Kurds. The campaign will also require a multi-layered intelligence effort in order to improve the operational effectiveness of the forces fighting the Islamic State.

c. *Establishing a framework for a multinational force.* Such a force should be established based on existing organizations such as NATO, in order to increase the order of battle taking part in the fighting against the Islamic State to achieve a critical mass, and to increase the coordination between the participating countries.

d. *Targeted killing of Islamic State commanders and the prevention of terrorist attacks.* Since the onset of coalition attacks, the United States has achieved a number of successes in targeted killing operations against leaders of the Islamic State.[11] This is an effective way of disrupting their activity and keeping them on the defensive. At the same time, it is necessary to include lower ranks among those being targeted, i.e., intermediate commanders and paid advisors, former Iraqi army commanders, and former members of the Baath Party, who today make up a sizable portion of the activists of the Islamic State. Such pursuit of the leading commanders and activists of the Islamic State must involve intelligence cooperation between coalition members around the globe.

e. *Starting to think in terms of a new state structure.* The dream of a "united Iraq" or a "united Syria" in the future Middle East is fading fast. The United States and the international coalition must demonstrate greater creativity and flexibility regarding the future borders of states and other entities in the region. One rule of thumb for the process must be to avoid a situation in which Shiites control Sunnis or vice versa. It will also be necessary to allow the establishment of autonomies based on ethnic, tribal, and cultural identity. In addition, ethno-national groups such as the Kurds must be allowed the right to self-determination, including the establishment of a Kurdish state in Kurdish regions, at least in northern Iraq and northeastern Syria.

f. *Iran is the problem,* as increased reliance on Iran will have detrimental effects. Washington and the West regard Iran more as a lever for solving the problems of the Middle East than as a subversive force fostering instability and operating Shiite militias and other proxies on its behalf.[12] The Sunni countries cannot come to terms with Iran playing a major part in the solution. Therefore, if a situation emerges in which Iran and its agents are fighting Sunnis and receive Western legitimacy and support for its hegemonic status in the region, these countries will employ the range of destructive abilities at their disposal, including the provision of indirect assistance to the Islamic State and Salafi jihadist groups.

g. *Mitigating the internal tension in the Sunni camp*, and in the process strengthening the more pragmatic forces that are willing to accept the rules of play of the international coalition, such as Jordan, Egypt, Saudi Arabia, and the Gulf states. To ensure that these states survive and are able to neutralize the internal emergence of groups and individuals supporting the revolutionary idea of the Islamic State, they must improve their governance, deal with corruption, work toward the separation of religion and state, insist on judicial systems, invest in education toward openness, and open routes of employment and self-fulfillment for the younger generation. They must also make a focused effort to improve the situation of the strata of the population that serve as recruiting grounds for Islamic State volunteers: poorer and weaker segments of the population, disgruntled young adults, threatened and isolated Sunni tribes, and those subject to extremist religious exhortation who lack the ability to contend with its arguments and its efforts to persuade.

h. *Stopping the flow of volunteers.* Also necessary is a comprehensive effort by different countries to stop the recruitment of foreign volunteers and prevent them from joining the Islamic State in Syria and Iraq. In late 2015, these volunteers were estimated at approximately 30,000.[13] The return of these volunteers to their countries of origin presents great danger to the internal security of Western states and Arab states alike. For this reason, the states of the West must halt the flow of volunteers to the Islamic State by means of strict border control practices, supervision of preachers in mosques and on the social media, and the formulation of ideas and ideologies that can compete with Salafi ideas. They must also prevent the transfer of funds and trade with the Islamic State.

i. *Nothing should be done to delay the effort to stabilize Syria and neutralize the influence of the radical forces there.* The strategy must address the fundamental problems of the Middle East that motivate large groups within the Sunni population to identify with the idea of the Islamic State. Defeating the Islamic State will require a sustainable solution for the problem of Syria. After all, although the Islamic State emerged in Iraq, Syria was the site of the declaration of the Islamic caliphate and has become a base for assisting in expanding its control. The brutal policy of the Assad regime pushes volunteers into the hands of the opposition, including the Islamic State. Moreover, the Sunnis in Syria would, if they could, presumably choose to fight Assad over the Islamic State.[14]

The opposing coalition of Russia, Iran, Assad, and Hezbollah causes a counter-reaction of support for the Islamic State. In addition, the confusion and chaos created by the different coalitions operating in Syria enable the Islamic State to thrive there. Therefore, the United States must deny accomplishments to the Russian-Iranian coalition against the other rebels fighting the Assad regime. On the other hand, it must promote cooperation with Russia in fighting the Islamic State.

j. *Intelligence and cyber warfare.* Also required is a combined effort of states and intelligence organizations against the Islamic State in the cyber realm and information warfare. This effort should be aimed at denying the Islamic State the element of fear achieved by displaying barbaric acts, and neutralizing its ability to engage in propaganda on the internet and influence masses and individuals through the social networks. At the same time, the internet facilitates the identification and neutralization of recruiters, volunteers, admirers and supporters, and communications media that serve to convey instructions. As such, the internet is part of the effort to neutralize Islamic State activity and its current expansionist trend. Also necessary is a focused effort to remove Islamic State propaganda immediately from the internet that aims to locate sources of support (ideological, economic, and financial), in order to block them and cut off the Islamic State from all external assistance.

Conclusion

The United States, along with other Western countries and the Arab world, must formulate a strategic concept for the fight against the Islamic State that integrates the ten components outlined above. This will require a sense of urgency, determination, and mobilization within the free world in order to bring about the collapse of the economic, social, and consciousness-oriented abilities of the Islamic State, stop the recruitment of volunteers into its ranks, and ultimately bring about its defeat. Perhaps the November 2015 terrorist attacks in Paris, which were aimed at Western civilization, will mark the turning point in the world's mobilization against the Islamic State.

Notes

1   Tom Cohen, "Obama Outlines ISIS Strategy: Airstrikes in Syria, More US Forces," *CNN*, September 11, 2014, http://edition.cnn.com/2014/09/10/politics/isis-obama-speech/; "Statement by the President on ISIL," The White House: Office of the

Press Secretary, September 11, 2014, https://www.whitehouse.gov/the-press-office/2014/09/10/statement-president-isil-1.

2   "Remarks by the President on the Military Campaign to Destroy ISIL," The White House: Office of the Press Secretary, December 14, 2015, https://www.whitehouse.gov/the-press-office/2015/12/14/remarks-president-military-campaign-destroy-isil.

3   Michael Weiss, "Why Some Secular Sunnis Support ISIS," *Business Insider*, March 14, 2015, http://www.businessinsider.com/why-some-secular-sunnis-support-isis-2015-3.

4   Aaron Mehta, "Odierno: ISIS Fight will Last '10 To 20 Years,'" *Defense News*, July 17, 2015, http://www.defensenews.com/story/defense/2015/07/17/odierno-isis-fight-last-10-20-years/30295949/.

5   Barbara Slavin, "Who has 'Boots on the Ground' in Fight against IS?" *al-Monitor: The Pulse of the Middle East*, July 8, 2015, http://www.al-monitor.com/pulse/originals/2015/07/us-kurd-shiite-allies-fight-islamic-state-iran.html.

6   "Operation Inherent Resolve: Targeted Operations against ISIL Terrorists," *US Department of Defense*, August 7, 2015, http://www.defense.gov/News/Special-Reports/0814_Inherent-Resolve.

7   Danny Kemp, "Allies Tolerate Turkey's Double Game to Boost ISIS Fight," *Daily* Star, July 30, 2015, http://www.dailystar.com.lb/News/Middle-East/2015/Jul-30/308909-allies-tolerate-turkeys-double-game-to-boost-isis-fight.ashx.

8   Lori Plotkin Boghardt, "Battling ISIS and beyond in the Gulf," *PolicyWatch* 2461, The Washington Institute, August 6, 2015, http://www.washingtoninstitute.org/policy-analysis/view/battling-isis-and-beyond-in-the-gulf.

9   Stephen M. Walt, "Top 10 Lessons of the Iraq War," *Foreign Policy*, March 20, 2012, http://foreignpolicy.com/2012/03/20/top-10-lessons-of-the-iraq-war-2/.

10 "Iraq's Ramadi Falls to ISIS after Army Deserts City," *al-Arabiya*, May 17, 2015, http://english.alarabiya.net/en/News/middle-east/2015/05/17/Iraq-Ramadi-falls-to-ISIS-after-army-leaves-city-.html.

11 Greg Miller, "U.S. Launches Secret Drone Campaign to Hunt Islamic State Leaders in Syria," *Washington Post*, September 1, 2015, https://www.washingtonpost.com/world/national-security/us-launches-secret-drone-campaign-to-hunt-islamic-state-leaders-in-syria/2015/09/01/723b3e04-5033-11e5-933e-7d06c647a395_story.html.

12 Barak Ravid, "Ya'alon: Israel Sees Iran as a Problem, U.S. Sees Solution," *Haaretz*, June 29, 2015, http://www.haaretz.com/news/diplomacy-defense/.premium-1.663506.

13 Peter R. Neumann, "Foreign Fighter Total in Syria/Iraq now Exceeds 20,000; Surpasses Afghanistan Conflict in the 1980s," *ICSR*, January 26, 2015, http://icsr.info/2015/01/foreign-fighter-total-syriairaq-now-exceeds-20000-surpasses-afghanistan-conflict-1980s/.

14 Jamal Khashoggi, "Who should Go First, Assad or ISIS?" *al-Arabiya*, August 17, 2015, http://english.alarabiya.net/en/views/news/middle-east/2015/08/17/Who-comes-first-ISIS-or-Assad-.html.

The Islamic State Challenge:
How Severe Is It?

Amos Yadlin

In June 2014, after crushing five divisions of the Iraqi army trained and equipped by the United States, a few thousand Islamic State soldiers conquered the city of Mosul in northern Iraq. This unexpected development, which took place before the name "Islamic State in Iraq and Syria" was replaced by "Islamic State" as an expression of a material change in the organization's strategy and goals, prompted the sense that a new militarily powerful and threatening enemy had arisen. The perception of a threat was also due to the barbaric fighting methods employed by Islamic State forces. The extensive and expert use of the social networks to disseminate horrifying images – kidnapping, beheading, burning prisoners alive, selling people into slavery, human trafficking, mass execution using a variety of cruel methods, and destruction of civil infrastructure and historical cultural treasures – greatly contributed to the fear, and to the belief that the Islamic State heads the list of threats to the West and Israel.

In the summer and fall of 2014, it appeared that the Islamic State was altering the balance of threats and alliances in the Middle East. It made al-Qaeda – the organization that was its original incarnation – look moderate. It positioned Iran as a country playing a stabilizing role, and even brought the United States back into the Middle East, only a few years after President Obama had withdrawn all American forces from Iraq, as he had promised during his presidential campaign. This reversal by the United States was supported by the American public – the same public that did not support intervention in Syria a year earlier, when Bashar al-Assad crossed the red line drawn by Obama and used chemical weapons against his own people. This support came only after the beheading of two American journalists by

Islamic State operatives, which brought the public in the United States to accept the campaign against the Islamic State with greater understanding.

I have already pointed out the tendency to overestimate the Islamic State's military and political power,[1] and I suggested removing "our hand off the siren button," at least in Israel. Analysis showed that the Islamic State posed four possible threats to Israel, all of which were unlikely to materialize: the Islamic State reaching the Golan Heights; its ideology taking root in the Palestinian territories; showcase terrorist attacks of the type committed by al-Qaeda; and a decision by the Islamic State to make the Kingdom of Jordan its main target. This final threat is the most significant theoretical possibility for Israel: Israel's longest border is with Jordan, and preventing the destabilization of Jordan is a leading Israeli interest.[2]

Consistent with this assessment, the Islamic State did not become a military threat to Israel in 2015. It consolidated its hold on areas in Iraq and Syria with strong Sunni populations, but was repelled wherever it waged war against communities and groups fighting for their country and their homes: the Kurds in northern Iraq, the Shiites on the outskirts of Baghdad (with Iranian and American aid), the Kurds in Kobani, and even the forces of Bashar al-Assad in areas where he invested sufficient combat energy. The Islamic State's efforts to expand into the heart of Iraq, Jordan, and Damascus have been unsuccessful. Its forces have repeatedly seized Sunni areas, such as Ramadi and Fallujah in Iraq and Palmyra in Syria, but its attempts to advance into the Shiite and Kurdish parts of Iraq encountered strong local opposition that brought their progress to a halt. The fears that the Islamic State would conquer the capital of Baghdad and take over all of Iraq also proved at an early stage to be unfounded. This likely occurred in part due to fear of a military clash with the Shiite population in the city, the Shiite militias, and Iranian al-Quds forces – ultimately prompting the Islamic State to avoid any attempt to attack Baghdad.

Moreover, from a military perspective, the Islamic State's mode of operation is not groundbreaking. It relies on the use of vehicles carrying explosives driven by suicide bombers timed to explode simultaneously, lightly armored vehicles, anti-tank weapons, and automatic weapons fire. Its attempts to use heavier and more sophisticated weapons captured in battle have not led to significant battlefield achievements. On the other hand, the use of light weapons has made the Islamic State forces highly mobile on the advanced road system in Syria and Iraq. It has thereby acquired the ability to concentrate forces quickly and surprise remote enemies. Still, these tactics and tools are not suitable for fighting a modern Western army, such as the US army or the IDF, which have reconnaissance-based air forces and for which the Islamic State's vehicles are relatively easy prey. In addition, the battle training of most of the Islamic State's soldiers and its decentralized command and control structure emerged from guerrilla warfare in an urban environment in Syria and Iraq and are unsuitable for a large scale conventional campaign against a country like Jordan, and certainly against Israel.

The main reason for the Islamic State's successes on the battlefield against the Iraqi army in the northwest of the country in territories with Sunni populations is that the units of the Iraqi army are composed mostly of Shiite soldiers who refused to defend territory populated by Sunnis and therefore abandoned the battlefield. The claims of global expansion by the Islamic State beyond Syria and Iraq to Libya, Nigeria, Afghanistan, and the Sinai Peninsula also require clarification. This alleged "expansion" consists mostly of declarations of loyalty by local terrorist organizations, whose activity and targets are primarily restricted to a defined and limited area.

Against this background, the question arises why, despite the Islamic State's limited military capabilities, it is still of such great concern among Middle East countries, the European Union, Russia, and the United States. The answer lies in the non-military aspects of the Islamic State's actions. In other words, it has become patently clear that the Islamic State is a much wider phenomenon than its territorial delineation and state structure established in northeastern Syria and northwestern Iraq. Rather, the Islamic State comprises four principal dimensions: it is a state; it is a collection of terrorist organizations from many places in the world, such as Sinai and Libya, that have pledged loyalty to it; it is a global terror entity that attacks in Paris and brings down a Russian airplane; and above all it is an extremist religious ideology that is spreading rapidly and wielding increasing influence on the internet and the social media. Thus beyond its military activity, the Islamic State is defined by its religious and ideological messages, the media tools it uses to disseminate these messages, and its psychological effect, including fear, aroused by its brutal acts against people and property.

The regional upheaval, which began with the so-called Arab Spring, reflected the scope and depth of the tension prevailing for decades between the public in Arab countries and the respective regimes. The chain of events that succeeded this upheaval reflected the height of the growing search for a new comprehensive ideological framework in the Arab world. Both the pan-Arab national ideology and the socialist-Communist ideology lost their attractiveness at the end of the twentieth century, and no longer serve as a political and value lodestone for Arab societies. The democratic-liberal-capitalist idea gave rise to disillusionment in the early twenty-first century, as did the political Islam advocated by the Muslim Brotherhood, which momentarily seemed to offer a viable alternative solution. The social-economic-political crisis has escalated, and the public, especially young people, has continued its search for a new guiding light. Salafi jihadist Islam offered a new-old idea of an Islamic caliphate existing in accordance with *sharia* law. This is the background for the insight and anxiety prevailing in the Middle East and beyond, i.e., that even if the Islamic State is stopped on the battlefield, the ideology it promotes will continue to stoke the social and political fire and agitate for violent change.

The Islamic State's organic ideology and its willingness to sacrifice in the name of jihad are a form of soft power that can be spread through the internet and the social networks. In this way, it threatens the stability of social structures and regimes in Arab countries. This threat can be realized through terrorist actions that will destabilize the status quo countries politically, socially, and economically, or through local popular revolutions inspired by the Islamic State.

An Islamic revolution and a military territorial threat are not realistic scenarios for European countries. On the other hand, the possibility exists of a wave of terrorism in European countries housing large Muslim populations. The likelihood of this scenario – and the accompanying fear of its realization – has grown given the possibility that citizens of those countries who left to fight in the ranks of the Islamic State will return to their home countries with battle experience and a heavy ideological payload calling on them to take action in the name of jihad. The European Union is having difficulty combating the problem of the foreign fighters, mainly due to legal, cultural, and political restrictions.

In contrast to Europe, the United States and Israel are better protected against the Islamic State, in part because of geographical factors. The United States is further from the Islamic State's region of activity, and Israel's borders are closed and defended. The composition of the two countries' populations, their immigration laws, and the fewer restrictions on their freedom of action in the name of "political correctness" – a principle that makes it very difficult for European countries to cope with Islamic extremism in general, and with its manifestation in their territory in particular – make its easier for the United States and Israel to deal with the challenges posed by the Islamic State. Moreover, there is extremely limited support for the Islamic State among Arab citizens of Israel. While the number of Muslim citizens of Israel is the same as in the UK, the extent of terrorist attacks carried out in Israel in the name of Salafi jihadism, and the force of the rhetoric supporting jihad ideas, are at a much lower level that what has prevailed in European democracies in recent years. Actually, rather than a direct threat, the United States and Israel regard the Islamic State as an indirect threat – one that results from the threat it poses to the stability, and perhaps to the very survival, of the Arab countries having common interests with the US and Israel, including Egypt, Jordan, Saudi Arabia, and the other Gulf states.

Iran, Turkey, and even Russia are more vulnerable to the threat posed by the Islamic State than Israel and the United States. The Islamic State regards Shiites in general as heretics, and Iran as an enemy country. Iranian forces are also the main factor in conflict with the Islamic State forces in Tikrit and Baghdad. Furthermore, Iran, which regards the continued existence of the Assad regime in Syria as a strategic asset, is expected to continue and even extend its involvement in the ground battles against the Islamic State, whether directly or through Hezbollah, its proxy in Syria and Lebanon.

For a long time Turkey turned a blind eye to the movement of jihad forces from its territory into Syria, until a wave of terrorist attacks began in Turkey in 2015 and the Islamic State derided Turkish President Erdogan as a heretic. Russia, which has a large Sunni Muslim minority that supplies many of the recruits to the Russian army, regards the Islamic State as an important enemy for several reasons: the Islamic State directly threatens Assad's Syria, a Russian ally, and also threatens Russia itself and that of the countries that were formerly part of the Soviet Union, which are considered Russia's sphere of influence. Clear evidence of this Russian attitude can be found in President Putin's decision to send air force units, air defense weapons, cruise missiles, and special ground forces from Russia to Syria. In effect, Russia has been directly involved militarily in fighting the Islamic State since October 2015.

If the threat posed by the Islamic State is so substantial and concerns so many countries, why has no significant solution been devised until now, and why has the Islamic State not yet been pushed back or defeated on the battlefield? In addition, why has the "broadest coalition in history" formed against the Islamic State, led by the United States – 64 countries, supported from outside by additional countries, including Israel and even Iran, as well as by non-state players, including the Jabhat al-Nusra Syrian opposition militia – not dealt successfully with it, and contained or defeated it?[3] This question does not refer to the eradication of Salafi jihad Islam as an ideology, or to fighting against a terrorist organization that has no strong organizational structure or control of a defined territory, such as al-Qaeda. On the contrary – what is involved is warfare against an entity in control of a defined territory, and which has created a state framework in it, maintains a regular government structure, operates courts and municipalities, produces oil from the territories it has conquered as its main source of income, and takes advantage of the area's topography for modern warfare. The armies of the West, Turkey, Jordan, and even Russia were designed for fighting against countries. The difficulty involved in fighting against an asymmetric enemy, however, is less valid for the Islamic State.

The reason why the Islamic State has not yet been defeated, despite being surrounded by countries that regard it as a threat, is that not a single one of the countries in the coalition against it regards it as the greatest threat to its national security. Turkey is more concerned about the Kurds attaining autonomy in northern Syria and the effect this would have on the national aspirations of the Kurds in its territory, and about Assad's regime being left in power in Syria. Russia is concerned first and foremost about the extension of NATO to Ukraine and the possibility that the Assad regime will fall. The Iranian regime regards the hostility of the United States and Israel as the biggest threat to its survival. Saudi Arabia is mainly concerned about Iran's strategic ambitions, in the Gulf in particular and the Middle East in general.

Furthermore, the Islamic State enjoys complex relations with its neighbors, Syria and Turkey, which can be called "hostile-friendly." Indications of this include purchases of oil from the Islamic State by the Assad regime and by sources close to the government in Turkey, and the fact that most of Turkey's attack missions, and those of Russia in Syria, were conducted against the Kurds and the "moderate" rebels, respectively, while only a few were against the Islamic State. The Assad regime is also operating according to a similar set of priorities. Its efforts are directed primarily against the secular Syrian opposition – Jabhat al-Nusra and other groups – while it regards the Islamic State as a marginal factor in the civil war.

Another reason why the Islamic State has not yet been defeated is the American strategy. On the one hand, this strategy is ambitious: "to degrade and ultimately destroy the Islamic State." On the other hand, this has not been translated into the political will to put boots on the ground and to allocate the necessary resources – political, financial, and military.

The Islamic State also poses a threat to Israel, but substantially less than the threat represented by Iran, Hezbollah, what remains of Syria's conventional army, and even Hamas. The Islamic State does not play by the rules of the game, such as those that have been observed for years between terrorist groups and hostile countries and Israel, but its ability to attack Israel is limited to individual terrorist acts that do not constitute a systematic or strategic threat, and certainly not an existential one. In addition, the Islamic State's activity is accompanied by efforts to exploit opportunities and achieve surprise in isolated well planned operations (such as the one in Sheikh Zayed in Egypt in July 2015), but it lacks strategically important weapons, such as long range rockets, ballistic missiles, an air force, and air defense. This inferiority on the part of the Islamic State results from its lack of military or diplomatic support from a powerful country, in contrast to Hezbollah, for example, which receives sophisticated weaponry from Iran, Syria, and Russia.

Israel currently has two possible points of contact with the Islamic State – in the Sinai Peninsula and the Golan Heights. The declaration of loyalty by Wilayat Sinai (formerly Ansar Bait al-Maqdis) to the Islamic State gave the local organization in Sinai better organizational capabilities as a result of the flow of money and weapons. Although the forces of this terrorist organization threaten Israel to some extent, mainly the border communities, including Eilat, and traffic arteries leading to southern Israel, most of its attention has been devoted to the struggle against the Egyptian regime, which is deploying for a decisive military campaign against jihadi groups.

The presence of groups identifying with the Islamic State on the Golan front is negligible, compared with the presence of combatants from Jabhat al-Nusra and other rebel organizations there. Israel's extensive intelligence familiarity with the border area, the IDF's precise and massive firepower, and the imposition of clear rules of the game for shooting into its territory have so far proved a correct policy. A takeover by Islamic State groups of the border area with Israel in the Golan Heights will require a revision of the Israeli strategy, but Israel has the intelligence capabilities and means to cope with this challenge.

For its part, the Islamic State is currently devoting most of its attention and resources to fighting the Assad regime and its allies, meaning the Shiite axis, as well as competing entities in the area, including Jabhat al-Nusra, other rebel organizations, and local tribal groups. The relative quiet in the Golan Heights highlights the fact that the Islamic State does not perceive Israel as its main enemy; it regards the "heretical" Arab regimes as its main adversary. If the Islamic State decides to act against Israel, this will presumably occur only at a later stage. Meanwhile, one of the unintended benefits for Israel from the Islamic State's activity is the bloody cost it has exacted from Hezbollah fighting at the side of the Assad regime. This has a negative impact on the standing of Iran, which backs the Assad regime and Hezbollah, and whose senior commanders are also under attack in Syria.[4]

After many years of warfare against diverse formations of terrorist organizations, as well as against the armies of hostile countries, Israel has no reason to be excessively alarmed or frightened at the rise of another terrorist organization operating far from its borders without any powerful support. At the same time, intelligence resources should be devoted to monitoring the Islamic State's development in order to gain a profound understanding of how it operates, its strong and weak points, and what tactics it is liable to develop against modern armies. In turn, Israel should devise an appropriate operational response to these tactics; closely follow development of Islamic State advanced military capabilities, such as anti-aircraft weapons, air defense, and surface-to-surface missiles; and closely monitor the Syrian Golan Heights and the Palestinian territories in order to spot initial signs of its presence there, design an appropriate operational response, and execute it at the right time. In addition, Israel should continue supporting Jordan in its struggle against the Islamic State's efforts to expand its influence there. Consideration should also be given to less likely but no less dangerous developments, such as a possible scenario of the Islamic State establishing an extremist Sunni state bordering Israel. While there is little likelihood of this scenario materializing, primarily because of Iranian and Russian support for the Assad regime in Syria, in the unpredictable and unstable Middle East, even scenarios that appear unfeasible must be taken seriously.

Finally, Israel should be alert and identify opportunities emerging from the current situation. In this framework, all parties should realize that Israel is an island of stability and clarity in the Middle East, and refute the allegation that the Arab-Israeli conflict is the main cause of instability in the region. The principal opportunity for Israel lies in the possibility of highlighting its status as a strategic asset and reliable ally for Western countries and the United States. Israel can help strengthen the Western coalition against the Islamic State and change the nature of its operations – particularly when Europe is faced with the massive flow of refugees, the United States is wary of any additional commitment in the Middle East, the Western coalition is stalled, and the Russian-Iranian coalition is occupied mainly with the question of the Assad regime's survival in Syria.

Israel has aerial reconnaissance capabilities and sophisticated cybernetic capabilities, as well as special forces of the highest quality. The ideological dimensions of the Islamic State and the content disseminated by its supporters on the social networks require the formation of a joint strategy by Israel and the countries with shared strategic interests to create cyber supremacy that will disrupt the Islamic State's ability to exploit the internet for the purpose of spreading dangerous messages. In addition, Israel is very familiar with the Middle East and can exert influence in this arena – assets likely to be extremely valuable to its allies in fighting the Islamic State.

In 2014 the Islamic State unexpectedly conquered northwestern Iraq and northeastern Syria, and consolidated the caliphate as a highly appealing ideal for the Arab world and Muslims in general, and as a substantive Salafi jihadist threat to countries in the Middle East and beyond. The territorial expansion was halted in 2015, and two global coalitions were formed for the purpose of combating the Islamic State. Israel has an opportunity to contribute to this global struggle, with the goal that 2016 will mark the end of the Islamic State's geographical and ideological expansion.

Notes

1   Amos Yadlin, "ISIS no Existential Threat to Israel," *Ynet*, Israel Opinion, September 3, 2014, http://www.ynetnews.com/articles/0,7340,L-4567128,00.html.

2   Itai Asher, "Should Israel fear ISIS?" *Liberal*, September 15, 2014, http://goo.gl/iha7ic.

3   "President Obama: "We will Degrade and Ultimately Destroy ISIL," https://www.whitehouse.gov/blog/2014/09/10/president-obama-we-will-degrade-and-ultimately-destroy-isil.

4   "Two More Iranian Military Commanders Killed in Syria," *Fars News Iran*, October 13, 2015, http://english.farsnews.com/newstext.aspx?nn=13940721001386.

Conclusion

Above and Below the Surface of the Islamic State

Yoram Schweitzer and Omer Einav

The volatile turbulence marking the Middle East since 2011 is the backdrop to the rise of the Islamic State and the context for its current vitality. The unstable state of affairs makes it impossible at this point to assess the Islamic State's historical importance and its long term ability to expand or even survive. Moreover, its singular nature and its stated ambitions defy a precise definition. Is this a multi-dimensional terror organization? Is it a religious-terrorist state entity? Or, perhaps, is it a mixed breed that intends on becoming a supra-national empire? One way or the other, it seems that the Islamic State is a phenomenon that does not fit the conventional definition of a non-state actor, and one that has succeeded in creating global repercussions that magnify its size and influence well beyond its actual scope and power.

Characteristics

The Islamic State is in essence an entity that defiantly decries the civilized world and its values. Its actions flout norms that have been institutionalized in the world over recent decades, including those relating to the laws of war, treatment of occupied populations and captives, protection of women's rights, avoidance of harm to children, and non-use of children as combatants. The Islamic State also challenges the established order within the global jihad camp headed by al-Qaeda, the organization from which it originally sprang. Its decision to establish an Islamic caliphate and crown Abu Bakr al-Baghdadi as caliph, without receiving the approval of senior Muslim clerics, essentially denied their religious authority and provoked all the rulers and leaders of the Muslim world, who automatically, as it were, became the subjects of the caliph.

With impressive determination and efficiency, the Islamic State exploited the disintegrating Arab regimes that had lost their legitimacy to continue to rule their countries and local populations. Against a backdrop of regional upheaval, the Islamic State conquered areas within the borders of certain states in the region and established its sovereignty in these territories. At the same time, it undermined the regional order by nullifying the borders defined in the Sykes-Picot agreement, and the erased border between Syria and Iraq signals the Islamic State's intention to continue in this vein and establish its rule in other failed states that suffer from chronic instability, such as Yemen and Libya. Indeed, it has extended its tentacles to other parts of Africa, the Caucasus, and Southern Asia. At the same time, the Islamic State, which successfully exploited the geopolitical state of affairs, is not only a product of regional volatility but is also an engine that furthers and fashions the instability.

The Islamic State believes in the imposition of Salafist Islam through violent jihad; it is in the name of this jihad that it rationalizes and justifies its actions. The Salafi jihadist ideology strives to destroy all other ideologies and ways of life, as the negation of the other lies at its root. This includes even Muslims – both Shiites and also Sunnis – who do not submit to it, and who are thus defined as infidels; it is of course all the more true of members of other religions, especially non-Muslim minorities. The vilification of rivals has become a central policy for the Islamic State, whereby any deviation from a pure and rigid form of Salafist Islam is considered straying off the correct path. The creation of this model by instilling fear and terror among its rivals as well as its supporters and subjects imparts an image of power to the Islamic State and casts it as a successful, unrelenting entity, in contrast to its rivals within and outside the Salafi jihadist camp. What it spouts as ethical superiority justifies in the eyes of its adherents acts such as ethnic cleansing, murder of civilians, rape, looting, robbery, and destruction of antiquities and historical sites.

Despite the Islamic State being in essence a fundamentalist Islamic entity striving to reestablish the Islamic rule of yore in accordance with the Salafist model, its leaders do not hesitate to use modern means to promote their goals. Their operatives make maximal use of technology and diverse forms of modern media. They document their brutality and distribute this testimony for everyone to see on social media, which impacts on millions of terrified viewers and enthused supporters throughout the world. The purpose of such conduct is to express open disdain and absolute rejection for the values of the world of the other, as well as to present Islamic State values as the proper alternative that must be imposed throughout the world.

How real and extensive is the threat the Islamic State represents? Whom does it endanger, and to what degree? In international discourse, it is difficult to find many people who would dispute that the Islamic State represents a clear danger to the stability of the Middle East, and even beyond that – to the world order. However, is the Islamic State a passing phenomenon, or an enduring Salafi jihadist state entity that will likely continue to foment unrest? Will it be capable of spreading beyond the regions it currently controls, even to non-Sunni areas, or has it, perhaps, exhausted its ability to expand? The results of the wars in Syria, Iraq, and maybe even Libya will serve as tests for assessing its strength and vitality.

Another major question regards the caliph and caliphate. A significant part of the Islamic State's power rests on its ability to preserve the status of the caliph, and to validate its audacity to establish a caliphate. Success in this regard has enabled it to recruit the masses and offer them an existing alternative regime with an attractive Islamic *sharia*-based character. The fate of the caliph himself, Abu Bakr al-Baghdadi, is closely intertwined with the caliphate's prospects for survival. His self-identification with the caliphate project contributed inestimably to the building of a powerful and authentic image for the Islamic State in the eyes of its supporters. This image depicts the caliph as the shepherd leading his flock and restoring the Islamic nation to its purest and most glorious state.

The image of the chosen caliph also plays a crucial role on the strategic-military level, as it helps present and implement the lofty vision, while providing support for the bravado required in making the vision a reality. Since declaring the establishment of the caliphate, al-Baghdadi has escaped a number of assassination attempts, after becoming the major target of all his enemies that came together in the Western-Arab coalition against the Islamic State. The basic assumption is that sooner or later, al-Baghdadi will be taken out of the game, as was his predecessor heading the Salafi jihadist camp, Osama Bin Laden. Consequently, it is important to understand to what degree the concept of the Islamic State depends on the existence and prevalence of al-Baghdadi the caliph, and to assess the consequences of his removal. This question is different from the general question of the effectiveness and justification of assassinating heads of terror entities, as the Islamic State has its own particular properties.

Observations

At the time of this writing, approximately a year and a half after the announcement of the establishment of the caliphate, the Islamic State finds itself in relatively stable condition. Its control over territories conquered in Syria and Iraq, which are administrated from regime centers in Raqqa and Mosul, has been maintained despite some territorial changes resulting from various achievements and failures on the battlefield. The Islamic State has deepened its hold over the population under its rule by establishing a mechanism of governance, and it has established an economic infrastructure for financing its operations. Fighting its enemies in Syria and Iraq, including the US-led international coalition and the coalition established by Russia, has hurt it but has not weakened it to the point of collapse. Moreover, the Islamic State has refrained from fighting in areas populated by communities that are not Sunni, and it has yet to be tested in fighting against an army of significant size. The loss of commanders from its ranks has not caused system-wide shock, due to the decentralized structure that gives independence to lower command ranks. Moreover, despite the losses, a large number of fighters, including foreign volunteers, still seek to join its ranks.

The challenge is, therefore, to identify ways of weakening the Islamic State and bringing about its decline. Political recommendations promoting these goals must be based on a number of crucial observations.

First, this is a multi-dimensional phenomenon that is not limited purely to the military realm. It is a phenomenon with roots entrenched deep within the societies from which it sprang, and it represents the ongoing failures of local Middle East politics. It is vital to fight it also with an understanding of the distress of the people who chose to adopt its precepts, whether regional residents or foreign volunteers. Beyond this, it would be a mistake to relate to the Islamic State as a military framework that works only with kinetic tools. Its power stems in large measure from a blurring of the boundaries between fighting and propaganda, between recruitment of fighters and recruitment of the masses.

Second, while treating the phenomenon as a framework built around a single, unified idea, careful attention must be paid to the differences and distinct modes of expression and nuances that it embodies. In other words, the different spheres in which the Islamic State operates possess different characteristics. First and foremost, this is true of the territories where the Islamic State has established de facto rule – portions of Iraq and Syria. Thus, for example, the social fabric in Iraq – where there is a Shiite majority and a Sunni minority that had the ruling power taken from it with no suitable compensation, a minority that is accustomed to violent inter-sectoral, as well as intra-sectoral, conflict – is quite distinct from the dynamic in Syria, where an Alawite minority ruled over a Sunni majority for over 40 years. Moreover, as to consequences for the expansion of the Islamic State, it is difficult to equate between the destabilization of Lebanon – with its sectorial society and its unique political balance – and the threat to the stability of Sunni Jordan, which has signed a peace treaty with Israel and enjoys American support. Another example of essential distinctions regards Islamic State actions against Iran and Saudi Arabia. These countries have different and opposing interests, and only an appropriately tailored plan of international action that takes into account specific geopolitical considerations and particular interests can lead to coordinated action to eradicate the threat.

Third, one of the dangerous side effects of the panic created by the Islamic State is the whitewashing of crimes and problematic actions perpetrated by other regimes and terror groups. Such groups have ruthlessly and violently murdered thousands of innocent civilians throughout the world, both before and after the Islamic State was founded. Thus, al-Qaeda and its partner the al-Nusra Front are sometimes presented as "moderate" Salafi jihadist organizations that are more pragmatic and thus worthy as potential partners for fighting the Islamic State. The campaign against the Islamic State has "redeemed" Hezbollah, designated as a terror organization; the Shiite militias in Iraq, partners in the war on terror alongside the regimes of Bashar al-Assad – responsible for the death of hundreds of thousands of his own people; and Iran, which more and more is perceived as a stabilizing factor in the Middle East. Despite the problem of perception, it must be remembered that in the fight against the Islamic State, a common enemy does not necessarily turn rivals into allies.

Based on these distinctions, the challenge is to formulate and implement a plan of action that will strike a balance among the various interests, and be based on an understanding that the nature and values of the Islamic State do not allow any compromise or agreement with it. It is clear that it will always act as a subversive element that forcibly disseminates its destructive ideology throughout the world. Thus, defeating it to deny its survival and proliferation are an historic necessity. This challenge is difficult to implement, but imperative.

A key question, which may be instructive regarding future trends in the struggle against the Islamic State, is to what extent Western countries will manage to overcome the stinging memories of the wars in Afghanistan and Iraq. In recent years, there has been a noticeable aversion among Western countries to direct military involvement in Arab and Muslim countries, including action against the Islamic State. Such reservations are understandable from an historical perspective. There exists a certain fatigue, accompanied by fear of being dragged into another Middle East war with high costs in life and treasure. In addition, the military involvement of Western forces in Muslim countries may play into the hands of the Islamic State, which will depict the Western forces as invaders who occupy and despoil Islamic lands and must therefore be fought by all Muslims.

However, all of these reservations are expected to change in light of the continued outrages perpetrated by the Islamic State – in its territory and throughout the world. Many countries, including Western – especially European – states are currently compelled to receive hundreds of thousands of refugees from the civil wars in the Middle East, some fleeing Islamic State barbarity. Syria is the main but not only example of a country experiencing a combination of a cruel, prolonged civil war alongside Islamic State terror against civilians. This has led to the migration of approximately half of the country's population to neighboring countries and Europe. This flow of migrants will change the demographic balance in Europe, which in turn will further intensify the already existing tensions between "old" residents of the European countries and the new and old Muslim immigrants, which may awaken extremist movements on the radical right. Developments in this direction may prove to be far worse than terror attacks, as dramatic and deadly as they are (such as the attack in Paris on November 13, 2015). Furthermore, the West has a clear interest in weakening the Islamic State to prevent a repeat of the phenomenon that took place with the "Afghan alumni" – but this time by "jihad alumni" in Syria and Iraq. In the past, some such alumni have returned to their countries of origin and raised the level of violence there; some migrated to other war regions; others founded and operated ad hoc terror cells and networks in the West; the highly skilled fighters among them were accepted into the ranks of al-Qaeda.

Another significant unfolding event, which provides an example of the unexpected turns that characterize the volatile era in the Middle East, is Russia's decision to intervene militarily in Syria, at the head of a coalition that includes Iran, the Assad regime, Hezbollah, and the Shiite forces in Iraq. This action is expected to impact on developments in the Syrian arena and beyond. Will this intervention save the Assad regime? Will it lead to solidifying its control only over the "vital" portions of Syria, or will it result in the re-conquest of the rest of the country currently ruled by Salafi jihadist organizations, including the territory now controlled by the Islamic State (and the end of its rule in Raqqa)? It is difficult to assess the results of this intervention and envision how Western states will react to the Russian involvement. Will they take significant steps toward military intervention, or work mainly through diplomatic channels to form a political-diplomatic settlement to stabilize the situation in Syria while dividing the country? Either way, a failure of the Western-Arab coalition in its war against Islamic State may result in making it stronger, and the Western-Arab coalition must be ready for such a scenario.

Recommendations

In the current age of turbulence and frequent change in the Middle East, more twists and turns are to be expected. Thus, for example, it is not impossible that countries of the region will experience further turmoil – including states whose regimes have thus far not collapsed. Such changes may not necessarily be connected directly with the Islamic State, but its influence on the development of such upheavals may be significant; it is certainly expected to attempt to exploit such events to promote its causes. Other unexpected turns of events may result from decisions of certain countries to change their policies regarding the Islamic State. For example, Western or Arab countries may become involved in Syria as a result of a major and highly lethal terror attack or exceptional action perpetrated against them.

The international community must thus accustom itself to the current Middle East zeitgeist – i.e., the undermining of the existing state order and the dissolution into individual communities – and develop flexibility regarding the state borders drawn in the region over the last century. The aspirations of various sectors in the Middle East can no longer be ignored, especially considering that their frustration in large measure led to the deterioration of internal stability and the growth of phenomena such as the Islamic State. In the current regional reality, new arrangements should be considered, as well as the formulation of alternative frameworks that will suitably address the sentiments forming among the various communities. Thinking in this direction may make it easier to contain the spread of the Islamic State.

The campaign should capitalize on a set of inherent weaknesses of the Islamic State in order to defeat it. For example, the Islamic State has amassed a great many enemies, and the number is growing steadily – enemies hungry for revenge among the occupied populations and the minorities that have been murdered, robbed, and exiled (in the Middle East, the blood feud takes on special meaning); international coalitions with an ever-growing number of countries joining the common effort to defeat the Islamic State; and bitter internal enemies from the global jihadist camp who want to help defeat it. The abundance of enemies opens potential intelligence channels for recruitment and actions against the Islamic State on an operational level. Similarly, the repeated promises of the Islamic State for victory and continual progress toward realizing the vision of the caliphate within a short time frame can serve as fertile ground for exposing its failures and harming its image as a victor. The Islamic State's eschatological vision, which holds that the world is about to face the final battle to ensure the victory of Islamic State-led Islam, enables the depiction of the caliph as a deceptive false messiah dragging Islam along a catastrophic path that will end with his own death and the deaths of leaders and followers alike – with whoever survives almost certainly living out life as a convicted war criminal.

In practical terms, the key to success for the struggle against the Islamic State is the conduct of a joint military-ideological-public relations campaign, to be led by combined Western and Arab-Muslim forces. On the military plane, the strategic goal must be to stop the spread of the Islamic State and strike at it with a proactive policy that combines kinetic tools with soft power. While it is impossible to completely eliminate the phenomenon in the short term, it is certainly possible to quickly contain it within a limited sphere. The Islamic State's successes in conquering territory were the result of the avoidance of direct conflict with regular, strong armies in hostile regions, along with its arrangement in a decentralized structure that made the command chain less vital. Thus, regular forces composed of special units should be formed against it under international direction, while at the same time, weak points and vital assets can be identified as future targets. This will help undermine the image of constant success and momentum that the Islamic State seeks to promote for itself.

Military action must be accompanied by the wielding of soft power. The Islamic State casts itself as a sovereign institution conducting itself as a state in all respects. This obligates the Islamic State's opponents to seek ways to undermine the foundations and influence of the alleged state. One possible way is to distance it from the oil reserves in its possession, and thus to significantly diminish its potential sources of income. On another level, an attempt can be made to reach the civilian population under Islamic State rule, as well as that under threat of being taken over, and provide them with alternative governance solutions in the areas of education, healthcare, welfare, employment, and other civilian realms. It will thus be possible to compete with the services offered by the Islamic State and puncture this critical image of a welfare provider. Taking a broader view, assistance should be given to threatened countries such as Jordan, Lebanon, and Egypt to address their social distress and reduce the danger of recruitment of young people in these countries by Islamic State.

Regarding the Salafist jihadi camp, the absurd idea of cooperation with elements wrongly depicted as "pragmatic," such as al-Qaeda and its partners – including the al-Nusra Front and others – must be abandoned quickly. Their inclusion as allies in the defeat of the Islamic State will only lay foundations for tomorrow's disaster. Therefore, it is actually best to exploit the split within the Salafist jihadi camp in order to deepen the rivalry and violence between the Islamic State and its allies, and al-Qaeda and its partners. Such a policy will help harm these organizations from within and disrupt their ability to create momentum for future actions. Assuming that this will be a long, drawn out campaign, it is crucial to ensure that responses to short term challenges presented specifically by the Islamic State do not contradict the long term solutions required in the struggle against the Salafi jihadist camp as a whole, including the al-Qaeda camp.

The ideological, public relations campaign must reach the potential target audience for support and recruitment, on the basis of two main messages: first, undermining the image of success and momentum radiated by the Islamic State; second, depicting it as a deviant element within the Muslim world.

In order to subvert the Islamic State's image of success, the campaign against it must focus on exposing its failures. Thus, for example, the mass exodus from Syria should be presented as the failure of the concept of *hijra*, which serves as a fundamental principle in al-Baghdadi's vision. This vision of *hijra* involves the caliphate centers in Syria and Iraq becoming magnets drawing in the believers. The emigration of millions of Muslims from Syria expresses their fear and revulsion of the Islamic State and its manner of conduct. Moreover, despite the relatively high number of foreign volunteers enlisting into the ranks of the Islamic State (which are compared in the West to the number of recruits drawn by the mujahideen in Afghanistan in the 1980s), it is still a small fraction relative to the number of Muslims in the world and the potential recruitment from among them. The implication is that al-Baghdadi's vision of the mass enlistment of Muslims into the ranks of the Islamic State is ultimately a failure.

At the same time, it is vital to enlist state and religious leaderships in the Muslim world, and include them in efforts to prevent the hijacking of Islam by a radical, unauthorized entity leading it to disaster in the name of an Armageddon-like fantasy. It is within the power of leaders of the Muslim states to enlist their spiritual leaders – recognized authorities – in providing religious authority and validity to the exposure of the religious and legal deviance of Islamic State. They must come together for a joint effort with parallel elements in the West who have the ability, talents, and tools to create an effective public relations framework that will turn the Islamic State brand and symbols from desirable to abhorrent. One example of what can be the focus of a joint effort is the exposure of the *sharia* prohibition on mass civilian executions – of minorities, Western civilians, and Muslims – which can thereby undermine the Islamic State's trademark, beheadings. Great value is attributed to authoritative and influential proof that such actions are not in the category of Islamic practice and are opposed to the spirit of *sharia*. The masses must be exposed to a clear, unequivocal message: judgment without trial, beheadings, and parading the heads on the bodies of the victim are a forbidden perversion, with no acceptable basis in *sharia*, and as such, acts of heresy.

In the ideological-public relations realm, there should be intensification of processes already underway in accessible internet platforms. An effective plan of action can become an inclusive multinational framework that operates as part of the international Western-Arab coalition working against the Islamic State. Such a framework will incorporate skilled marketing campaign managers from the West and Arab world, combined with recognized *sharia* authorities with standing in the Muslim world. This will create a counterweight of public relations arrays with messages tailored to an audience of young Muslims and Muslim converts, who see the Salafi jihadist interpretation as the undisputed and clear truth. These messages will be disseminated in a manner customized for the various target audiences, through the diverse formats of social media, guided by the use of the Islamic State's own methods against it. This is an ongoing challenge that will require constant attentiveness to changes underway in the methods and ideological messages of the Islamic State, enabling the development of an overall campaign against it that adjusts to changes within the various target audiences.

Finally, attention must be paid to the connection between Israel and the Islamic State phenomenon. At this stage, Israel does not represent a central element in the international struggle against the Islamic State. The relatively significant distance of Islamic State forces from Israel's borders and its regional standing position it as a contributing, but uninvolved, factor. Indeed, any involvement by Israel may discourage cooperation by some essential Muslim partners. Thus, the main activity for Israel regarding the Islamic State must be assisting the international coalition with intelligence sharing and at the same time focusing on basic preparations for future escalation vis-à-vis the Islamic state and its allies, and on concerns of destabilization of neighboring countries. This reflects, inter alia, a basic Israeli assumption that holds that the greatest threat to its security is the Iran-Assad-Hezbollah axis. Despite the many arguments supporting this claim, it is possible that this order of priorities will change as a result of dynamic developments in the region in general, and in the Israeli-Palestinian conflict in particular. While the Iranian threat is familiar and plays out as part of the "old order," the potential future entry of the Islamic State into the arena likely to occur on one of Israel's borders may change the situation. Moreover, Iran and Hezbollah represent Shiite interests in the Middle East, and thus their influence on Palestinian society, and Arab society in Israel, is limited. The Islamic State, however, has already proven (though still on a small scale) that there exists potential support for its ideas among certain parts of this population, most of which is Sunni. This potential is most likely to play out more aggressively in the case of a violent escalation in the Israeli-Palestinian arena. Thus, Israel must prepare to meet the evils expected from the direction of the Islamic State – evils that may appear both within its borders and without.

Contributors

Keren Aviram is a research assistant in the Law and National Security program at INSS. She specializes in international law, constitutional law, administrative law, minority rights, and research into the political process between Israel and the Palestinians. Ms. Aviram holds a Bachelor's degree in law from the Kiryat Ono College and a Master's degree in law from the Hebrew University, focusing on public and international law.

Afik Barak is an intern in the Terrorism and Low Intensity Conflict Program at INSS. His research deals with the anti-terrorism policy of the United States, Canada, Australia, and China. He holds a Bachelor's degree in Middle East Studies from Ben Gurion University, and is studying for a Master's degree in the Security Studies program at Tel Aviv University.

Av Baras is an intern in the Terrorism and Low Intensity Conflict Program at INSS. His research covers terrorism in Egypt, the Gaza Strip, Libya, and Tunisia. He holds a Bachelor's degree in Middle East and African history from Tel Aviv University.

Ofra Bengio is a professor emeritus of history of the Middle East and a senior researcher at the Moshe Dayan Center for Middle Eastern and African Studies at Tel Aviv University. Prof. Bengio's principal fields of research are Iraq, Turkey, and the Kurds. She also translates from Arabic and Turkish.

Benedetta Berti is a research fellow at INSS, lecturer at Tel Aviv University, TED fellow, and independent consultant. Dr. Berti has published three books, including *Armed Political Organizations: From Conflict to Integration* (2013). Her research has been published in numerous journals, including *Foreign Policy, Foreign Affairs, Studies in Conflict and Terrorism, Mediterranean Politics,* and *Middle East Journal.*

Shlomo Brom is a senior research fellow and head of the Israeli-Palestinian Relations Program at INSS. Brig. Gen. (ret.) Brom served in the IDF as head of Strategic Planning in the Planning Directorate of the IDF General Staff. He has taken part in peace negotiations with the Palestinians, Jordan, and Syria, and served as deputy head of the National Security Council. His main areas of research are Israel-Palestinian relations and national security doctrine. Co-editor of *The Second Lebanon War: Strategic Perspectives* (2007) and the annual *Strategic Survey for Israel*, he also edited *The Lessons of Operation Protective Edge* (2014).

Udi Dekel is the Managing Director of INSS. Brig. Gen. (res.) Dekel served as head of the negotiating team with the Palestinians under Prime Minister Ehud Olmert during the Annapolis process. In his last position in the IDF he served as head of Strategic Planning in the Planning Directorate of the General Staff. He was head of the Israel-UN-Lebanon committee following the Second Lebanon War, and was head of the military committees with Egypt and Jordan. He also served as head of the working groups on strategic-operational coordination with the United States; on developing a response to the threat of surface-to-surface missiles; and on international military cooperation. He was a member of the committee to update Israel's security concept (2005/6), where he coordinated the formulation of IDF strategy.

Omer Einav is a research associate at INSS, and a doctoral student in the Department of History at Tel Aviv University. His research at INSS focuses on the Israeli-Palestinian conflict, Syria, and Lebanon. Mr. Einav is the editor of "Shorty," the INSS blog. His doctoral thesis deals with football as a tool for examining relations between Jews and Arabs in Mandatory Palestine. He has a Bachelor's degree in Islamic and Middle Eastern Studies and International Relations from the Hebrew University.

Oded Eran is a senior research fellow and former director of INSS. Before joining the Institute, he served as the World Jewish Congress representative in Israel and Secretary General of the WJC Israel branch. Dr. Eran has served as Israel's ambassador to the European Union (covering NATO as well), Israel's ambassador to Jordan, and head of Israel's negotiations team with the Palestinians (1999-2000). Other previous positions include deputy director general of the Ministry of Foreign Affairs, and the deputy chief of the Israeli embassy in Washington. He also serves as a consultant to the Knesset Subcommittee on Foreign Affairs.

Shmuel Even, a senior research fellow at INSS, holds a Ph.D. from the Technion and Haifa University. Alongside his work at INSS, Dr. Even engages in research and consulting in the business sector through a company he owns and serves as a professional Board member for other companies. At INSS he has authored studies on the Israeli economy, intellectual property, the gas and oil economy, strategy in foreign and security matters, defense costs, cyber issues, intelligence, and the political process with the Palestinians.

Sarah Fainberg is a research fellow at INSS and Visiting Professor at the Harold Hartog School of Governance and Policy at Tel Aviv University. Dr. Fainberg holds a doctorate in Political Science from Sciences Po Paris and is a graduate of the École Normale Supérieure in Paris. She was a guest lecturer at the Foreign Service School at Georgetown University in Washington (2009-2012), and is the author of two books: *Les Discriminés: L'antisémitisme Soviétique après Staline* (2014), and *Secularism on the Edge: Church-State Relations in the US, France and Israel* (2014, with Jacques Berlinerblau and Aurora Nou).

Zack Gold is a former visiting research fellow at INSS and a fellow at the American Security Project in Washington. He specializes in security of the Sinai Peninsula, and in relations between Egypt, Israel, the Gaza Strip, and the United States. He holds a Master's degree in Law and Diplomacy from the Fletcher School at Tufts University, and a Bachelor's degree from the University of Delaware.

Yoel Guzansky is a research fellow at INSS. Before he joined the Institute, he was in charge of strategic issues at the National Security Council in the Prime Minister's Office, coordinating work on the Iranian nuclear challenge. He specializes in issues of security in the Gulf and strategic issues in the Middle East, and advises and lectures on these subjects in Israel and abroad. Dr. Guzansky is a member of the INSS management team and head of the internship program. He manages the Institute's forum on strategic issues and ideas, is a member of the editorial board of the INSS journal *Strategic Assessment*, and is the Institute's representative at the Euro-Mediterranean

Study Commission (EuroMeSCo). He is the author of *The Arab Gulf States and Reform in the Middle East* (2015).

Yotam Hacohen is a joint founder of DoAlogue Strategic Consulting, a researcher at the Institute for Intelligence Studies, and a consultant on behalf of the Shitufim company in the framework of the reform in the Civil Service Commission. He was previously head of the team that reviewed Israel's national security concept at the Reut Institute, and was also joint leader of the effort to examine Israeli strategy in view of the crisis in Syria. Mr. Hacohen is a reserve officer in the Intelligence Corps and holder of a Bachelor's degree with distinction in sociology and the multi-disciplinary program from the Hebrew University.

Adam Hoffman is a Neubauer research associate working in the Terrorism and Low Intensity Conflict Program at INSS, and a doctoral student in the Department of Political Science at Hebrew University. His research focuses on the use of social media by Salafi jihadist organizations. He specializes in Salafi jihadist ideology, the Islamic State, radical Islamic movements in Iraq and Syria, and the use of social media for jihad purposes.

Ephraim Kam is a senior research fellow at INSS, and was deputy head of the Institute from 1995-2013. Before joining the Institute, Dr. Kam served in the IDF Intelligence Research Division, where his last position (with the rank of colonel) was assistant to the head of the division. A graduate of the Hebrew University in Middle East Studies and Economics and holder of a Master's degree and Ph.D. in government from Harvard University, he has written two books: *Surprise Attack* and *From Terror to Nuclear Bombs: The Significance of the Iranian Threat*. He teaches in the Security Studies Program for M.A. students at Tel Aviv University.

Gallia Lindenstrauss is a research fellow at INSS, specializing in Turkey's current foreign policy. Among her other areas of expertise are ethnic disputes, the foreign policy of Azerbaijan, the Cypriot issue, and the Kurds. She holds a Ph.D. from the Department of International Relations at the Hebrew University. Her opinion pieces and commentaries have been widely published in Israel's leading media outlets, as well as in *National Interest, Hurriyet Daily News*, and *Insight Turkey*. Dr. Lindenstrauss lectures at the

Interdisciplinary Center in Herzliya, and formerly lectured at the Hebrew University.

Meir Litvak is the head of the Alliance Center for Iranian Studies and an associate professor of Middle East history at Tel Aviv University. His primary research areas are the history of Iran and the modern Shia, as well as modern Islamic movements. Among his publications are *From Empathy to Denial: Arab Responses to the Holocaust* (with Esther Webman. 2009); and *Shi'i Scholars of Nineteenth-Century Iraq: The 'Ulama' of Najaf and Karbala'* (1998).

Zvi Magen, a senior research fellow at INSS, joined the INSS research staff following a long career in Israel's intelligence and foreign service. From 1993-1997 he served as Israel's ambassador to Ukraine, and in 1998-1999 he served as Israel's ambassador to Russia. From 1999-2006 he served as head of Nativ, the liaison group for the FSU and Jewish diaspora affairs at the Prime Minister's office, and in 2006-2009 he was head of the Institute for Eurasian Studies at the Interdisciplinary Center, Herzliya.

Aviad Mandelbaum, an intern in the Terrorism and Low Intensity Conflict program at INSS, holds a Bachelor's degree in political science from Tel Aviv University and is a graduate of the Seminar on Arabic Language and Culture at Givat Haviva. In his internship he researches Salafi jihadist terror organizations (including al-Qaeda and the Islamic State), Hamas, Palestinian Islamic Jihad, and other terror organizations operating against Israel.

Kobi Michael is a senior research fellow at INSS, and was formerly on the faculty at Ben Gurion and Ariel Universities and a guest lecturer at Northwestern University. His main fields of research include strategy and security studies, politics and the military, the Israeli-Palestinian conflict, and peacekeeping and state building campaigns. He has written and edited twelve books and monographs, and some fifty articles in his fields of expertise. Dr. Michael served as a senior officer in GHQ Intelligence Branch, and in 1994, following the Oslo Accords, was one of the founders and commanders of the Israeli-Palestinian Security Coordination Mechanism in the Gaza Strip. In 1999-2000 he commanded the Security Coordination Mechanism in the West Bank. In 2007 he was head of the Palestinians and peacekeeping forces desk at the National Security Council, and from 2009 to 2013 was Deputy Director General and head of the Palestinian and Neighboring Countries Branch in the Ministry of Strategic Affairs.

Meirav Mishali-Ram is a lecturer in the Department of Political Science at Bar Ilan University and a research fellow on the International Conflict Behavior (ICB) project. Dr. Mishali-Ram has published several articles in journals on international relations, most recently on the conflicts in Afghanistan and Pakistan. Her research focuses on ethnic and sectorial conflicts, regional studies, non-state actors, and civil wars all over the world, particularly in South Asia.

Orit Perlov, a researcher at INSS and expert on social media matters, analyzes opinions and trends expressed through new social media in Arab countries. Her work, which involves daily dialogue with Palestinian, Egyptian, Jordanian, Syrian, Lebanese, Libyan, and Tunisian civil society, seeks to understand and characterize in depth processes in Arab civilian societies and the use of new media to influence public opinion in those countries. Ms. Perlov is also an advisor and guest lecturer at various research, security, and government bodies. From 2002-2008 she worked in the Foreign Ministry and served as a political advisor in Israeli embassies in Jordan and the Gulf states.

Eyal Propper is deputy head of the Strategic Issues Division in the Foreign Ministry, and a visiting lecturer on Chinese foreign policy in the East Asia Studies group at the Hebrew University and at the Interdisciplinary Center, Herzliya. Dr. Propper served in the Israeli Embassy in Beijing for over seven years, in two positions: after Israel-China relations began in 1992, he was the first advisor on communications, culture, and academic issues in China, and he returned there in 2002-2006 as political envoy and deputy ambassador.

Yoram Schweitzer is a senior research fellow and and head of the Terrorism and Low Intensity Conflict Program at INSS. He served in the intelligence community in Israel and was head of the international terror section in the IDF, and was a member of the task force dealing with Israeli prisoners and missing persons in the Prime Minister's Office. Mr. Schweitzer was an advisor on combating terror in the Ministry of Defense and the Prime Minister's Office. His publications include An *Expected Surprise: The September 11th*

Attack and Its Ramifications; Al-Qaeda and the Globalization of Suicide Terrorism, and *Al-Qaeda's Odyssey to Global Jihad.*

Smadar Shaul, an intern in the Terrorism and Low Intensity Conflict Program at INSS, researches terror organizations in Nigeria, Somalia, Yemen, and Saudi Arabia. She holds a Master's degree in social psychology from Haifa University. She was formerly a research assistant at the Interdisciplinary Center in Herzliya and in the Shmuel Ne'eman Institute for Research into National Policy. Ms. Shaul was also a member of a research team at the Center for National Security Studies at Haifa University.

Shaul Shay is a lecturer at the Interdisciplinary Center in Herzliya, where he is also the head of research at its Institute of Policy and Strategy. Dr. Col (res.) Shay served for 25 years in the IDF Intelligence corps, where he filled senior positions and won the head of the Intelligence division's Prize for Creative Thinking (1995). In the Yom Kippur War he was a combat soldier in the paratroopers, and in the First Lebanon War he was the intelligence officer of a military formation that fought on the eastern front in Lebanon. From 2000 to 2007 he was head of the IDF History Department, and from 2007-2009 he was deputy head of the National Security Council.

Ilan Shkalrsky is an officer in the IDF regular army and an intern at INSS, working in the Terrorism and Low Intensity Conflict Program. He holds a Bachelor's degree in political science and history from Tel Aviv University, and is currently studying for a Master's degree in Security Studies at Tel Aviv University.

Gabi Siboni joined the INSS staff in 2005 as a senior research fellow. At INSS he heads the Military and Strategic Affairs Program and the Cyber Security Program, and is editor of the INSS journal *Military and Strategic Affairs.* In the course of his military career, he served as a fighter and commander in the Golani Brigade, and in the IDF reserves he served as head of the Golani Brigade HQ and as head of the Divisional HQ. Dr. Col. (res.) Siboni holds B.Sc. and M.Sc. degrees in Engineering from Tel Aviv University and a doctorate in information systems from Ben Gurion University of the Negev. He is a consultant to state organizations, corporations, industry, and start-ups in the fields of cyber security and information, business development, and managing security-operating-technological risks on computer and communications systems.

David Siman-Tov is a researcher in the fields of intelligence and cyber security at INSS, where he is also involved in central learning processes. He was involved in conceptual and organizational changes in the IDF and GHQ Intelligence Branch, such as formulating the concept of the Inter-War Struggle (IWS), and setting up the IDF Cyber HQ. Mr. Siman-Tov is a consultant to companies in the security sector. For 25 years he served in research and collection positions in the IDF GHQ Intelligence Branch, and in the Strategic Planning Section in the Planning Division, where he was responsible for formulating the reference threat and was engaged in formulating the IDF's military strategy. In recent years he served as a researcher in the GHQ's Intelligence Research Institute. Together with Shai Hershkowitz, he wrote *Military Intelligence Comes to Light* (2013), and together with Shmuel Even, wrote the monograph *Cyber Warfare: Concepts and Strategic Trends* (2012).

Shimon Stein, a senior research fellow at INSS, served as Israel's ambassador to Germany (2001-2007). Prior to this appointment he served in the Ministry of Foreign Affairs as deputy director general for the CIS, as well as Eastern and Central Europe. Ambassador Stein held additional MFA posts in Washington, Germany, and Israel, and was a member of Israeli delegations to multilateral negotiations on arms control.

Asher Susser is a Professor Emeritus of Middle East history and senior researcher at the Moshe Dayan Center for Middle Eastern and African Research at Tel Aviv University, as well as Professor at the University of Arizona in the United States. Prof. Susser was head of the Moshe Dayan Center for twelve years, and taught for over thirty years in the Department of Middle East History at Tel Aviv University.

Carmit Valensi is a research associate at INSS and a researcher in the Military Intelligence Research Division. Dr. Valensi specializes in the study of the contemporary Middle East, terror organizations and political violence, and strategic studies. Her doctoral thesis at Tel Aviv University deals with the appearance of "violent hybrid actors" and the test cases of

Hamas, Hezbollah, and FARC. She has published on the regional upheaval in the Middle East, the development of military concepts among extreme Islamic organizations, and the governance capability of armed groups.

Ophir Winter is a Neubauer Research Associate at INSS and a lecturer at Ariel University and in the Jezreel Valley College. Dr. Winter's research focuses on the Arab-Israeli conflict, relations between religion and state in the Arab world, and contemporary Muslim practice. His doctoral thesis deals with the struggles of the regimes in Egypt and Jordan on the legitimacy of the peace agreements with Israel in the years 1973-2001.

Amos Yadlin was appointed Director of INSS in November 2011, following forty years of service in the IDF, nine of them as a member of General Staff. From 2006-2010 Maj. Gen. (ret.) Yadlin served as head of Military Intelligence, following a term as IDF military attaché to the United States. In 2002 he earned the rank of major general, and was appointed commander of IDF colleges and the National Defense College. Maj. Gen. (ret.) Yadlin served as deputy commander of the Israel Air Force. Prior to that he was a commander of two combat squadrons and two IAF bases, as well as head of the IAF Planning Department. He served as a fighter pilot in the Yom Kippur War, Operation Peace for Galilee (the First Lebanon War), and Operation Tammuz (the raid on the Iraqi Osirak nuclear reactor). Maj. Gen. (ret.) Yadlin holds a Bachelor's degree with honors in Economics and Business Administration from Ben Gurion University of the Negev, and a Master's degree in Public Administration from Harvard University. He is the co-author of *Regime Stability in the Middle East: An Analytical Model to Assess the Possibility of Regime Change* (2013).

Ronen Zeidel is a senior researcher at the Moshe Dayan Center for Middle East Research at Tel Aviv University, specializing in Iraq and the Islamic State. Dr. Zeidel coordinates the Iraq and Islamic State Forum at the Moshe Dayan Center and teaches courses on this subject at Haifa and Tel Aviv Universities, as well as at the Interdisciplinary Center in Herzliya.

Eyal Zisser is the vice-rector of Tel Aviv University and was the Dean of the Faculty of Humanities at Tel Aviv University from 2010-2015. Before that, Prof. Zisser was head of the Moshe Dayan Center for Middle East and African Studies (2007-2010) and head of the History of the Middle East and Africa Department (2004-2008), both at Tel Aviv University. His areas of expertise include the modern history of Syria and Lebanon, and the Arab-Israeli conflict. Among the books he authored: *Assad's Syria at a Crossroads* (1999); *Faces of Syria: Regime, Society, and State* (2003); *In the Name of the Father: Bashar al-Assad's First Years in Power* (2004); *Lebanon: The Bleeding Cedar, from the Civil War to the Second Lebanon War* (2009); and *Syria: Protest, Revolution, Civil War* (2014).

INSS Memoranda, May 2014–Present